**PRAEGER SPECIAL STUDIES IN
INTERNATIONAL ECONOMICS AND DEVELOPMENT**

The New Elite
in Asia and Africa

A COMPARATIVE STUDY
OF INDONESIA AND GHANA

Thom Kerstiens

FREDERICK A. PRAEGER, Publishers
New York · Washington · London

The purpose of the Praeger Special Studies is to make specialized research monographs in international economics and politics available to the academic, business, and government communities. For further information, write to the Special Projects Division, Frederick A. Praeger, Publishers, 111 Fourth Avenue, New York, N.Y. 10003.

FREDERICK A. PRAEGER, PUBLISHERS
111 Fourth Avenue, New York 3, N.Y., U.S.A.
77-79 Charlotte Street, London W.1, England

Published in the United States of America in 1966
by Frederick A. Praeger, Inc., Publishers

Library of Congress Catalog Card Number: 65-24728

Printed in the United States of America

CONTENTS

PART I. INTRODUCTION

6. THE NEW ELITE AND POLITICAL
      INSTITUTIONS.   141

        The Social Background   142
        The Elite and the Political Parties . . .   144
        The Elite and the Opposition.   153
        The Elite and Local Government.   156
        The Elite and the Presidency.   161
        The Elite and the Army.   169

7. THE NEW ELITE AND SOCIAL INSTITUTIONS . . .   181

        The University and the Elite.   182
        The Trade Unions and the Elite.   187
        The Press and the Elite   193
        The Civil Service and the Elite   196

8. THE NEW ELITE AND INTERNATIONAL
      CONCEPTS.   202

        Communism and the New Elite   202
        Christianity and the New Elite.   208
        International Politics and the
          New Elite   210

9. THE NEW ELITE AND THE CHALLENGE OF
      THE FUTURE.   220

        The Challenge of Democracy.   222
        The Challenge to the West   228
        The Challenge to Christianity   233

APPENDIXES:

PART

INTRODUCTION

CHAPTER **1** THE ELITE GROUP
IN THE
DEVELOPING COUNTRIES

In our democratic age, it has become rare to
use the term "élite." In a period which seems to be
marked by a striving for equality amongst all men on
the political and socio-economic, as well as the cultural level, the term "élite" has acquired a bad connotation, as belonging to a period when the climate of
opinion was hostile to the modern ideals of equality
and democracy.

Nevertheless, one notes of late, especially
among the social sciences, a revived interest in the
phenomenon of the élite. This to a large extent is
due to the increasing attention given to the problem
of development of socio-economically backward regions. It is more and more realized that in the
socio-economic processes of change which are taking
place in the developing countries, the élite has a
preponderant role to play.

In this chapter we intend to give a very brief
history of the term "élite" with the various connota-
tions it has had through the centuries.

The three main notions linked to the term are
those of superiority, prestige and power. Although
in modern society, various groups exert power (politicians, clergy, industrialists, military, intellectuals, etc.), in developing countries, especially
during the period of decolonization, a general recognition of the need for political leadership has
overshadowed that for economic or social leadership,
and it is in the political élite that the great
power resides. But, as we shall try to show, this
political élite was at the same time an intellectual

élite and was largely drawn from the middle class, a
class born in the cities under the influence of Western rule. Elite groups do not remain stable and it
is their mobility which often can give an insight
into the changes which are taking place on the socio-
economic and political levels. This is particularly
true for the developing countries.

Although the term "developing countries" has
passed into common usage, we think it useful in this
chapter to define the criteria which we wish to apply to this term. It then becomes clear that both
Indonesia and Ghana in all aspects fit into this
category. The fact that they were the first countries in their respective continents to accede to
independence after World War II (under, however,
quite different circumstances) offers the possibility of studying over a longer period the role played
by the élite, not only in the achievement of independence but also in the difficult period of the social
revolution which must necessarily follow that of the
political upheaval. It is for these reasons that we
have chosen Indonesia and Ghana as examples for our
study.

THE CONCEPT OF ELITE[1]

Etymologically speaking, the term "élite" is derived from the Latin "eligere," to choose. It came
into use in the French language around the 14th century. The French substantive "élite" had the meaning of choice. It was applied to a choice of persons, first of all in military terminology--"hommes
d'élite" and "compagnie d'élite"; but already in the
15th century Froissart applied it to "meilleurs des
meilleurs" (best of the best). In the 18th century
this became the general meaning. For instance Racine
in Iphigénie (verse 2) speaks of "Patrocle et quelques chefs, qui marchent à la suite de mes Thessal-
iens vous amènent l'élite."[2] In English we find the
term for the first time in Byron's Don Juan, "at
once the 'lie' and the elite of crowds."[3] Gradually,
the emphasis of the term changed from choice to
eminence.

In sociology, Pareto was one of the first to coin the term "élite" in his <u>Trattato di Sociologia Generale</u> (translated into English as <u>The Mind and Society</u>). For Pareto, however, "élite" and "class" were, practically speaking, synonymous, as is shown by the following statements:

> Let us suppose that, in every branch of human activity, each individual is allotted an index number, corresponding to his abilities, in much the same way as marks are given in examinations on the different subjects taught in schools.

> Let us then take a class of people who have the highest indices, in the branch of activity with which they are concerned, and give <u>that class the name of élite</u>. [my underlining.][4]

To define, however, exactly who belongs to the class of élite is easier said than done. Pareto realized this himself when he remarked:

> In reality, there is no examination by which each individual can be assigned his place in these different classes of society. Instead, other methods are used; certain labels are applied, taking--more or less satisfactorily--the place of examinations.[5]

In fact, therefore, his method of selection is that of the traditional social classification.

THE NOTIONS OF SUPERIORITY, PRESTIGE AND IMITATION

If Pareto, in his time, was still rather free to take a certain class with certain qualifications and put on them the stamp of "élite," today it is more difficult to make such an arbitrary choice. To define the term "élite" as used in the social sciences, it is useful to examine certain notions which are generally implied when speaking of an élite.

In the first place, it is hardly necessary to
remark that "élite" does not apply to only one or two
people, but always to a plurality, a collectivity of
some kind, within society. Secondly, it is generally accepted that such a collectivity stands out in
society, has certain qualifications or skills which
give it a certain superiority; "high status" is the
term generally used. This leads us to the question:
do all people who share the same high status--be-
cause of wealth, social background, etc.--belong to
the same élite? If we would follow Pareto, the
answer would be yes, and a certain class of people
with superior qualifications could be termed "élite."

There is, however, another line of thought,
which sees in the élite a group which is properly organized, which has some degree of exclusiveness, and
of corporateness. This has been expressed in the
following way by Nadel:

> They must form a more or less self-conscious
> unit within society, with its particular en-
> titlements, duties and rules of conduct in
> general. Above all, the pre-eminent posi-
> tion must be regarded, by the members of
> the élite as well as the rest of society,
> as belonging to the former, not fortuitous-
> ly because of some possession, experience
> or interest they happen to share, but by
> right--by a corporate right which is not
> within the reach of everyone.[6]

Thirdly, the notion of superiority is always
linked with that of "élite." Kolabinska states: "The
outstanding idea in the term élite is superiority."[7]

Nadel states that the élite is intended to refer
to an objective empirical fact, namely: "The existence in many, perhaps most societies of a stratum
of the population which, for whatever reason, can
claim a position of superiority, and hence a corresponding measure of influence over the fate of the
community."[8]

C. Easton Rothwell puts it this way: "The

concept of élite is classificatory and descriptive,
designating the holders of high positions in a given
society."[9]

Closely linked with the notion of superiority
on the part of the élite is that of deference on the
part of the non-élite towards the former. Now, the
term "deference" is generally used to describe a
situation whereby respect is paid to someone or some
group, because of superior qualities--skills, knowledge, virtues, possessions--which are generally
recognized and the possession of which is generally
sought after as a benefit. It is, however, essential that deference should not be paid to an élite
for one particular quality, whether this is their
superior knowledge or their wealth, but that their
superiority is more widely generalized and that they
are respected for the other qualities and even, in
an ideal situation, for their general pattern of
living.

It is only in such a situation that an élite
can exert its superiority in a true sense, because
it can set an ideal pattern of life which society
regards as an example to be followed. This last
point is, again, essential. To exercise an influence, the qualities of an élite must be, to a certain extent, imitable. If this is not the case, the
élite could be equated with any other group which
has superior qualities or power, and which, therefore, always exercises some direct command over
others. This, in my opinion, would be a weakening
of the true concept of élite. Nadel puts it this
way:

> The élite influences the conduct of others
> by merely being what it is, a body judged
> to be superior in numerous ways. It is
> looked up to and imitated, because it is
> credited with important gifts and desir-
> able attributes. Thus, the élite, by its
> very manner of acting and thinking, sets the
> standard for the whole society, its influence
> or power being that of a model which is ac-
> cepted and considered worth following.[10]

THE POLITICAL ELITE, THE INTELLECTUALS,
THE MIDDLE CLASS

It is the notion of superiority that in many
cases leads to the identification of the term "élite"
with one particular élite, which is superior in the
political sense, that is, the governing élite.
Pareto had already made a division between "a governing élite, comprising individuals who directly or
indirectly play some considerable part in the government, and a non-governing élite, comprising the
rest."[11]

In the Hoover Institute Studies, dealing with
"a comparative study of élites," we also note that,
in fact, consideration is confined to the political
élite--the governing classes--as is shown by the
monographs which have appeared so far: The Politbureau; the Nazi Elite; the German Executive; the
Kuomintang and Chinese Communist Elites. The identification of the political leadership group with
the élite is particularly pertinent in the case of
the developing countries which have recently acceded
to independence. This is understandable for the following reasons:

(a) the striving for independence becomes the
    central idea for the people of the country
    and the leaders who give political expres-
    sion to this striving for independence are
    awarded with "high status";

(b) the new political élite, after independence,
    claims special solidarity acceptance because
    of its leadership in the struggle for liber-
    ation, and it tends to widen its leadership
    from the political to the economic and social
    fields. It tries "to direct all the social
    developments of the country, especially the
    raising of the standard of living and the
    development of new occupations and the mobil-
    ity within them."[12]

It is therefore to this political élite that we
shall refer in our study when using the term.

One qualification which in all societies has received recognition is that of education. It is for
that reason that very often the term "élite" has been
given to the intellectual class of society. Education of necessity gives authority and power to the
holder, and brings in its wake deference from the
uneducated. This is more clearly the case in those
places where education is still the privilege of the
relatively few. History abounds in examples of this.
The clergy in pre-reformation times certainly constituted the educated élite in European society, and
its superiority was not restricted to its religious
function, but can be attributed just as much to its
cultural influence, the fruit of its educational
position. Geiger, in his book <u>Aufgaben und Stellung
der Intelligenz in der Gesellschaft</u> gives a series
of other examples.[13]

He points to the cultural influence of the intelligentsia which was grouped around the Italian
courts, during the period of the "Rinascimento" and
which introduced the cultural wave, termed the "Re-
naissance." He also points to the influence of the
German universities and Patrician class, with their
emphasis on a rationalistic attitude of mind, thereby serving as pioneers for the Baroque period with
its new philosophies of a Spinoza, a Descartes and a
Leibnitz. The intelligentsia as an élite group has
given a new orientation to society by developing in
particular the notions of rationalism and the sovereign state.

Also in this new period the intelligentsia, according to Geiger, played the first fiddle:

> Die Politische Aufklärung der Barock ist
> somit aristocratisch und institutionell
> in der Sinne, das nur eine schmale Elite,
> die Intelligenz und durch sie der Furst,
> mit seinem Beamtenstab der Staatsweisheit
> teilhaftig ist.[14]

In our day, we note that in France the term
"elite" is, practically speaking, used solely to refer
to the intellectual élite. This is probably due to

the fact that since the revolution of 1789, no particular group, military, clergy or parliamentarians,
has (except the intellectuals) ever managed to obtain a truly national prestige.

In our modern pluralistic society, it is much
more difficult to consider the intelligentsia as one
élite group. The most one can say is that the intellectual element among the different élite groups existing in our society is growing rapidly. Lasswell
goes so far as to suggest in a bold hypothesis that
"the most significant fact of our time is the rise of
the intellectual, whose capital is knowledge."[15]

It is clearly noticeable, for instance, among
the political élites. Whether one can speak here of
a sudden rise, or of a phenomenon which is slowly
rising, but which has existed in many countries for
a long time, is another question. Maxwell E. Knight,
in his study on the German executive from 1890-1933,
came to the conclusion that, under the Monarch 59.2%,
under the Weimar republic 70.4%, and under the Hitler
regime 75.8% of the Cabinet members had been at a
university or a technical college.[16] If one takes
into account that, for instance, the years before
the Second World War, with the highest university
enrolment being reached in 1931, had less than 2.5%
of the population between 18 and 21 years of age in-
clusive in the universities, we must recognize that
the intellectual element has, for the last 70 years,
played a dominant role in the German political élite.

Even more interesting in the light of Lasswell's
hypothesis is the rising number with a university
education among the business élite. Reinhard Bendix
and Frank W. Hawton discovered for the United States
that if, in the period from 1801 to 1830, 16% had
been at college, of whom 8% had graduated, for the
period 1891 to 1930, the figures were 57% and 39%
respectively.[17]

But even if this tendency were to continue so
that, in future, an academic degree might become a
prerequisite for entering an élite group, it still
will not be possible to speak of the intelligentsia

as the élite of modern society. They lack the sense
of exclusiveness of corporation which we defined
above as the prerequisite of an élite. The higher
the number of university trained people will ascend,
the more also Boll's statement will hold true, that
"en aucun cas, les diplômes ne peuvent conférer un
privilège exclusif, notamment en ce qui concerne la
sélection des élites."[18]

        Nevertheless, in modern times, sociologists
have tried to define the specific role which the intelligentsia could play as an élite. For instance,
Karl Mannheim in his book Ideologie und Utopia exam-
ines the role which the intelligentsia could play in
our pluralistic society, in which there is a contin-
uous conflict between the classes. He sees the importance of the intelligentsia in the fact that they
are socially an independent group--sozial frei-
schwebend--that is to say, a group which is not bound
up with a particular social class--aristocratic,
labor, peasant, middle class. It is, therefore,
this group which should best be able, after a critical analysis of the different class ideologies, to
come forward with a synthesis which would take in
the best of everything and therefore, would be the
best for society. Raymond Aron in his L'Opium des
Intellectuels has clearly exposed how uncritical and
full of prejudice an intellectual group can be.
Mannheim's concept, therefore, remains an Utopia, unless it is applied to that part of the intelligentsia
which is actively engaged in the working out of a
three, five or seven-year plan for a certain country.
In that case, however, the results in those countries
which have the longest experience of this kind of
state planning, i.e., the communist countries, show
so far that their planning does not take into account
the different class ideologies, but is based on a
particular one. Milovan Djilas has shown this with
forceful clearness.[19]

        Although in our modern society, therefore, the
intelligentsia cannot any longer be considered as
one élite group in our definition of "élite," our
study will show that the most important element of
the political élite in the developing countries has

been made up of those who could be called the intellectuals of their country. This is not surprising
considering the fact that, given the high rate of
illiteracy, the few with education are practically
predestined to be looked upon as the future leaders.

Finally, there is little doubt that, in Europe,
the middle class has for a long time taken over the
position of the clergy and nobility as the class
from which the new élite has come forward. The rise
of the middle class in Europe as an élite group is
earmarked by the rise of the cities as important industrial or commercial centers. However, it took
some time before the middle class became the holders
of political power. In Great Britain, the middle
class was enfranchised in 1832, but did not penetrate the political élite until after the second
Reform Act of 1867. In France, a revolution was
needed to take the power away from the aristocracy.

In the developing countries, we see a similar
process. If, originally, political power rested in
the hands of the indigenous aristocracy, while a
middle class did not exist, the impact of the West
is causing changes to take place. It is in the cities with the growing urbanization resulting from
western influences that a middle class is slowly
growing up. It is this group, the most westernized
in its outlook, which is sending its sons to western
schools; and it is from this group that the new
ideas of nationalism and political independence have
sprung.

The new élite in developing countries, as we
will endeavor to explain, is made up of the political leaders who, to a large extent, have come forward
from the middle class and who have a relatively high
degree of education.

ELITE AND MOBILITY

The great value of a study of the élite lies in
the role this group can and does play in a society
undergoing change. It is in such a society that

rival élite groups come into conflict. We have seen,
for instance, cases where the aristocratic élite was
slowly pushed aside by a new élite whose claims to
superiority were based on wealth. Such a new emerg-
ing group can, of course, only be considered an
élite when it manages to prove its superiority by
setting new standards which are accepted by the
others.

This dynamic character of the élite, reflected
in the processes by which it emerges or changes, has
been given a good deal of attention from social
scientists. Pareto labelled this process "the circulation of élites."

Changes in the recruitment of an élite are also
dealt with by Karl Mannheim. In his Mensch und
Gesellschaft im Zeitalter des Umbaus he points out
the dangers in the recruitment of an élite in a liberal society. He sees a danger not only in a too
rapid growth in the numbers of the élite in a certain society with, as a consequence, the fact that
none of them can become the standard-bearer for the
whole of society, but he also points out that the
élite lost its exclusiveness, which he believes
necessary to enable it to be effective.

> Geht ein bestimmtes Mindestmass an Exclu-
> sivität verloren, so kann es zur zielbewus-
> ten Ausformung eines Geschmacks, eines
> führenden Stilprinzips nicht mehr kommen.[20]

On the other hand, Mannheim agrees that, for
the continuity of an élite, it is essential to have
a certain openness in recruitment.

> Deshalb ist eine relative Offenheit dieser
> Elite Gruppen neben der soeben besprochenen
> Exclusivität gleichfalls Vorbedingung echter
> Kulturlebendigkeit.[21]

Is there, therefore, a problem in regard to the
recruitment and emergence of an élite which can be
solved to a certain extent by studying the principles of selection effective in society, and analyzing

the social origins of those who form the élite in a
given time? Much more difficult is the problem of
the change of orientation of the élite.

Here we find the problem: does the cultural
outlook of society and its human ideals change because of a change in the élite or the other way
around?

There is much talk about the new technico-
scientific era in which we are living. Has this
change been brought about by the new élite of scientists or technicians, or is this latter group rising
in status and becoming an élite because of the increasing technicality of our times? Everybody will
agree that an answer is not easily given if, indeed,
it can be given at all in our pluralistic society.

A similar question can be asked with regard to
the effect western technical civilization has had on
the growth of a new élite in the developing countries,
and what role this élite is playing in changing the
cultural pattern of those countries. We hope to give
an analysis of this in the following chapters.

                THE NOTION OF DEVELOPING COUNTRIES

Before entering into the field of the élite in
developing countries, it is necessary to make clear
what we understand by the term "developing countries."
The term refers directly to countries where, through
socio-economic processes, one tries to raise the
standard of living of the people, which is considered by international standards as being below an
acceptable minimum.

A second question which immediately rises is:
what do we understand by the term "standard of living of a people"? At a meeting of experts organized
by the United Nations in 1953, the following definition was agreed on:

The idea of a standard of living must be applied to the needs and desires of all categories.

It goes without saying that this idea must
incorporate the evaluation of the well-
being, which constitutes a generally admitted need of man; it should also include
the connected material elements, as in the
case of consumption. The committee nevertheless emphasized that we should also take
into account certain non-material factors,
such as the degree to which the people realize their cultural needs, and the need for
instruction, how far they appreciate art
and music and make use of its political
rights, which can be of great significance
in the interpretation and comparison of different standards of living.[22]

What is important in this definition is that it
refers not only to economical factors such as consumption, but takes into consideration socio-cultural
factors such as the need for instruction, the use of
political rights and the appreciation of art and
music.

What the definition does not bring out, and
which is equally important, is the psychological factor. It is very doubtful whether the Neanderthal man
had any idea about, or interest in his standard of
living. Modern man has, and increasingly so, and it
is this awareness of the existence of such a standard, and its comparison to that of his neighbors,
which makes him realize that his own is either high
or low. This realization of having too low a standard of living in the developing countries has first
been arrived at by the new élite of those countries
who, among other things, have used this notion most
effectively in their striving for independence, as
well as in their claims for foreign aid, as we will
see later on.

The terms "standard of living" as well as "developing country" are comparative notions and therefore it has become of great importance to work out a
system based on the notion of the standard of living
which allows us to make a distinction between phases
of development in different countries.

The experts of the United Nations have tackled
this problem, and have come up with the following
system of classification based on four indices, two
of an economical character (per capita national income and fuel consumption in kilograms of coal equivalent per head), and two of a social character (the
infant mortality rate and the rate of increase in
school enrolment). For each set of indices, six
categories have been worked out, which have a certain correlation with each other. The result has
been the following:[23]

	A. National Income Per Capita	B. Fuel consumption per head in kgs. of coal equivalent	C. Infant Mortality Rate	D. Rate of Increase in school enrolment
I.	$1,000 upwards	3,150 upwards	less than 28	more than 92
II.	$575 to $1,000	1,675 to 3,150	28 to 44	81 to 92
III.	$350 to $575	800 to 1,675	44 to 65	69 to 81
IV.	$200 to $350	350 to 800	65 to 100	54 to 69
V.	$100 to $200	120 to 350	100 to 160	38 to 54
VI.	less than $100	less than 120	more than 160	less than 38

Developed (I, II, III); Developing (IV, V, VI)

If we now apply this scheme to the different
countries in the world, at least those where--with
regard to our four indices--reliable statistical
material exists (which unfortunately excludes the
greater part of Africa)--we come to the following
categories:

In Category I, that of the most developed countries, we only find two countries, which, under each

of the four headings, fall into this category: the
United States and Australia. Canada, Great Britain
and New Zealand are close runners-up, with three out
of the four indices. At the other end of the scale,
in Category VI, we find the least-developed countries.
Here notably we find the Asian countries such as Pakistan, Burma and Indonesia, with all four indices in
Category VI, and India and Thailand with three out
of four. Although not mentioned in the United Nations report, because of the lack of reliable statistical material, there is little doubt that most of
the countries in so-called "black Africa" will also
fall into this category.

Generally speaking, and according to the United
Nations experts who estimate that the dividing line
between what we can call developed countries and developing countries lies between Category III and
Category IV, we may conclude the following. The
countries of North America and Europe, with the exception of Greece, Spain, Bulgaria, Yugoslavia and
Albania, can be considered developed. On the other
hand, practically the whole of Asia, with the exception of Israel (three indices in the developed categories) and Japan (two in the developed categories),
and the whole of Latin America, with the exception
of Venezuela, Argentina, Puerto Rico and Trinidad
(three indices in the developed categories), and Cuba
(two in the developed categories) can be considered
as developing countries.

With regard to Africa, with the exception of
South Africa (two indices in the developed categories and one, infant mortality, unknown) it can be
considered as falling entirely into the categories
of developing countries, with--probably--"black
Africa" mostly in the lowest Category VI, and North
Africa in IV and V.

In making such a classification, there is one
point which we should not lose sight of. The term
"developing country" does not imply a judgment on the
cultural standing of that country. If the United
States ranks in the highest category and Indonesia
in the lowest, this does not mean that the American

cultural pattern rests at a higher level than the
Indonesian. If India and Dahomey fall, in our system, into the same category, this again does not
mean that their cultural pattern is on the same plane.
One of the greatest mistakes the West continues to
make is to judge a culture solely by its material
and technical aspects and, as the West still has a
lead in these, to believe that the economically less-
developed areas of the world are at the same time
culturally backward.

THE CHARACTER OF, CHANGE IN, AND
STRIFE AMONG THE ELITE GROUPS

There is a general pattern regarding the character and the change among the élite, which holds true
for nearly all developing countries which have
passed through colonial rule.

In most Asian countries, before the arrival of
the European colonial powers, two classes could be
distinguished in society: the great mass of rural
population and a small group of aristocracy, which
was often concentrated in the so-called cities and
which, in most cases, also represented a true élite
in the sense that it was an exclusive group with a
superiority based both on descent or caste and on
cultural qualifications, among which the religious
factor played an important role. In Africa, the
situation was similar in the sense that the aristocracy, in general, was formed by the tribal chiefs
and their village Councils. Although kinship relations differ greatly among different tribes, and the
composition of the ruling group changed accordingly--
from forms wherein the chieftancy was hereditary, to
those where kin-right and election were combined,
and to those where democratic forms of electing the
wisest and strongest were the pattern--nevertheless,
the Chief and Council formed a true élite, whereby
the deference paid to them was singularly reinforced
by the fact that, in most cases, the Chief held a
religious position, in the sense that he was to a certain degree representative of the dead ancestors.

It was this élite in primitive society which
was the guardian of ancient traditions and customs,
and the standard-bearer of the cultural pattern of
society. Its prestige was singularly enhanced by
the fact that in most cases it was entrusted with religious functions and had obtained a kind of sacro-
sanct standing. It was--and it is important to
underline this--a unified élite in the sense that it
combined religious, cultural, economic and political
values in one group, similar to what we have seen
with the aristocracy in Great Britain in the 17th
and 18th centuries. That its authority was questioned by no one can be shown by the fact that the
predecessors of European colonization, embodied in
the big trading companies such as the British East
Indian, British West African or the Dutch East India
Company, hastened to conclude treaties with it, so
as to ensure an undisturbed and respected trade.

However, with the development of a colonial policy, we see a growing influx of Europeans into those
areas. After the merchants and soldiers came the
European missionaries and civil servants, and later,
the white trader, plantation manager and settler.

Seen from a European point of view, these
groups, with the possible exception of the missionaries, could hardly be considered an élite, unless
it was an élite of adventurers. In Europe, they belonged to different social classes; in the colonies,
however, they became a new class--that of the "white"
man. Although not always the best representatives
of European civilization, they became slowly but
surely--and automatically--the standard-bearers of
this civilization in the colonial countries.

In the beginning, from an Asian or African
point of view, these "white" men could not be considered as an élite, since they had--with the exception
again of the missionaries--little contact with the
indigenous masses, and enjoyed only the superiority
which is based on a "gun-in-hand" approach. Slowly,
however, with the increase in numbers and with the
change in colonial policies, demonstrated, for instance, by the British "White Man's Burden," and the

Dutch "Ethical" policy, which gave greater attention
to the welfare of the countries, they became an
élite whose prestige grew increasingly and whose
standards, in every walk of life, became the ideal
for a growing number of Asians and Africans. Since
the twentieth century--and more particularly after
the First World War--the European element in those
countries can be considered as a group which increasingly fulfilled the function of an élite, as we defined this function at the beginning of this chapter.

The need to establish their colonial power firm-
ly forced the European nations rather early in their
colonial history to erect and develop an administrative apparatus which could work above or alongside
the old indigenous aristocratic élite. This forced
them to train young Asians or Africans as lower-
grade civil servants, clerks, policemen, etc., as
auxiliaries to keep the colonial administrative and
commercial system going.

Apart from the colonial administration, in many
countries the European missionaries--Catholic and
Protestant--right from the beginning consecrated a
good deal of their effort to education. In this way,
a beginning was made in the creation of a new
western-educated, indigenous élite.

This tendency was further reinforced when, in
Europe, the realization grew that colonial people
were not only a benefit to, but also a responsibility of, the so-called Mother country. Faidherbe's
declaration of 1860 gives a good indication of these
tendencies.

> Everyone can reach the same goal when he
> satisfies the conditions required of all
> of you alike, conditions which we are today
> putting within your reach. You see young
> men from the Christian families of St. Louis,
> who, after a good start in the mission
> schools, go and continue their studies in a
> secondary school in France, came back fit
> for filling the highest positions in the
> colony. That road is open to you all alike.

> We are ready to facilitate access to the
> liberal professions of every child who
> shows exceptional talent at school.[24]

Thus we have seen the creation of a new élite, educated according to a western pattern and, in many cases, in schools and universities in Western Europe, and which has become the leading force for independence.

In our study, therefore, we will have to deal with the above-mentioned three élite groups--the old aristocratic élite, the European élite and, specifically, the new western-educated élite.

The three groups still exist in most developing countries and in most of them we see growing strife between the three groups, strife between the old aristocracy and the new educated élite on the one hand, strife between the educated élite and the European élite on the other. Generally speaking, one can say that the new élite has managed to achieve political power after independence, and is in conflict with the old aristocratic élite to gain the social prestige of the latter, while the aristocracy wants to cling to the political power it possessed in former days.

The strife between the European élite and the new élite is essentially one of strife for political power. After independence, this has fallen into the hands of the latter group, but economic power has still remained, to a great extent, with the European groups, which might cause further conflict as the case of Indonesia shows.

There is one group which plays an important part in the life of the developing countries, and has in many cases all the aspects of a commercial élite. We refer here to the Chinese minorities in many Asian countries, and to the Indian, Syrian and Lebanese minorities in Africa. We will not deal with them, however, in this study as this would take us too far, and their role and attitudes are similar to those of the European commercial elements.

In our study we hope to pay particular attention to the third of the three élite groups mentioned above--that of the new educated élite. We
will, using the examples of Indonesia and Ghana,
study in particular the questions of recruitment of
this élite, the methods whereby it has been, or
still is, trained, and the concepts it has as to its
role in these countries. With regard to the last,
we will give particular thought to the attitude of
the new élite towards government, an attitude derived from concepts greatly influenced by the fact
that this élite was developed with the aid of and in
juxtaposition to the European élite.

A particular phenomenon which we note in the developing countries is the rise to power of the "mass"
or "heroic leader." Generally one of the leaders in
the struggle for independence, gifted with "charismatic" qualities, the heroic leader has managed to
obtain a general popularity and a mass following
which has enabled him to become a kind of Father of
the "Vaterland." It is the heroic leader who more
than any other factor is responsible for a new trend
in government in those countries of late, away from
democracy towards dictatorship.

THE FIELD OF STUDY--INDONESIA AND GHANA

Having previously defined our notion of developing countries, we will restrict ourselves in our
further studies to those which are on the lowest
step of the developing ladder, those of Category VI,
as we might expect that in those countries with a
relatively simple social and economical structure,
it will be easier to follow the process of the emergence and role of the élite.

As has been noted above, this restricts our
field of research to a number of countries in Asia
and in "black Africa." This has another advantage
as it is in those regions of the world that the decolonization process has taken, or still is taking
place. It is, therefore, in those areas that it
will be best to study the result of the impact of

European civilization on the indigenous socio-
economic and cultural patterns, as it shows itself
in the emergence of the new élite groups.

The field of research, taking in a good part of
Asia and Africa, and having to consider the influence
of European civilization as manifested by English,
French and Dutch colonial policies in Asia, and
English, French, Belgian, Portuguese and Spanish policies in Africa, is still too vast for the scope of
our study. We will therefore restrict ourselves in
the following chapters to an analysis of the role
and the emergence of the new élite in two countries,
Indonesia and Ghana.

We have chosen these two countries as they both
belong to Category VI, that is, to the category of
least-developed countries, and because they each represent to a certain degree a different continent,
and therefore have had considerable different backgrounds, particularly from a cultural point of view.
In addition, they have undergone different experiences of colonial power: for Indonesia, the Dutch,
with their system of indirect rule; for Ghana, the
British, also with a system of indirect rule but of
a different character.

Although the British and Dutch concepts of colonization were not identical, as will be shown, the
difference was not so great as would have been the
case if we compared British and Portuguese colonization, which would make it difficult to draw any com-
parisons with regard to the emergence and character
of the new élite. In addition, we have chosen a
country rich in resources and manpower, in the case
of Indonesia, which was colonized by a small European country, to compare with a relatively small
country, possibly rich in resources, but relatively
poor in population density--Ghana--which was colonized by the world power of the time, Great Britain.
Finally, we have chosen two different examples of
processes of decolonization--Indonesia, through
strife and with effective interference from the United Nations; Ghana, through peaceful means--differ-
ent processes which have had a great influence on

the attitude and role of the new élite, as will be
shown. Moreover, both countries were the first in
their respective continents to obtain independence
after the Second World War; Indonesia in 1945, Ghana
in 1957--and thus in both cases there is a chance to
see what role the élite has played after independence.
For Indonesia we will follow the development until
1958, for Ghana until 1960.

We hope through our study of the emergence and
role of the new élite to shed some more light on the
intricate social and political processes which are
taking place in those countries, the outcome of
which in our modern times concerns us all.

Footnotes to Chapter 1

1. For an analysis of the élite concept see:
Th. Geiger, Aufgaben und Stellung der Intelligenz in
der Gesellschaft (Stuttgart: Enke, 1949); Interna-
tional Social Service Bulletin (Paris), VIII, No. 3,
1956; Gaetano Mosca, The Ruling Class (New York:
McGraw-Hill, 1939); Vilfredo Pareto, The Mind and
Society, ed. Arthur Livingston, Vols. 1-4 (New York:
Jonathan Cape, 1935).

2. E. Littre, Dictionnaire de l'Académie. La
Langue Francaise (Paris: Hachette, 1873).

3. J. Murray, A New English Dictionary, Vol. III
(Oxford: Clarendon Press, 1897).

4. Pareto, op. cit., p. 9 1297/1298.

5. S. F. Nadel, "The Concept of Social Elites,"
International Social Service Bulletin, VIII, No. 3
(1956), 415.

6. Maria Kolabinska,"La Circulation des Elites
en France. Etude Historique depuis la fin du XIe
siècle jusqu'à la Grande Révolution," thesis, Lau-
sanne, 1912.

7. Nadel, op. cit., p. 413.

8. Harold Laswell, Easton Rothwell, and Daniel
Lerner, The Comparative Study of Elites: An Intro-
duction and Bibliography (Hoover Institute Studies;
Stanford, Calif.: Stanford University Press, 1952),p.2.

9. Nadel, op. cit., p. 417.

10. Pareto, op. cit., p. 1423.

11. S. N. Eisenstadt, "Changes in Patterns of
Stratification Attendant on Attainment of Political
Independence," Transactions of 3rd World Congress of
Sociology (London, 1956), III and IV, 36.

12. Geiger uses the term "intelligentsia" in
such a way that it comprises not only the academical-
ly educated group, be it A or B faculties, but also
the artist. He states himself: "Der Name 'Intelligenz' will deutlich in erster Linie auf die wissen-
schaftlich und technisch Schaffenden ab, umgreift
aber in erweidertem Sinn auch die schönen Künste.
Der rationale Geist gibt so der ganzen Schicht der
Geistig Schöpferischen den Namen. Das entspricht
seiner Vorherrschaft in der Kultur der Neuzeit."
Op. cit., p. 37.

13. Ibid., p. 54.

14. Lasswell, et al., op. cit., p. 18.

15. Maxwell E. Knight, The German Executive 1890-
1933 (Stanford, Calif.: Stanford University Press,
1952), p. 36.

16. Reinard Bendix and Frank W. Hawton, "Social
Mobility and the American Business Elite," British
Journal of Sociology, No. 9 (1959), p. 367.

17. Marcel and André Boll, L'Elite de demain
(Paris: Calmann-Lévy, 1948), p. 52.

18. Milovan Djilas, La Nouvelle Classe dirigeante
(Paris: Plon, 1957).

19. Karl Mannheim, <u>Mensch und Gesellschaft im</u> <u>Zeitalter des Umbaus</u> (Leiden: Sythof, 1953), p. 65.

20. <u>Ibid</u>., p. 67.

21. United Nations, Report on <u>The Definition</u> <u>and Evaluation of Standards of Living</u>, E/CN 3/179 - E/CN 5/299, p. 5.

22. United Nations, Report on <u>The Social Situa-</u> <u>tion of the World</u>, E/CN 5/346, pp. 144-145.

23. Quoted from P. Mercier, "Evaluation of Senegalese Elites," <u>International Social Science</u> <u>Bulletin</u>, VIII, No. 3 (1956), 444.

PART II

THE EMERGENCE OF THE ELITE

CHAPTER **2** THE COLONIAL ERA:
INDONESIA

The two countries we intend to study in particular show marked differences with regard to their
geographic, demographic and economic potentialities,
as well as with regard to their historical and cultural backgrounds. A certain comparison is only possible when they both enter that phase of history
which can be termed the "colonial era." The influence of the European colonial powers, however different their method of colonization may have been, has
introduced a series of processes, as far as the emergence of new élite groups is concerned, which have
followed the same pattern. One should, however, not
underestimate the influence of cultural and religious
traditions on the orientation of the élite groups, an
influence which has not subsided with the introduction of western ideas and cultural patterns.

In this and the following chapter, therefore,
we will briefly outline the history of both countries
up to the beginning of the twentieth century. Although, unfortunately, not much material exists except from Dutch sources, we have tried to sketch the
development of the indigenous Indonesian society up
until 1500.

Further, we hope to gain an historical insight
into the process of colonization. While the pre-
colonial era was signified by the operations of the
trading companies, colonial policies were worked out
only at the end of the eighteenth century. We have
dwelt at some length on the operation of the Dutch
East India Company, as we think that Dutch historians have tended to exaggerate the role it has played
in Indonesia, especially during the first century of
its operations. The importance of the company for

our study lies in that it has introduced the system
of indirect rule of government which has been of
great importance for the development of the new
élite.

   In the nineteenth century, we note everywhere a
change in colonial policies under the influence of
the new social philosophies which held sway in Europe. The results of those policies led to the
social changes in colonial societies which are
studied in this chapter.

                 INDONESIA'S HISTORY UP UNTIL 1500

   Geographically speaking, Indonesia forms the
largest group of islands in the world (1,491,562 Km^2).
With the Philippine Islands it forms the Malay Archipelago. This Archipelago is divided between two regions: the Asiatic and the Australian, and this is
evident in various branches of its geography--zoolog-
ical, botanical and anthropological. The equator
passes through the middle of the Archipelago cutting
the big islands of Sumatra, Kalimantan (Borneo),
Sulawesi (Celebes) and Halmaheira, and most of the
islands belong to the great equatorial forest belt.
In the later part of the secondary epoch there was
in all likelihood a land connection between Asia and
Australia.

   Indonesia's[1] history is that of an anthropological and cultural melting-pot. Populated from earliest known times, as shown by Dubois' findings of the
"pithecanthropus erectus," dated in the Paleolithi-
cal period, and the remnants of a neolithicum found
on all the main islands, it has received various
population waves coming from the Asian continent.

   Its possession of articles in great demand in
India and the Chinese and Roman Empires--spices,
silks, precious stones, gold and ivory--caused early
contact through trade with the outside world. Such
trade was not restricted to material goods, and the
Indonesian population has in the course of history
been influenced by a great number of religious and

cultural ideas.   There was Brahmanism and Buddhism
of the Mahayana type, imported from India between
the fifth and fifteenth centuries.   Both religions
blended into one--"syncretism"--and developed, notably in Java, a Hindu-Javanese society of an original
character with, as the highest deity, Ciwa-Buddha.
The Hindu influence was not restricted to religious
concepts.   The organization of the state and jurisprudence were greatly influenced by Hindu concepts.
Linguistically speaking, a great many Sanskrit words
were introduced and in the so-called "old Javanese"
language, we note, for instance, that for objects of
everyday life Javanese expressions are used, but for
notions dealing with religious concepts, governmental organizations, etc., Sanskrit words are employed.[2]

    The metric system, as well as the use of coins,
are the results of the Hindu period.   Architecture
also underwent strong Hindu influence, as can be
seen by the tjandis[3] of Mendoet, Ngawen and Borobudoer,
while the popular Wajang[4] stories show many traces of
Sanskrit literature.

    During this period we note for the first time
the emergence of some important kingdoms, such as
the Kingdom of Criwidjaya (Palembang), in the
seventh century and especially that of Majapahit in
Java in the thirteenth and fourteenth centuries.[5]

    Was Hindu culture brought to Indonesia because
of the trade relations existing between that country
and India?   A great deal of speculation took place.
On the one hand we find viewpoints such as that of
Mookerji who believes there was a Hindu empire which
from the fourth century until the Muslim invasion
was spread over India and parts of Indonesia.   He believes in a kind of colonization process because of
ethnic and/or class groups with political motives.
On the other hand, a great number of Dutch historians, like Krom and Berg, believe that the Hindu civilization is the result of a pacific penetration of
traders who settled for long periods or permanently
in Indonesia, mixed with the population, and later
induced other trading groups to come to that country.
It seems dangerous to me, however, to give too much

weight to the trader as disseminator of such a refined culture as the Hindu one. Van Leur rightly
points out that trade in those days was carried on
by a mixture of people and that trade between India
and Indonesia was not necessarily in Indian hands:
"The majority of the traders in the peddling trade
belonged to the lower social groups, and foreigners
from all sorts of countries were intermingled with
them."[6] This is hardly a group who would introduce
the refined ritual, the magic establishment of the
ruler's ancestry, and the classical mythological
genealogy of the ruling house, the intricacies of
the offering, etc., so characteristic of the Indian
culture which we find in Indonesia.

Moreover, although from earliest days, the various trading nations had their own trading stations
in the main port cities, as later the western companies would have, traders had little or no contact
with the ruling house. It is therefore more logical
to assume that the introduction of the Hindu civilization came from the Indonesian ruling group, who, as
van Leur suggests, invited Brahman priests and Indian
court artificers to their Kratons.[7] This implies,
however, that already before the Hindu period a high
civilization must have existed, at least in Java.
The latest findings seem to confirm this. In the
neolithic age, stone agricultural instruments including pachuls[8] were known, which indicates already a
cultivation of rice on sawahs[9] with all the social
implications of water supply and distribution, fixed
seasons of harvest, etc. The Brahman priest then
brought to Indonesia the magic elements. Stapel mentions in this regard, the preaching of Goenawarman,
a Buddhist prince from Kashmir, as well as in Java
in the fifth century the reign of Cailendras who
probably came from abroad and through marriage managed to become the rulers of the Kingdom of Mataram.[10]

Moreover, it is known that Balapoetra, one of
the kings of Criwidjaya, founded a monastery near
Nalanda, on the Ganges river, for students from his
kingdom who went to study there.

It is certain that, from the fifth century

onwards, a new élite, the <u>prijaji</u>, which was Hindu
in cultural outlook, developed around the royal
<u>Kratons</u>, and strongly influenced the Indonesian com-
munity. Hinduism remained, however, restricted to
an élite and never became part and parcel of Indonesian <u>dessah</u> (village) life, as was to be the case
later on with Mohammedism. In the <u>dessah</u>, the Indonesian animist continued to live according to old
traditions, although the nearer he came to the
<u>Kraton</u>, the more he became influenced by Hindu con-
cepts. This new élite is somewhat similar to the
new élite we find in the Italian or German courts of
the later middle ages. Patronized by the kings, it
shone with the lustre of its artistic and cultural
achievements.

     The introduction of Islamism to Indonesia is,
in many ways, analogical to that of Hinduism. Again,
it was introduced from India, this time mainly by
the Gujarat traders. Marco Polo who, during his
trip to China in 1292, stayed in Northern Sumatra
for some time, mentions that the main port, Perlak,
was already a center of Islamic culture.

     An important role was played by Malaya, which
in the fourteenth century gradually assumed the
place of the former Criwidjaya empire. It became a
center for Islamic penetration into Indonesia. Its
traders and preachers spread via Palembang, Toelan
and Grisee, from Java, up to the Maluku islands.[11]

     When the kingdom of Majapahit fell to pieces be-
cause of internal strife in the sixteenth century,
it was the little state of Demak which took the lead,
later in its turn to be overpowered by the Muslim empire of Mataram. At about the same time, the kingdom of Bantam arose in Western Java. Rather quickly,
Islamism spread over the whole of Indonesia, with
the exception of Bali, which until today has managed
to keep its Hindu-Javanese cultural pattern.

     The direct participation of the trader in the
spreading of Islam has certainly been much greater
than in the time of the penetration of Hinduism.
Islam, in contrast with Hinduism, is a much more

expansive missionary religion in which all the faithful can and have the duty to participate. The Muslim
trader, as we see still today in Africa, is therefore,
a natural missionary.

Van Leur believes that political motives are
foremost in explaining the spread of Islam among the
Indonesian nobility.

> Commercial and other motives of Gujarati
> Moslems regarding the trade of the Javanese
> ports and the lords of the trade there, the
> Javanese patriciate, political motives of
> that patriciate regarding the international
> trade and the government of Majapahit--those
> two factors together brought about the Islami-
> zation of Indonesia.[12]

This might be true and it certainly was a big
factor later in the struggle against the Portuguese
and Dutch trading companies, but nevertheless the
political reasons for change must be found to a great
extent in the fact that Islam was penetrating the
masses, or had an appeal to them, and this made it
attractive for the aristocracy to follow suit and
thereby bind their followers closer to them. The
rapidity with which Islam spread throughout Indonesia can therefore partly be explained by its appeal for equality among all men, which brought it
into direct opposition with the Hindu concept of
caste. Islam, thereby, became right from the outset
more of a people's religion and often the royal
courts became converted later to strengthen the popular support, necessary in the growing struggle
against the new colonial powers.

While Hinduism exerted an enormous influence on
the cultural plane, as is shown through drama, architecture, dancing and literature, Islamism exerted a
strong influence on the social plane.

It is clear, therefore, that the European traders who came to Indonesia in the sixteenth century
found on most islands there a population of high cultural standards, and living according to a well-

ordered social system centered around the <u>dessah</u>.
It was an agricultural society--in Java based on the
irrigated rice-fields, the <u>sawah</u>, and outside Java
based on shifting agricultural plots, the <u>ladang</u>.
The head of the <u>dessah</u>--<u>Lurah</u>--and the elders, ran
the village and cultivation was, in general, com-
munal.

     Seen from a socio-economic point of view, the
village was a closed unit. Its chief purpose was to
produce for its own consumption. Nevertheless, especially in Java, it was certain that it also produced for the maintenance of the higher authorities,
or for export. The village passed these products
upwards in the form of tribute or rent. Such a system later made it easier for the trading companies
to obtain the products they wanted as they placed
themselves at the top of the hierarchical ladder.
The products--so to speak--moved only one more step
upwards.

     In the village there had appeared a new force
which had taken over the sacred functions formerly
performed by the headman. This was the Muslim priest
or the holy man (<u>Hadji</u>) who had been to Mecca. He
was in general responsible for education (teaching
the Koran).

     Along the coast we find a trading people with a
long tradition of contact with the outside world.
There was also a nobility which lived in the cities
and there were many of those city states, some of
which--like Mataram and Bantam--had managed to extend their sovereignty over large areas. For a long
time the nobility had been Hindu in cultural outlook
and was just shifting to Islam at the time of the
arrival of the white man--a process often hastened
by the coming of the European.

     This nobility was generally called <u>prijaji</u> in
Java. It formed only a small part of the Indonesian
population and was very self-conscious of its status,
which it managed to keep by following a rigid system
of social identification. It was this group who provided cohesion to Javanese society above the local

level, and supplied the political, intellectual, cultural and religious leaders. In other words, it fulfilled all the functions of an élite and we will
refer to it as such for the rest of this chapter.

THE PRE-COLONIAL ERA: THE TRADING COMPANIES

Authors dealing with the colonial policies of
the European powers often attempt to make a compre-
hensive examination of them. It is difficult to
undertake such studies as they must--in order to be
complete--take into account the large range of factors which have, in the past, determined the direction of these policies. The influence of the Treaty
of Tordesillas, the French Revolution, the abolition
of the slave trade, and the invention of the steam
engine are just as much a part of the colonial policies of the European powers as the depression of the
thirties or the manifestation of international interest in the future of colonies, as these latter found
expression, first in Geneva, and later in the organization of the United Nations.

We should not forget, however, that in the very
beginning of the colonial era, many European powers
had no policy. Colonialism was often the result of
the keen trading sense, the leaning towards discov-
ery or the missionary zeal of a few individuals.
This pre-colonial period is embodied in the activities of the early trading companies as the history
of those operating in Indonesia and Ghana will show.

A greater difficulty in dealing objectively
with this period stems from the fact that, in general,
Dutch historians judged it purely from a Dutch point
of view. Indonesia's life was, so to speak, observed
from the lookout on the mast of a Dutch ship or the
ramparts of a Dutch settlement. This leads to an
exaggeration of Dutch influence on Indonesian life
in the seventeenth and eighteenth centuries.

We should not forget that, when the Dutch arrived in Bantam, they formed just another new foreign
trade element. "There came such a multitude of

Javanese and other nations as Turks, Chinese, Ben-
gali, Arabs, Persians, Gujarati, and others, that
one could hardly move,"[13] one reads in the journal of
the first Dutch ship landing in Bantam. Asia in
that period was neither politically nor economically-
speaking inferior to Europe. The Asian ships, their
armaments, their way of trading, were all much the same
as those of the Portuguese, Spanish, Dutch or English.
If, nevertheless, the Dutch company managed to get
the upper hand in Indonesia, it must be attributed
to the fact that "the thorough organization of the
Dutch company constitutes an institution of a considerably higher development"--compared with the Portuguese or Asian traders--"with its completely carried
out separation of merchant officials and goods and
strongholds, its centralization of affairs, its
bureaucracy, for that time elaborate."[14]

     It was the Portuguese who, under the far-
sighted leadership and stimulus of Henry the Navigator, first found their way into Indonesia. In 1512,
their first ships arrived in the Maluku Islands, and
the Sultan of Tidore did not hesitate to offer them
a monopoly on cloves in exchange for political support, which was granted through the building of a
fort in 1521.

     In those days, the Dutch were content to obtain
tropical products in Lisbon in exchange for goods
brought from the Baltic ports, and they thus became
the distributors of tropical products in large areas
of Europe. However, when in 1585 Philip II suddenly
confiscated all Dutch ships in Portuguese and Spanish ports, the Dutch traders realized that it might
be more profitable to try to obtain the goods directly in the country of origin than to be dependent on
the whims of a Spanish sovereign.

     Thus, a company was formed by some merchants in
Amsterdam--the "Compagnie van Verre"--which sent
four ships to Indonesia in 1595, under the command
of Cornelis de Houtman. It took them fifteen months
to get there and another fourteen passed before
three of the ships returned, but the aim was achieved.
One result was that suddenly a number of new companies

were founded to get into the same market.[15]

Before 1601, more than fourteen fleets, making
a total of 65 ships, had left for Indonesia and the
Dutch did not hesitate to build trading centers in
different parts of the Archipelago as in Bantam,
Amboina and Ternate.

All these different companies worked without
any collaboration or coordination among each other;
on the contrary there was often open animosity, and
they tended to run each other into the ground.[16]

To remedy this situation, the great statesman
of Holland, Johan van Oldenbarneveld, proposed to
give a monopoly to one company in which all the
others would merge and, with the aid of his good
friend, Prince Maurits, he managed to convince the
"Staten-Generaal"[17] to grant a Charter, in 1602, to
the "Vereenigde Nederlandse Geoctroyeerde Oostin-
dische Compagnie," usually called the V.O.I.C. (the
Dutch East India Company), to carry out trade in all
countries East of the Cape of Good Hope up to the
Straits of Magellan. Even more important was that
Article 35 of this Charter gave the company a right
within the territory consigned to it to conclude contracts with the rulers of states or territories and
to build fortresses and other strongholds; furthermore, it could appoint governors, soldiers and judges.
Clearly, the mandate granted the company not only the
usual trading rights but conferred upon it the status
of a sovereign. This is also shown by the stipula-
tion in the Charter "to care for the promotion and
spreading of the true Christian religion."

The V.O.I.C.[18] had a lively career. In 1605,
it concluded its first contract with the ruler of
Hitoe (in N. Amboina). New trading stations were
founded in Grissee, Makassar, Djohar and Patani as
well as in India--Mazuli, Patnam, Petapoeli and
Suratbe--and in Japan--Firando. Nevertheless, those
were difficult years for the company. However, the
difficulties were overcome and by 1650 one could say
that the V.O.I.C., at least in theory if not in practice, had a monopoly over the whole of the Indonesian

archipelago, but this only for a few products like
cloves and nutmeg.[19]

What policy did the V.O.I.C. have towards the
Indonesian people and what influence did it have on
Indonesian society?

In considering this question, we must not forget that first and foremost the V.O.I.C. was a trading company. From its charter, as well as from the
Ordinances of 1650 concerning the aims of the company, it is clear that three principles were the
bases on which it was built: (a) to liquidate competition; (b) to buy products as cheaply as possible
in Asia; (c) to sell them as dearly as possible in
Europe.

Amsterdam never set a policy-line for the governors of the company on how to deal with the Indonesian rulers. This was left almost completely in
the hands of the Governor-General and his Council of
four to six members. The policy followed, in practice, was that of divide and rule. Coen's policy,
for instance, to try and play the two States in
Java--Mataram and Bantam--off against each other and
to prevent one from becoming preponderant, has been
followed down the line by his successors. The family
quarrels which often ensued over the right of succession to a throne generally gave the V.O.I.C. a
chance to step in and, by throwing its support behind one of the contenders, bind him through loyalty
to the V.O.I.C. Nearly always, the new prince had
to grant the V.O.I.C. a monopoly position in the buying and trading of tropical products. Moreover, once
he was in power he often had to pay in money or in
goods for the expenses of the V.O.I.C.'s armed support.[20]

Two systems were in use by the V.O.I.C. to obtain the products it sought. The system of "Contin-
genten" was practised in those regions over which
the company had obtained sovereignty. The Indonesian
rulers under this system were forced to deliver a
certain yearly contingent of a specified product.
For this the V.O.I.C. paid either nothing, especially

to those rulers it had helped to the throne, or only
a very small sum which disappeared into the pockets
of the Indonesian rulers. This system could be considered as taxation in kind. The system of "ver-
plichte leverantien," or forced deliveries, was used
with those rulers who still had their full sovereignty. Here, the V.O.I.C. concluded contracts by which
the rulers promised to deliver exclusively to the
company against fixed prices the yearly yield of a
certain product.[21]

A proof that trade policy did not in any way
take into account the welfare of the population is
found in the fact that, if a certain territory
yielded a greater quantity of any product than the
company could consume, it did not hesitate to extir-
pate a number of the trees producing the crop. The
ruler got a so-called extirpation premium; the producers of course got nothing.

In the eighteenth century, when the V.O.I.C.
managed to expand its sovereignty over most areas,
the system of "contingents" replaced more and more
that of "forced deliveries." The animosity of the
population towards the V.O.I.C. and its own rulers
grew accordingly and the number of uprisings increased greatly.

The results of the V.O.I.C.'s policy, judged by
Dutch historians like Stapel, were not very benefi-
cial for the population, particularly in those areas
where products were grown in which the company was
interested. These historians talk about a general
impoverishment which worked even against the company
itself which in the eighteenth century ran into difficulties in selling products imported from Europe
or from India--like cotton, linen, batikwork etc.[22]

Another disastrous effect mentioned is that
through its trading monopoly and its relentless pur-
suit of smugglers, it killed the market for the Indonesians. It is difficult, however, to take such
broad statements at their face value. They give too
much importance to the influence of the Dutch company. If one can assume that the plight of the

Indonesian people on the Spice Island--like Ternate,
Tidore and Amboina--where the company exercised effective power, was bad, this represents only a small
percentage of the Indonesian people. Moreover, it
should not be forgotten that the so-called monopoly
of the Dutch was never fully effective. Smuggling
went on on a much larger scale than the Dutch company commanders cared to admit. Van Leur, describ-
ing the situation of trade around 1650, and after a
careful analysis, concludes that "there was no question of a European preponderance in trade, either in
volume or in organization."[23]

On the positive side, the list is also short.
Undoubtedly, the company--by its interference--pre-
vented prolonged warfare between States like Bantam,
Mataram on Java, or when a succession problem arose
in a kingdom. However, it also saw to it that no
state became too important so as to jeopardize the
position of the V.O.I.C., and its own "police actions"
were not less bloody.

A positive factor also was the introduction of
coffee in the Preanger hills in Java, a product
which remains an important export article up to the
present day.

Direct contact with the population was restricted to those places where the V.O.I.C. had a depot,
or where the company troops came into action--neither
of which was the cause of any increase in mutual appreciation. The V.O.I.C. dealt only with the Indonesian rulers and even then, contact was sporadic
and shunned by both sides. The small Dutch colonies,
insofar as they existed, lived on their own, and the
presence of Indonesians in their compounds was generally restricted to slaves. No real attempt at
starting European colonies was ever made except in
the Cape.[24]

The Governor-General was the key person upon
whom success or failure depended. One must recognize that, seen from a Company point of view, by and
large they were competent and capable people, generally selected from among V.O.I.C. employees with a long

experience in the business, experienced merchants
who knew how to handle a fleet, and reliable administrators. But there were with a few notable exceptions, such as Coen, Diemens, Maetsuyker, van Imhof,
no empire builders or diplomats who took any interest in the people who produced the products they
were after. That they nevertheless managed to leave
the embryo of a colonial empire behind them was more
accidental than planned. Their policy was to obtain
and transport goods needed in Europe, but wasn't
Leopold II of Belgium credited with saying that
"coloniser, c'est transporter"?

We have dwelt at some length on the activities
of the V.O.I.C. as the aims and methods of this company are typical of many others, were they Dutch,
French, Danish or English in origin. The English
competitor in Indonesia was the English East India
Company, founded by Queen Elizabeth in 1600, when
she gave a charter to the "Governor and Company of
Merchants of London Trading with the East Indies."
With a starting capital of £30,313, it became a
joint-stock concern. Outdone by the Dutch in Indonesia, although it had concluded an agreement for
merchant cooperation with the V.O.I.C. in 1619, so
as to withstand the pretentions of Indonesian rulers
and to stabilize the prices of the products sold in
Europe, it was more successful in India itself. In
1702, the company was enlarged into the "United Company of Merchants of England, Trading to the East
Indies," and it was this company which, like the
V.O.I.C., obtained sovereignty in India until the
Government took over in 1858.[25]

These trading companies--precursors of the colonial regimes which followed on their heels (the flag
followed the trade)--were not only active in Asia,
but just as much so in the Americas and Africa, as
we will see from the history of Ghana.

It is clear that the history of the trading companies is quite different depending on whether one
judges them from a European or an Asian point of
view. From a European standpoint they are the true
precursors of a colonial regime which was to follow

and which brought immense benefits to the European
home countries. In the framework of oriental history, however, the appearance of the trading companies takes on another aspect. The Dutch East India
Company, especially in its first century of operations, carried on trade at different trading points
much in the same way as the oriental traders. Like
the Javanese trader it bought cloves in Amboina;
alongside the Chinese trader it obtained pepper in
Sumatra. It paid tolls on many ports as the others
did and it used Chinese labor to build its strong-
hold on Batavia.

What is important for our study, however, is
the fact that the trading companies, by their methods of operation, opened the way to a system of
colonial rule which the Dutch later followed in Indonesia, that is, the system of indirect government.

DEVELOPMENT OF COLONIAL POLICIES: DIRECT AND INDIRECT RULE

The development of a truly colonial policy as
part of a national policy has been influenced by
three circumstances in the nineteenth century.
(a) The industrial revolution in Europe. The development of the cotton mills, sugar refineries, etc.
in England and on the continent led to a great need
for raw materials which were to be imported from the
colonial countries. The introduction of steamships
and the opening of the Suez Canal in 1869 ensured
technical means of transport on a large scale. However, it became necessary to have a more direct and
coordinated system of colonial administration which
would ensure that the goods were being produced in
sufficient quantities and sold cheaply.

Later on, with the extension in output of European industry it became necessary to look for new
markets where cheap products in great quantities
could be sold. Here again, the colonial countries
formed an ideal market which could be protected, provided a well-coordinated colonial policy existed.
To this economic reason should be added a political

one. (b) The division of the world into spheres of
influence among the European powers. This process
of empire-building led--in the second half of the
nineteenth century--to an enormous amount of competition for those areas where no colonial power was yet
entrenched, or not sufficiently entrenched. In Indonesia, it led to efforts to establish the "Pax Neerlandica" over the whole of the Indonesian archipelago--
an operation which was mostly accomplished under the
rule of the soldier-statesman van Heutz (1904-1909).

The third factor is (c) the development of a new
social philosophy in Europe, with its emphasis on
social justice, democracy and nationalism, of which
we will speak later.

Nations throughout the whole of history have encountered fundamentally the same problems regarding
the administering of a territory brought under control either by conquest or otherwise.

In principle, two ways were open. One was to
recruit among its own nationals a body of subordin-
ate agents, large enough to carry out the functions
of local rule. This system can work well in those
places where the cultural pattern of the home country and the new territory are akin. However, where
no such affinity exists, this system has always shown
itself to be a source of friction and, moreover, puts
a great financial burden on the home country.

Therefore, governments in such circumstances
have generally sought to recruit from among the subject population itself the agencies through which
they can administer local affairs. The methods of
recruitment, as well as the conditions under which
these agencies have been employed, have varied widely. Here we come to the difference between direct
and indirect rule.[26]

Under the system of direct rule we understand a
system whereby political administrative authority is
handed down from the mother country directly to the
people in the subjugated territories along proper
channels which are directly controlled by the colonial

power. This means that from the lowest loci of power,
the village head, to the Governor General, a system
of civil servants is introduced which is directly in
the service of the colonial power. This can be done
either by enlisting the existing indigenous political
élite from high to low in the civil service or by
training other people for such positions. Such a
system ensures certainly a much greater and more
direct control of the country, but it generally
means a disruption of the indigenous way of life,
and is more costly. Indirect rule is the system
whereby the sovereign power recognizes the existence
of a political élite as constituted by tradition.
It leaves this system untouched at the lower echelons but it puts political advisors next to them at
the middle and higher levels, to ensure that the policy of the colonial power is being carried out. Such
a system obviously disrupts much less the indigenous
society and is easier to put into practice. In a
way this was the system introduced by the trading
companies who concluded treaties with the local
rulers whereby the sovereignty of the company was
recognized, certain levies in money or goods were
paid, but the administration was left to the local
rulers.

In Java both methods have been tried. After
the take-over of the V.O.I.C. by the Dutch Government, which was in those days the Batavian Republic,
little was changed in the way in which the new government monopoly carried out its work in Indonesia.
The instruction given to a commission to reorganize
the Civil Service in "the Asiatic possessions" mentioned as its aims: to ensure (a) the highest possible well-being to those possessions, (b) the greatest possible profit in trading with the Republic,
and (c) the highest possible income for the finances
of the Republic.[27]

Governor-General Daendels tried to put these instructions into practice. He reorganized the administration, centralizing all power in Djakarta. The
Indonesian political élite, consisting of rulers and
regents (heads of regions) and lower, Indonesian traditional civil servants, remained the administrative

link between the Indonesian population and the Dutch.
Daendels, however, placed alongside the Indonesian
élite Dutch administrators to control the former and
prevent abuses of power. He retained the system of
"forced deliveries" and extended it considerably in
Java, but he also saw to it that the payment for
goods came directly into the hands of the population.

Important also was his reorganization of the
juridical apparatus by the introduction of Peace
Courts (Vredesgerecht) which were entirely in the
hands of Indonesians. Jurisprudence was based on
the Indonesian traditional law--adatrecht. Daendels
was, finally, the first person to work for public
welfare, although in general his aim was military.
His first road of more than 1,000 kilometres in Java
provided a better link between Surabaya and Djakarta.
The extensive use he made of compulsory labor, his
harshness towards the Indonesian rulers whom he
treated as lower civil servants, put him, however,
in a bad light with the Indonesian political élite
and hastened the take-over of Indonesia by the
British (1811).

Thomas Stanford Raffles was the typical representative of that class which combined the qualities
of merchant, statesman and scholar in one person--a
class which has built the British Empire.

He wanted to introduce into Java the same direct
system of government which the British had introduced
in Bengal. He abolished the system of compulsory labor and forced deliveries and introduced a general
tax, the so-called "land-rent." Under this system,
about two-fifths of the produce of all cultivated
land had to be paid as taxes. He did away with the
indirect system of government through the Indonesian
ruling class and appointed European residents who
were directly responsible for the levying of the
taxes.

Although he hoped by this system to lighten the
burden of the Indonesian people by making them less
dependent on extortions by their own political élite,
he remained in power for too short a time to see his

system generally introduced.   In 1816, the Dutch
were back in the saddle.

William I, King of the Netherlands, was at the
same time--according to the constitution of 1814--
"sole ruler of the colonies and other possessions
outside the Netherlands in other continents."[28]

William I, and with him the Dutch nation, hoped
that Indonesia would soon return to the status of
the hen who lays the golden egg.   This did not seem
likely in the beginning.   The Dutch had lost their
status as an important maritime nation and it was
British ships which took care of transport.   Moreover, difficulties in Indonesia--notably the Javanese
war[29]--forced the Government to spend money instead
of receive it.

It was then that Governor General van den Bosch
came up with his suggestion for the "Cultuurstelsel"
(forced system of cultivation) in 1830.   Like Raffles,
he considered the Government the sole possessor of
all land and the population only the "renters."   Instead of paying as tax two-fifths of the crops they
grew, van den Bosch decided that they should culti-
vate an export crop on one-fifth of their land.[30]
For instance, in the Preanger area, coffee and indigo
were to be cultivated; elsewhere, sugar, tobacco,
pepper, tea, etc.   Such a system evidently demanded
good administrative control and he again returned to
the Indonesian political élite to look after this.
To stimulate its interest, it received a certain percentage of the crop, planted, and delivered (cultuur
procenten).

Immediately after Raffles, the Indonesian political élite was returned to its position of command,
and this new system augmented its power--and its possibility of misusing it--considerably.

Van den Bosch's system very much helped to fill
the Dutch Treasury.   In 1831, the Dutch made a profit
in Indonesia for the first time, to the extent of
fl.200,000 which grew in the following years to an
amount of about fl.20,000,000 a year.   The whole

trade was again in the hands of one company which
had a monopoly--the "Nederlandse Handel Maatschappy."
When the system was revoked in 1870, and private enterprise was given a chance, it was due to opposition in the Netherlands to a system which by then
was felt by many to be unethical. Undoubtedly, although there never had been any open opposition in
Java to the system--probably because the Indonesian
élite profited too much by it--the system and the
many abuses which went with it led to an impoverishment of a vast portion of the population.

Van den Bosch's administrative system was a typical example of an indirect system of government.
The administrative build-up was the following:

(a) Village head
(b) Sub-district officer (<u>Assistant Wedana</u>) com-
    prising about 20 villages
(c) District officers (<u>Wedana</u>)
(d) Regent--head of township
(e) Assistant Resident (leading an area compris-
    ing several regencies)
(f) Resident
(g) Governor--head of province
(h) Governor-General

For the lower ranks--(a), (b), (c) and (d)--the
Indonesian political élite was used. The office of
Regent was in general a hereditary function assumed
by the Indonesian aristocracy.

The highest positions--from (e) to (h)--were
filled by Dutch civil servants. The Assistant Residents were considered advisers to the Regent. Their
influence grew with time[31] and they held magisterial
power. Later, the functions of <u>aspirant controleur</u>
(assistant cadet) and <u>controleur</u> (cadet) were introduced and were also reserved for Dutch civil servants.
These held no magisterial, judicial or administrative
powers, but were there to advise the native administration and protect the population against abuses.
Their task was to hold frequent Councils to explain
government policy to the native administrators. According to Furnivall, this system offered a way of

practical training.   "It is a form of government
through social education."[32]

Another important aspect of indirect rule was
the operation of the legal system.   Here again we en-
counter the recurring problem of which path to follow
when a conquering or colonizing power finds the need
to integrate the law of different peoples with different habits or standards of social behavior into
its own legal system.   We know that in the beginning
of its existence, the Roman Empire confined the operation of its legal system to those indigenous peoples
who had the status of "citizens"; the "subjects" were
left with the operation of their own courts where
such existed, as in Sicily or Greece, or to tribal
custom in other areas.   The Dutch applied much the
same system, and the Ordinance of 1854--like the
later one of 1925--stated: "Everywhere that the native population is not left to enjoy its own system
of law, law will be administered in the Netherlands
Indies in the name of the King."   Native law was
based on custom (adat) and administered by the Indonesian rulers.   The Europeans, Chinese and others
were judged according to Dutch Common Law.   In the
beginning, this was meted out by the administration;
only after 1869 do we see the development of an independent judicial apparatus.

Both Raffles' "land-rent" system, and van den
Bosch's "forced cultivation" system were introduced
only in Java and later in some areas of Sumatra.
Dutch policy with regard to the other islands of the
archipelago was to leave them alone as much as possible, provided the rulers there recognized Dutch
sovereignty.

The year 1869, which saw the opening of the
Suez Canal, was an important one for the development
of Indonesia.   The distance between Indonesia and
Europe was shortened and transport became cheaper;
this had a direct influence on the export market for
tropical products.   The agrarian law of 1870 had
opened the possibility of developing free enterprise
in tropical products.   The results were soon to be
seen.   While Java in 1870 produced 152,950 tons of

sugar, in 1885 it doubled the cypher to 380,346 tons.
The total value of tobacco exported in 1870 was fl.
3,600,000; in 1890 it was fl. 32,300,000.[33] New capital started to pour into Indonesia: banking houses
were founded such as the Handelsvereeniging Amsterdam, the Nederlandsch-Indische Handelsbank, etc. At
the same time the government made great efforts to
promote the introduction of new crops as rubber,
kinine, etc.

With this development a new type of European--
the "planter"--appeared in Indonesia. While in 1872,
the number of Dutch, including the Indo-Europeans,
was estimated at 36,000, in 1892 the number had risen
to 58,000.[34] Moreover, great efforts were also undertaken in the field of mining. The exploitation of
tin and oil was started--in 1890 the famous Royal
Dutch Shell Company was formed. The liberal-minded
rulers of that period had hoped that the income
gained from this development through taxes, import
and export duties, would more than offset the loss
in income from the liquidation of the forced cultivation system. They thought, especially, that since,
beginning in 1877, no more of the national benefits
had to be transferred to the Netherlands, it would
be possible to give greater attention to the needs of
Indonesians and that investments could be made in order to build up an infrastructure in the form of
roads, rail and waterways, education, sanitation, etc.

However, they had not counted on two factors:

(a) The open market policy which was introduced
    and which made Indonesia totally dependent
    on the world economic situation and, es-
    pecially, on world prices for tropical
    products. Boom and slump years made a long-
    range policy of economic development look
    like a poker game;

(b) As was mentioned before, the general colon-
    ial policy and the scramble for "open"
    spaces after 1870 forced the Dutch to imple-
    ment the Pax Neerlandica as quickly as pos-
    sible to the whole of the archipelago, and

forced them into a series of police actions,
of which the war with Atjeh was not the
only, but certainly the most spectacular
and costly, one.[35]

Finally, growing economic development had also
its consequences as far as the administration was
concerned. Although officially the system of indirect government was followed, in practice the European advisers became more and more the real rulers.
To this must be added the fact that, with the development of new government services, such as income
tax, land-rent, cooperatives and health services,
more and more civil servants were sent into the
field and this led to considerable friction between
the indigenous authorities and the European special-
ists.

CHANGES IN COLONIAL POLICY--
THE ETHICAL POLICY

It is clear that, in the first period of colonization, the era of the trading companies, economic
considerations were the propelling factors. At the
end of the eighteenth century, and for a good part
of the nineteenth, these factors still held a preponderant position, although purely political concepts
came more to the fore, as can be seen clearly by the
attitude of the Dutch towards Indonesian territories
outside Java. All this should, however, not make us
forget the influence that social philosophy--as it
developed in Europe--had exercised on the development
and change in colonial policy. During all phases of
the colonial era, there have been people who have
stood up for high moral and ethical conceptions of
colonialism and, as Furnivall rightly remarks, "The
inspiration of colonial policy by humanitarian
ideals is no modern invention, but as old as western
rule."[36]

However, the logical consequences of colonial
practices have, in general, differed widely from the
humanitarian aims set forth in colonial policy,
which is the reason why each new phase of colonial

development brought with it a condemnation of the
former one, as being one of exploitation.

The general and often narrow-minded condemnation in our days of all aspects of colonialism is
therefore no new phenomenon, except that it now
seems to be the sole prerogative of many of those
who have most benefited from it, i.e., the new political élite of the colonial countries.

In nineteenth-century Europe, the liberal economic theory of "laisser faire, laisser passer" held
full sway. It exercised a very strong influence on
colonial policy and was, for instance, responsible in
Indonesia for the ending of the "forced cultivation
system" and the development of free enterprise. It
also demanded a more intensive and active form of
colonization and led to a considerable extension of
colonial administration.

At the same time, we note in Europe the development of a social philosophy influenced by Rousseau
and the French Revolution. It also encompassed Dar-
win's notion of the survival of the fittest as a
justification of efficient--be it drastic--action in
the colonies. And it finally included the ideas of
social justice developed by St. Simon, Robert Owens
and in the encyclica Rerum Novarum as well as other
sources.

Those new ideas were responsible for forcing a
change in colonial policy which aimed at giving the
native his fair share, and which found expression in
British policy in the term "the white man's burden,"
and in Dutch policy in the term "Ethische Koloniale
Politiek"[37] (Ethical Colonial Policy).

In the Netherlands, it was such people as a Member of the Second Chamber of Parliament and Indonesian expert, Robert, Baron van Hoëvell (1857), and
the Minister for Colonial Affairs, Isaac van der
Putten (1862), and more particularly, the author
Multatuli (E. Douwes Dekker) with his book Max
Havelaar (1860), who shocked the country into a
realization of the unethical aspects of colonial

policy, as expressed by the forced cultivation system.   This new trend was encouraged by the Liberal
cabinets which governed the Netherlands in the second
half of the nineteenth century, although their aims
were not entirely devoid of self-interest.   The growing textile industry in Deventer increasingly was on
the lookout for an export market in Indonesia.   However, the welfare of Indonesia had to be ascertained
if the products were to be sold.   Other private companies and business concerns also looked more and
more to Indonesia and they got their chance with the
gradual abolition of the forced cultivation system
and the lifting of the monopoly position of the
"Nederlandse Handel Maatschappy."   All sides clam-
ored for a more intensive administration, as we remarked earlier, and there was a growth in the Dutch
colony of civil servants, as well as the number of
private citizens.

As long, however, as the Indonesian budget was
coupled with the Dutch, and profits were transferred
from Indonesia to the mother country, nothing very
great could be accomplished.

It was C. van Deventer[38] who launched the first
attack in 1899 with an article "An honor debt."   In
this he suggested that all profits transferred to
the Netherlands Treasury after 1867 should be considered a debt and should be reimbursed to Indonesia.

In 1901, the ethical colonial policy won out
and the Queen's message for the Opening of Parliament spoke of an "ethical obligation and moral responsibility to the people of the East Indies."   The
Liberal party, after a long period of government,
was replaced by a coalition of Conservative and Religious parties, determined to introduce Christian
principles into colonial policy.[39]

New difficulties, however, soon arose as to the
practical application of the ethical policy.   Several
options were advanced which can best be explained by
the terms: unification, assimilation and association.
The term unification originally referred around 1900
to the attempt of codification of all legal systems

and legislations in all parts of Indonesian society
into a single codified law. Later, however, this
term was expanded to include other facets of social
relationships, such as the Civil Service, education
and taxation. All discrimination on the social plane
had to cease. The terms "assimilation" and "association" are subheadings of the term "unification." Unification by assimilation would mean unity on a European
basis; unification by association would imply unity
wherever possible and without harming one group or
another. In the latter case, diversification would
be preferable. The last two terms have, however, a
strong cultural connotation; assimilation means here
all efforts to make a brown Dutchman out of the Indonesian, and a displacement of Indonesian culture by
a western (Dutch) civilization. Association, however,
stood for all efforts to make western civilization
available to the Indonesians, insofar as it would
help them to advance in prosperity and well-being,
but without trying to force any change, and with a
strong inclination to respect Indonesian culture.
This difference of opinion with regard to a policy
to be followed among the "ethical" school gave the
opposition its chance to oppose any reform at all.
This opposition came particularly from Indonesia,
and more specifically from those groups who harbored
strong racial prejudices, and were afraid of economic competition, such as the European lower-middle
classes and certain sections of the Indo-European
group. In the Netherlands, the opposition was more
against introducing the new policy too speedily.
There were the "pushers"; there were those who
wanted a more gradual change.

The important results of the ethical policy were:

(a) a decentralization of the colonial govern-
    ment (1903) and the introduction of local
    citizens' Councils, which did become a
    political training ground for the Indonesian
    élite;

(b) an effort to introduce education for the In-
    donesians themselves, a field which had, up
    until then, been left almost entirely in

the hands of the missionaries. In 1900,
the O.S.U.I.A. type of school was introduced which aimed at training native administrators. While in 1900, the expenses for
the European schools (European population
about 80,000) were still double that for
the Indonesians (population in Java,
40,000,000) in 1925, Indonesia had about
11,000 Government schools for natives, plus
a couple of thousand private schools;

(c) to cope with the population explosion in
Java[40] efforts to improve the irrigation
system and promote emigration to other
islands;

(d) the organization of a credit system for the
Javanese peasant;

(e) the development of a health service for the
Indonesians.

SOCIAL CHANGES: THE EUROPEAN ELITE: NATIVE
"BOURGEOISIE" WESTERN-EDUCATED ELITE

The new colonial policies which after 1850 were
strongly influenced by a sense of responsibility towards the dependent people had a very great influence
in many fields:

(a) as a consequence of the economic system of
laissez-faire, a sizable number of Europeans not directly engaged in administration were drawn towards the colonies;

(b) with the development of trade (small crafts,
and the introduction of export crops produced by the native population) a native
middle class, or native bourgeoisie, was
growing up;

(c) with the extension of the administrative
apparatus and the emphasis on education
for native civil servants in the lower

categories, a new Western-educated élite began to appear which was soon to show itself
a good pupil of Western nationalism and
democracy, and to start to claim greater
measures of self-rule.

All these measures, therefore, caused changes in
the social structure of the dependencies.

If Indonesian society, when the white man arrived,
could be divided into three classes--(a) the Prijaji
(political élite), (b) the free farmer, and (c) the
slaves--this situation was considerably changed by
the end of the nineteenth century. First of all,
the slave class had practically disappeared, under
the influence of the colonial power. The position
of the head of the dessah--as primus interparis--and
that of the Prijaji class, had been maintained and
even strengthened because of the colonial policy of
indirect rule, whereby these men were drafted into
the Civil Service. This class even grew in number
and showed signs of losing its unity, as we shall
see later. Apart from the Prijaji, the religious
Muslim leaders maintained and even strengthened
their position, as the Dutch government never tried
to introduce Christianity on a large scale.

However, a new class had come into being--that
of the white man. If the European colonies were
small during the period of the trading companies,
and did not exercise any significant cultural influence, the nineteenth century changed this considerably as the numbers of European civil servants grew;
but, even more important, the moral qualities of
those going to Indonesia were much greater. Apart
from that, the number of traders, planters and busi-
nessmen grew rapidly. Most important, however, was
that more and more European women came and thereby,
European family life--although with too much luxury
and glamor--was introduced. The role European women
have played in colonial life would be an interesting
subject for further study. From personal observa-
tion both in Indonesia as well as in African colonial
countries, I am inclined to believe that their general conduct has greatly contributed to the psycho-

logical resentment which grew up among indigenous
people against European rule. Whatever can be said
of the European men who went to the colonies, in general they had to work intensively under often trying
conditions of climate. The European wives, however,
who came to the colonial countries, and who often
were from the lower middle class, found themselves
suddenly at the top of the social ladder. Living in
large houses with plenty of servants, inhibited in
their activities by all kinds of social taboos, they
often could find little else to do but to engage in
intrigues and tea parties. Thereby they often set
the worst example of European conduct and their treatment of the indigenous people rightly was the cause
of growing resentment. In the beginning, however,
the arrival of the Dutch wife created a new style of
living.[41]

All this had far-reaching consequences. "The
extension of the white man's power over the coloured
races in the 19th century was accompanied everywhere
by a marked rise in the social standing of the whites
and great regard socially for all the outward characteristics, such as language, dress and colour of skin,
which symbolized the white race."[42] The European
group, therefore, although coming from different social strata, melted slowly into one élite group
whose cultural tastes became the criteria of Indonesian society. This is clearly borne out by the
fact that, in the urban Indonesian communities, a
social stratification developed, based on the individual's nearness to the symbols of power and authority. The highest level was formed by the house servants of leading European families, and was followed
by those who worked in a government service, while
those Indonesians who had small private business or
enterprises and who were, therefore, generally
wealthier, were nevertheless considered as belonging
to a lower category.[43]

Apart from the pure white, there arose another
class--that of the half-caste or Indo-European (Singo).
They formed an expanding group which tried as much as
possible to act and behave like Europeans. Their
status depended a lot on the degree of whiteness of

their skin and their European style of living. So
marked was their tendency to identify themselves with
the whites, that apart from the individual cases they
upheld Dutch colonial policies right to the bitter
end, and never wholeheartedly identified themselves
with the cause of Indonesian independence.

Most significant, however, was the gradual rise
of an Indonesian bourgeoisie, especially in the cities, where they lived as civil servants, craftsmen,
merchants and small entrepreneurs. It was this group
that first wanted to organize its own movement, and
to start making an Indonesian voice heard--as we will
see later. Closely linked with this was the growth
of a European-educated Indonesian élite. They came
in general from the existing political élite (the
Prijaji class). However, we see a separation slowly
appearing between them. In view of the guarantee of
hereditary rights for the higher Prijaji group, and
the existence of the Pax Neerlandica, the younger
sons of the Prijaji, or their near relatives, had
very little chance of ever holding a high position.
However, the expansion of the civil service, which
meant the taking in of people who had had a certain
measure of European education, gave them their chance.

This group was to take an increasingly critical
attitude towards their seniors who held higher positions, but a lower standard of education, and later
it was to form a new élite, more Western in training
and at the same time more critical towards the West.

A social stratification of the different classes
existing in Indonesia around 1900 revealed, therefore, the following situation:

    I. the European whites

   II. the half-whites (Singo's): in this cate-
       gory we might also include the Chinese
       and Arabs

  III. the Prijaji class, which was divided into
       an elderly, hierarchical, more conservative
       component, and a younger, more Western,
       more dynamic component

IV. the Indonesian bourgeoisie

V. the Indonesian peasant class.

Footnotes to Chapter 2

1. For the history of Indonesia, we refer the reader to the following books, which we have used extensively in this chapter: C. C. Berg, Hoofdlijnen der Javaansche Literatuur Geschiedenis, Inaugural lecture University, Leiden (Groningen: Bos, 1929); N. J. Krom, Hindoe--Javaansche Geschiedenis (Den Haag: Nyhoff, 1931); J. C. van Leur, Indonesian Trade and Society (The Hague: W. van Hoeve, 1955); Radha Kumund Moukerjis, Indian Shipping, A History of the Seaborne Trade and Maritime Activity of the Indians from the Earliest Times (London: Longmans and Co., 1912); F. W. Stapel, Geschiedenis van Nederlandsch Indie (Amsterdam: J. M. Meulenhoff, 1943); Bernard H. M. Vlekke, Geschiedenis van den Indischen Archipel (Roermond: Romen en Zonen, 1947), trans. The Story of the Dutch East Indies (Cambridge, 1948).

2. The written languages of Balinese, Madurese, Javanese, Sudanese, Makassaars, Bataks and Lampongs, have been based on Indian scripts, while Malayan, Atjehs, Ternatese have been modelled on the Arabian script.

3. Tjandi-temple, as one finds them, especially in East and Central Java.

4. Wajang are popular stories told with the help of dolls, manipulated in such a way that their shadows are projected on a screen.

5. Chinese texts of the 7th century mention the existence of the Kingdom of Criwidjaya (Palembang) on the Musi river in Sumatra. Because of its geographical position, it controlled all maritime traffic between India and China, and it extended its power over Malaya and other parts of Sumatra. In

the 8th century, we hear about a kingdom in Central
Java, later overshadowed in the 11th and 12th centuries by the State of Kediri, East Java. The most
famous of the Hindu-Javanese states, however, was
the kingdom of Majapahit which was ruled in the 13th
and 14th centuries by such famous personalities as
King Hayam Waeroek (Young rooster) and his counsellor, Gadjah-Mada. In the 14th century, it expanded
its rule over Sumatra, Tandjoengnegara (Kalimantan),
Malaya, the lesser Sunda islands, Makassar, Boeroe,
Ceram, Amboina, the Maluku islands, and even parts
of South and Southwest New Guinea (Irian). Science
and the arts flourished in this kingdom; the tandji of
Panataran and the famous poem Nagarakertagama, mark
the heights of architecture and poetry of the Hindu-
Javanese period. The Kingdom of Majapahit was well-
governed. Foreign visitors praised the honesty of
the governing class. Agriculture was based in Java
on a dense irrigation system and the population had
to do compulsory service. (See Stapel, op. cit.)

6. Van Leur, op. cit., pp. 98-99.

7. Kraton is the Javanese term for the Royal
Court, also used to indicate the compound of the
ruling monarch.

8. Pachul is a kind of hoe, still used in
Indonesia.

9. Sawah--irrigated rice field, in contrast
with ladang--non-irrigated rice field.

10. Stapel, op. cit., pp. 6-10.

11. Tradition claims the spreading of Islam on
Java was due to the nine Saints or Walis; one of the
greatest was Raden Rahmat who founded the famous
school in Ampel (Surabaja).

12. Van Leur, op. cit., p. 115.

13. G. P. Rouffaer and J. W. Yzerman, De Eerste
Schipvaart der Nederlanders Naar Oost Indie onder
Cornelis de Houtman, 1545-1597. Journalen, Documenten

en Andere Bescheiden, Linschoten Vereniging, pp. 83-89.

    14.   Van Leur, op. cit., p. 263.

    15.   Two other companies were founded in Amsterdam, two in the province of Zeeland and two in Rotterdam.   Moreover, in 1601, the towns of Hoorn, Enkhuizen and Delft also started to form their own companies.   (Stapel, op. cit., pp. 40-42.)

    16.   This competition gave the Indonesian rulers the chance of increasing their prices.   In a few years, the prices for cloves and other spices rose from four to eight times.

    17.   In those days, the highest legislative organ.

    18.   The V.O.I.C. was ruled by a board of 17 people, the so-called "Heeren XVII," and started with a capital of about 6,500,000 guilders, which was obtained through the issue of shares in various cities.   The Charter was granted for a period of 21 years and has been prolonged several times--the last time in 1798--until on December 31, 1799, the State took over the V.O.I.C. with all its debts to an amount of 140,000,000 guilders and thus acquired in return a considerable colonial empire.   The rulers were elected from the different cities where the company had its offices.   The distribution was: Amsterdam 8, Middelburg 4, Delft, Rotterdam, Hoorn and Enkhuizen, one each.   The 17th member was chosen in rotation from one of the last four cities to prevent an Amsterdam majority.   In general, Amsterdam provided about half the capital.   Subscriptions ranged from fl. 60 to fl. 97,000.   (Stapel, op. cit., Chap. III.)

    19.   One cannot say that in the Netherlands, the majority of the people were enthusiastic about the working of the V.O.I.C.   Shareholders repeatedly complained about the secret way in which the books were kept.   Hugo de Groots' famous Mare Librum, first published in 1609, can easily be interpreted as an attack on the monopoly position of the V.O.I.C.

Other traders made contact with France to obtain
help to found another company to compete with the
V.O.I.C. (Stapel, op. cit., Chap. III.)

    20. It was often stipulated that such payments
did not have to be carried out as long as the ruler
did not tamper with the monopoly position of the
V.O.I.C. It thereby helped to prevent the Indonesian
rulers from trying to conclude secret contracts with
English or Portuguese companies.

    21. An elaborate system of bribery through
gifts or yearly premiums to the Indonesian rulers
guaranteed that the fixed prices were very low indeed. If the population tried to sell its products
to the Spanish, Portuguese or English for better
prices, they were severely punished. That under
such circumstances, smuggling was nevertheless the
order of the day is only too easy to understand.
During the whole period of its existence, therefore,
the V.O.I.C. found a rich field in pursuing smugglers
and sinking their boats. Eastern Indonesia, Makassar
and Java (Bantam) were the smuggling centers, as it
was in those places that the British and Portuguese
companies had their depots.

    22. See Stapel, op. cit., Chap. IV.

    23. Van Leur, op. cit., p. 189.

    24. Some of the Governor-Generals, such as
Coen and Imhoff, suggested such a policy which would
have brought several advantages to the V.O.I.C. Amsterdam, however, never took up such suggestions.
The Dutch community, therefore, remained restricted
to soldiers, sailors and civil servants, and never
grew to very great dimensions. By the end of the
18th century, there were about 12,000 on the Company's payroll. As far as moral qualities were concerned, they were certainly not the best men the
Dutch nation could produce, although the V.O.I.C.
rules forbade the enrolment of "die gefailleert, van
de paepsche religie ofte van eenige delicten betigt
en met infamie genotieerat syn" (those who had gone
bankrupt, were of the Roman Catholic religion or

accused of crimes, or had behaved in an infamous
way). Stapel, op. cit., p. 86.

25. Stapel, op. cit., Chap. IV.

26. For opinions about the systems of direct
or indirect rule, see also J. S. Furnivall, Colonial
Policy and Practice--A Comparative Study of Burma
and the Netherlands Indies (rev. ed.; New York:
New York University Press, 1956), and Lord Hailey,
An African Survey (rev. ed.; London: Oxford University Press, 1956).

27. Stapel, op. cit., p. 187.

28. The constitution stipulated that: "De
souvereine vorst heeft bij uitsluiting, het opper-
bestuur over de kolonien en bezittingen van den
Staat in andere Werelddelen." (The Sovereign Ruler
reigns solely over the colonies and other possessions in other continents.)

29. The Javanese war was a typical example of
a war of succession. When in 1814 Amengka Buwono
III died, his younger brother Djarat succeeded him.
Raffles seems to have promised his half-brother Dipo
Negoro the right of succession in case Amengka
Buwono died prematurely. When this happened, the
Dutch did not know about Raffles' concession and
recognized Buwono's two-year-old son as the legitimate heir; because of this, and the tactless attitude of the Dutch Resident, Nahuyis, an uprising was
started by Dipo Negoro which took the Dutch much
time and money to suppress. (Stapel, op. cit.,
Chap. XIX.)

30. In other colonial areas the system in use
was that the population had to work a certain time
for the government, for instance, 20% of their normal
labor time. Van den Bosch's system is a variant on
this, in that he took as basis not the time put in
working for the government, but the area cultivated
for the government.

31. A famous expression was that the Dutch Resident should act as the "older brother" to his Indonesian colleague, the Regent, who was of the same standing. Soon, however, these "older brothers" became real "bullies."

32. Furnivall, op. cit., p. 239.

33. Vlekke, op. cit., p. 355.

34. Ibid., p. 358.

35. The system introduced was to have Indonesian rulers sign the so-called "short declaration" which stipulated that the territory would (a) be a part of the Dutch East Indies, governed by Her Majesty the Queen and Her representative, the Governor General; (b) not make any contact with foreign countries and, recognizing that the enemies of the Dutch were to be their foes too, and the friends of the Dutch their friends; (c) obey all directives given by the Queen or her legal representative, the Governor General, or his representatives. (Stapel, op. cit., pp. 293-294.)

36. Furnivall, op. cit., p. 289.

37. This term was first used by Mr. P. Brooshooft, an editor of the Dutch newspaper De Lokomotief, in Indonesia, in a publication entitled De ethische Koers in de Koloniale Politiek (The Ethical Orientation in Colonial Policy).

38. C. T. van Deventer has often been called the father of the ethical policy. He wielded great influence with such writings as De eereschuld in het Parlement (February 1900) (An Honor Debt in Parliament), and Indie en de democratie (April 1902) (The Indies and Democracy).

39. This was also made possible through the fact that the constitution was changed and the King was not the sole ruler in Indonesia, but the Minister of colonial affairs bore the responsibility to Parliament.

40.   In a period of around 140 years, the population in Java had grown from 4 to 44 million people.
The European population, at the same time, had grown
from 4 to 193,000 of which about half were Indo-
Europeans.   (Boeke, "Van vier to vierenveertig mil-
loen zielen op Java" [From Four to Forty-four Million
Souls on Java], in W. H. van Helsdingen and H. Hoogenberk, Daar werd wat Groots Verricht, Nederlandsch
Indie in de XXste eeuw [Amsterdam: Elsevier, 1941].)

41.   Some idea of life of the Dutch family in
Indonesia can be obtained from the novels written
about life in Indonesia like those of Bep Vuyk, M.
Szekely Lulofs, E. Breton de Nys, etc.

42.   W. F. Wertheim, Indonesian Society in Transition, a Study in Social Change (The Hague: W. van
Hoeve, 1956), p. 136.

43.   R. van Niel, The Emergence of the Modern
Indonesian Elite (The Hague: W. van Hoeve, 1960),
p. 58.

CHAPTER **3** THE COLONIAL ERA:

GHANA

    As in the previous chapter, we shall here treat
subsequently Ghanaian society before the arrival of
the white man in the fifteenth century; in the pre-
colonial era; colonial policies as they developed
through the eighteenth and nineteenth centuries, and
the changes these wrought in society. As in Indonesia, the pre-colonial era arrives with the appearance of the European trading companies. However,
Ghana had not the same value for them as Indonesia,
as can be noted by the ease with which emplacements
were sold from one country to another. The main interest in those days was the slave trade and, after
its abolishment, we immediately see a slackening of
interest in this region.

    While colonial policies in the nineteenth cen-
tury were largely determined by economic, political
and social ethical factors, in contrast with Indonesia the first factor did not play a big role in
Ghana. The "scramble for Africa" as the period from
1884-1890 is called was not--at least so far as
Ghana was concerned--determined by European economic
trends, but by political relations between Britain,
France and Portugal, which were complicated by the
arrival on the scene of two new Pretenders, the King
of Belgium and Bismarck.

    British colonial policy in Ghana, as Dutch pol-
icy in Indonesia, but unlike British policy in India,
was based on a system of indirect rule. We have
given some attention to this as it has had far-reaching consequences even to our time.

    As in Indonesia, we also see in Ghana at the end
of the nineteenth century a change in policy because

of ethical motives.   The new term was "the white
man's burden."   This change in policy had its consequences on the social level where we see the growth
of a native middle class and the rising up of a
western-educated indigenous élite.

GHANA'S SOCIETY BEFORE 1500

Ghana[1] is, compared to Indonesia, not only a
much smaller country, relatively sparsely populated,
but its history remains to a great extent in darkness.

Of the earliest population of Ghana, little is
known.   One thing is sure however: the actual state,
Ghana, has nothing in common with the Ghana Empire
of the tenth and eleventh centuries, except for the
name and possibly the aspirations of its present
leaders.[2]   The old kingdom of Ghana was probably
situated for most of the Middle Ages where now we
find the Sudan.   Bonnel de Mézières and Mauny[3] believe that the capital of Ghana was Khoumbi Saleh,
the location of which they think they have determined.
Hailey maintains that its location is still uncer-
tain.[4]   It saw its greatest extension in the eleventh
century when it spread from Senegal to Timbuctoo,
taking in parts of Mauritania, as well as Upper Volta.
Documents mention the extraordinary security which
reigned in this kingdom as well as its richness, and
it was--with the thirteenth century empire of Mali
and the later empire of Benin (Nigeria)--one of the
strongest states in West Africa.   However, it never
touched the actual frontier of present Ghana.

The populations of the two tribal kingdoms in
our present-day Ghana, namely those of Ashanti and
Gondja, seem to have come from the north.   They were
only discovered in the seventeenth century, when
Kumasi was established as the capital of Ashanti,
and the coastal people were brought under tribute
during the leadership of Osai Touhou.

The Ashanti were good fighters and Cornevin remarks: "esprit très indépendant, l'Ashanti n'est
pas volontiers main-d'oeuvre ni militaire, il veut

etre son maitre; c'est un bon guerrier et un mauvais
soldat."[5]

The kingdom of Gondja was founded by a prince
named Mande. This kingdom was known for its importance as a center for the growth of Kola.

At the time of contact with the West, the majority of the population of Ghana belonged to the Akan
and Fanti-speaking people. Both had a well-developed
political organization consisting of states controlled
by a Head--or Paramount Chief.[6] Contrary to the situation in Indonesia, it was not the village which
formed in Ghana a territorial, as well as a geneologi-
cal unit. The great stress here was on kin relationships. The important kin-group was the lineage or
group of males tracing descent from a common ancestor
for several generations in either the male and patri-
lineal or female and matri-lineal line.

Among the Akan and Fanti, each village had its
Council, chosen from among the elders of the different
kin groups. They were then united in divisions, with
a Divisional Chief, and a Council representing the
village councils.

The head of the chiefs was the intermediary between them and their ancestors and, therefore, performed a sacred function. His authority among the
Ashanti was symbolized by the possession of the
sacred stool[7] and the council was known as the
"Stool Council," while the land they held in common
was called "Stool Countries." The Ashanti, by far
the most powerful tribe, were a mixture of patri-
and matri-lineals.[8]

They were further known for their human sacri-
fices and, each year, a large number of slaves was
offered in honor of the ancestors.

Unlike the situation in Indonesia, one could not
speak of the existence of a nobility which formed a
class apart, although the paramount Chiefs and the
State Council had many of the characteristics of a
political élite group. Generally speaking, and

compared with the situation in Indonesia, the Europeans found in Ghana a people of relatively low cultural standards.

THE PRE-COLONIAL ERA:
THE TRADING COMPANIES

It was the search for India which brought the
European traders along West Africa's coast. Cornevin
could rightly remark that during the Middle Ages
"l'Afrique n'intéresse personne sauf les curieux, les
géographes et quelques chrétiens à tempérament mis-
sionnaire."[9] Henry the Navigator financed the first
expeditions; Pedro de Cuna reached Sierra Leone in
1462 and 1471 saw Portuguese ships under Diago d'Azom-
buja reaching Ghana, where they soon built a strong-
hold at El Mina. Sixteen years later, Vasco da Gama
sailed around the Cape to reach Calicut in India.

For the next four centuries, until Suez offered
other possibilities, West Africa with its coastal
stations was to play an important role on the route
to India.

In the meantime, Ghana's wealth in gold, ivory
and, later, in slaves had been discovered and made
it a rich territory, for which Portuguese, Danish,
Dutch, French and English traders were willing to
risk each other's necks, and sometimes lost their own.

The Portuguese monopoly lasted until the end of
the sixteenth century. Then, as in Indonesia, the
Dutch moved into the picture with the "Vereenigde
West Indische Compagnie" (United West Indies Company) founded in 1621.[10] Although especially interested in the Americas, this company could not ne-
glect West Africa as a source of the manpower needed
for the American plantations. Soon a fort was built
in Ghana--Fort Nassau--and in due course, the Portuguese fort of San José del Mina was taken over
(1637).[11]

But, as in Indonesia, the Dutch were not the
only arrivals. Frederick William of Brandenburg

sent an expedition in 1677; the Danes built a fort-
ress--Christianborg[12]--where the city of Accra now
stands; a French company settled in Takorady.

   However, it was the British Royal African Company[13] which finally managed to get the upper hand
and, out of the gold of Ghana, found their Gold Coast,
although the Dutch and Danish forts remained in place
until the middle of the nineteenth century.

   The Royal African Company immediately erected a
number of forts in Ghana, such as Sekondi, Dixcone.
In the beginning, the main trade product was gold
which was to be later overshadowed by slaves. Because of the development of such industry in England
as sugar refineries, cotton mills, etc., the British
Government was forced to expand its plantations in
the Americas in order to produce the necessary raw
materials. As cheap labor was in short supply in
those countries, slaves were imported from the African coast and, in this way, a kind of triangular
trade developed which brought wealth to Liverpool,
Glasgow and Bristol as well as to Nantes and Bordeaux, or Middelburg and Amsterdam.

   Trade was lively. After the Treaty of Utrecht,
for instance, in 1713, the Royal African Company got
the "asiento" or contract to supply the Spanish colonies with a yearly contingent of 4,800 African
slaves. In the meantime, the Dutch West Indies Company traded about 6,000 slaves a year.[14] The abolition of the slave trade in 1808 considerably crippled
the Company's activities and in 1827, it was forced
to dissolve itself and the Government took over. In
1817, however, the Company had managed to come to an
agreement with the Ashanti chiefs, whereby the latter
recognized British rights on the coast. The first
step towards British sovereignty in Ghana was thus
taken.

   Trading again took place through the chiefs, especially those of the Ashanti tribes, who had always
used a great number of slaves themselves.

   In general, gifts or donations were made to a

certain chief, who then allowed the company to trade.
Gold or slaves were traded for a great variety of
goods--from mirrors, salt and old uniforms, to liquor,
powder and cotton goods. Guns were particularly
sought after as barter goods, owing to the warrior-
like temperament of several African tribes.

What has been the effect of the trading companies on the people in the Gold Coast? Unlike the situation in Indonesia, there was practically no African
sea trading before the arrival of the Europeans and
the exchange of products remained limited to ivory,
gold and especially slaves. The interest of the
foreign companies in this region of Africa remained
limited for the following reasons:

(a) a very unhealthy climate dominated the area (in
    the period 1637-1852 not less than 85 Dutch Gov-
    ernors were sent to the Gold Coast of whom 40
    died on the spot. Few stayed longer than 3
    years);[15]

(b) the trade in ivory and gold became very soon a
    limited affair and, as far as the slave trade
    was concerned, the whole African coast was able
    to supply this "material." It is therefore un-
    derstandable that often certain strongholds were
    sold from one country to another.[16]

The effect the slave trade has had on the population is difficult to analyze. Neither having
slaves nor trading them was a European invention,
but long-standing practices among many African
tribes, especially those in contact with Moslem
states. This is also borne out by the fact that
none of the companies had great difficulty in obtaining slaves and they did not engage themselves in
rounding them up, one reason why no efforts were
made to penetrate the interior of Ghana.

Finally, although one is abhorred today when
visiting the fortresses of El Mina or Goree to see
under what circumstances slaves had to live, one
must not forget that the slave trade was a business
and that, therefore, reasonable care was taken to

ensure that the slaves reached their destination in
fairly good condition. Van Hulsen has calculated
that over a number of years the death rate of slaves
during a trip to the Americas was 15 percent, while
that of the crew of the ships was 25 percent.[17] The
large scale on which the slave trade was carried on
must, however, have had a disastrous effect, not
only on the demographical level, especially as the
young African in the prime of his life was the more
favored object of trade, but also on the sedentary
agriculture practiced around the villages. In whole
areas, people did not dare to stay long in the same
place for fear of being noticed by slave traders.

For the purpose of this study, it is interesting to note that the slave trade led to the emergence
of a certain bourgeois trading class among the
Fanti's on the coast, as Macmillan has remarked.[18]

As the Europeans themselves did not engage in
rounding up slaves, this was left to Africans who
raided villages in the inland and brought the people
to the coast where they were sold to the companies.
A whole class of relatively rich traders developed,
in this way. They were on good terms with the European traders and fulfilled the role of intermediary
between the chiefs in the inland and the European
companies. We find here the first beginning of a
middle class.

Precursors of the colonial era, the trading companies of North Western Europe, followed the same
simple policy of all good merchants: that is, to obtain as many goods as possible for the lowest of
prices and the least costs. To achieve this, the
acquisition of a monopoly position was important.
The states generally helped to give such a monopoly
as far as the home country was concerned. Through
warfare or international agreements between companies, attempts were made to obtain such a monopoly
also in the areas in which the products were found.
For this, however, the collaboration of the population was needed. In general, this was obtained by
concluding contracts with the rulers in those areas.
In this way, the trading companies maintained and

sometimes even strengthened the political power of
the political élite already established, as in Indonesia.

In Ghana such contracts were concluded with the
Head Man or with the intermediary Fanti trader mentioned above. As we have seen in the previous chapter, the companies in general did not try to exercise influence on the social structure in those countries by introducing new ideas or cultural values.
This was even more true of Ghana where European influence remained strictly restricted to a few strongholds. Nevertheless, a difference must be made here
between the Spanish and Portuguese companies on the
one hand, and the Anglo-Saxon on the other. With
their particular emphasis on conversion to the Christian faith, the Portuguese and Spanish traders had
more in common with their Moslem counterpart. That
they met with considerable success can be seen in
the Christianization of Latin America, the Philippines and the Christian communities on the Malabar
Coast. This has had far-reaching consequences in
later colonial policy. Not only was there a marked
absence of racial discrimination, compared with
Anglo-Saxon colonial practices, but the new élite
which grew up was automatically much more westernized and problems of assimilation or association, as
we met in Indonesia, never occurred. Assimilation
was the logical policy.

For the trading companies belonging to the
Protestant nations, such as England, the Netherlands,
or Denmark, religion was not an export article which
could bring in any profit and they were quite happy
to content themselves with a reference in their constitution to the propagation and dissemination of
the Christian faith. Although there were chaplains
to be found on board the ships of both Portuguese
and Dutch traders, the former saw their mission
among the indigenous people; the latter limited themselves in general to the crew and company employees.
This difference in policy started by the companies
was to have far-reaching effects up to the present
day on the religious level of the people. Another
important effect of the trading companies has been,

as we mentioned in the previous chapter, their introduction of indirect rule as a system of colonial
policy.

DEVELOPMENT OF COLONIAL POLICIES--
DIRECT AND INDIRECT RULE

Ghana's interest in the beginning of the nineteenth century lay, as we noted before, in its ex-
porting of slaves. After the abolition of the slave
trade in 1808,[19] the trading companies soon ran into
difficulties and in 1821, the "African Company of
Merchants" was dissolved and the British Government
took over.

A curious period ensued. Many in Great Britain
had no interest at all in Ghana and felt that there
were other more important things to do on the colonial front. To this must be added the continuously
conflicting situation existing because the Fanti on
the coast felt themselves menaced by the Ashanti in
the interior. The Fanti sought the help of the
British who declared the coastal region a protectorate in 1821. But in 1824, a British column was [20]
wiped out by the Ashanti in the battle of Insamanku.
This caused such consternation that the British Government was seriously considering, under the influence of a Liberal and anti-colonial opinion, a complete withdrawal from Ghana. A compromise was found,
however, whereby (rather uniquely in history) the
British Government handed over its possessions to a
committee of merchants, who received a yearly subsidy of £4,000. Their capable leader, Maclean, managed to come to terms with the Ashanti and a treaty
was signed in 1831.

In the meantime, two important developments
were taking place in Europe. There was the industrialization process with its growing need of export
markets; there was above all Bismarck's new policy
after 1878 to push French colonial interests in
Africa, and in this way make them less dangerous in
Europe. In Africa the run on the "open spaces" took
place at the end of the nineteenth and beginning of

the twentieth century.   The Conference of Berlin
(1884-85) and the ensuing scramble for Africa (1884-
1890) gives perhaps the most typical example of
empire-building, whereby spheres of influence were
neatly divided off with complete disregard for the
geographical or ethnic divisions of the populations
concerned.

Nevertheless, it would be one-sided to see, for
instance, British interest in Ghana as prompted purely by considerations of political advantage and prestige.   Even if the welfare of the people in Africa
was not the main concern, there were many people who
were led by high ethical motives such as the extirpation of the slave trade and who forced the British
Government to intervene.

In 1843, the Colonial Office took over again
and set out to extend British influence.   Through
the purchase of the Danish fort in 1850 and a treaty
with the Dutch in 1872, the British became the sole
rulers in Ghana.   In 1874 the British overran the
coastal territory and after a further series of expeditions against the Ashanti,[21] the latter country
was simply annexed by Royal Decree in 1901, while
the Northern Territories were at the same time
placed under a protectorate.

The system of a native authority, introduced by
the British in many African territories, was, again,
a typical example of a system of indirect rule.   It
recognized the existence of traditional indigenous
authorities (whether chiefs, or tribal councils, or
similar bodies) and allowed them to exercise a wide
range of traditional powers, the use of which was
subject to statutory regulations and administrative
supervision.   However, this native authority system
was not applied to Ghana until after the Second
World War, and was soon to be followed by a new pat-
tern--that of local government.

At the outset, the relationship between the
British Government and Ghana was most complex because of the political history of the multiple dependencies, which comprised the Gold Coast (trans-

ferred to the Crown in 1821), Ashanti (annexed as a
colony in 1901), the northern territories (declared
a Protectorate in 1901), and the mandated territory
of British Togoland. As Hailey remarks:

> The Gold Coast, preoccupied with its
> political problems, neglected for many
> years any attempt to integrate into the
> machinery of government the organisa-
> tions headed by the traditional native
> authorities and was--compared to many
> other territories--noticeably backward
> in the expansion of local economic and
> social service.[22]

In fact, in the early history of Ghana, it was traditional government policy to respect the political independence of the Akan and Fanti confederations.
The native jurisdiction ordinance, which remained in
force until 1927, empowered chiefs and their councillors authorized by native law to enforce by-laws, to
form tribunals to try breaches of those laws, and to
exercise minor civil and criminal jurisdiction.
Moreover, administrative officers had no supervisory
powers over the native tribunals.

When we speak of indirect rule in Ghana in its
early days, it is of an extreme form whereby the ex-
istent political élite is left in place, but no attempt is made to incorporate it into the Colonial
Civil Service, as the Dutch had done in Indonesia.
But, if the Dutch drew the local élite into the
colonial service, they were eager not to interfere
too much in indigenous society, and therefore took
care to study this society and to spend a good deal
of money in anthropological and ethnic research.

> The [British] administration in Africa
> exhibited far less interest in investi-
> gations of this nature than was shown by
> the Dutch in Indonesia. There was, how-
> ever, a special reason for the interest
> shown by the Dutch; from the outset they
> had determined to exercise local rule en-
> tirely through indigenous authorities,

and they were anxious, as a matter of
policy, to protect Native customs from
any form of foreign encroachment.[23]

Another difference between the British and
Dutch systems was that, because of the strong tradition in Britain of the rule of law, British policy
always tended to emphasize the judicial aspect of
native authority. It tended--so to speak--to make a
magistrate and judge of every native official. The
Dutch, however, were much more prone to emphasize
the aspects of peace and order (orde en rust) and
made a policeman and a nightwatchman of even the
European official.

The system of indirect rule versus direct rule
had one extremely important consequence as far as
the emergence of a new élite was concerned. Under
the system of indirect rule, the bulk of the civil
servants were recruited from the indigenous political élite who were already present and whose positions were only confirmed. Such a system, therefore, only needed a relatively small number of European civil servants for the higher echelons of the
administration, and to control or advise the indigenous ruling class. It was, moreover, not necessary
to train great numbers of native civil servants for
the lower functions.

The system of direct rule, however, as the
British practiced it in large parts of India and
Burma, demanded a greater number of European civil
servants, at the same time, the training of a great
number of indigenous civil servants.

Both systems--that of direct and of indirect
rule--had far-reaching consequences for the educational policy to be followed. In the case of indirect rule, little attention needed to be given to
the education and training of a new class of indigenous civil servants, but with a system of direct
rule--unless one wanted to introduce a large staff
of civil servants from Europe--one had to put emphasis on schooling and training. The Dutch system of
indirect rule, therefore, is largely responsible for

the fact that education was introduced much too late
into Indonesia and that the building of a western-
educated élite had still made relatively little progress when the struggle for independence was on, as
we will see later.

Moreover, as we have seen in the previous chapter, during the latter years of Dutch rule, when
more emphasis was given to education, a split appeared in the Prijaji class. The old nobility, less
educated in a western sense and through tradition
assured of their position, were attacked by the lower
Prijaji class who, in general, were more western-
educated but not assured of a position in the colonial administration.

The case in Ghana was similar to that of Indonesia. The clash which occurred here was between
the traditional political élite, which was incorporated into the civil service much too late on the
one hand, and the offshoot of a middle class of
traders and cocoa growers who went in for western
education.

One can therefore rightly remark that the
colonial regimes based on a system of indirect rule
and therefore in those days much less "imperialistic"
in outlook than the regimes based on a system of
direct rule, considerably augmented the difficulties
at the time of the turnover from a colonial to an
independent state, this because of the negligence of
western education and therefore the tardiness in
creating a western-educated political élite large
enough in number and long enough incorporated into
the administrative system to get acquainted with
western democratic processes of government. The
modern history of Indonesia and India forms a living
proof of this.

CHANGES IN COLONIAL POLICY:
THE WHITE MAN'S BURDEN

In Indonesia we have seen under the impulse of
new philosophical trends in Europe a change in policy

which was called the "Ethical Policy."   In Britain,
we note a similar change, which was termed the
"White Man's Burden."   The white man's burden was a
burden of guilt, the sense of a debt to be repaid.[24]

Here, as in Indonesia, under the influence of
the new policy, one soon ran into the dilemma of
assimilation or association.   French colonial policy
pursued the first system for a long time, while the
British in West Africa--notably under the influence
of Lugard, the builder of Nigeria--favored that of
association.[25]   In this, anthropologists played a
large part with their insistence that the African
was a tribesman who should be allowed to develop his
own institutions according to his own character.

It should be added that such a policy, for a
country like Ghana--which in comparison with so many
other British possessions offered neither the possibility of white colonization nor profitable trade--
was the most advantageous from a Treasury point of
view.   As Hanna remarked: "No compelling sense of
urgency, therefore, inspired the administration;
they dealt as best they could with the problems of
the day, with such meagre financial resources--and
consequently of personnel--as were available."[26]
The revenues which could be collected were not even
adequate to pay for the rudimentary functions of government.   Grants of aid, therefore, had to be sought
from the metropolitan country for an initial period
of some twenty to thirty years.   However, "these
grants were kept to the bare minimum and were in no
circumstances made available to finance development,
still less to provide any kind of social service."[27]

It was only in 1930 that the British changed
their policy and started the "Colonial Development
Fund."   In 1940, the Colonial Development and Welfare Act was passed and, as the name indicated, it
became policy then to finance welfare services such
as education and health, besides the development of
economic resources.[28]

Education in Ghana, as in many other parts of
Africa, was left to missionary societies almost until

the Second World War. "As in the countries of Western Europe, so in their African colonies, popular
education was first conceived as a function of the
Christian Churches."[29] The earliest schools were
started by Portuguese missionaries in the eighteenth
century and, with the European settlements on the
coast, came other Mission schools.

> It was, however, neither the Dutch nor
> the British settlers who were responsible
> for the penetration of tropical Africa by
> Christian teachers, but the societies es-
> tablished in European countries by several
> Christian sects. They found the money;
> they appointed the missionaries; they were
> responsible for establishing the mission
> stations which, in many parts of Africa,
> are still the most prominent evidence of
> Western civilization.[30]

Boyon cites some interesting statistics.[31] Of
the 139 schools which existed in 1881, three were
government schools (2 in Accra and one in Cape
Coast). The Basel missions had 47; the Methodists
84; the Bremer mission 4 and the Catholic mission 1.
In 1914, the Minister of Education was still responsible for only 8 percent of the schools.

SOCIAL CHANGES: EUROPEAN ELITE, NATIVE BOURGEOISIE, WESTERN EDUCATED ELITE

In Indonesia we noted during the period of the
ethical policy the growth of a European élite. In
Africa, during the same period, the European colony
in some areas has grown to such an extent that it is
likely to become a permanent part of the population,
but at the same time cannot be considered as one
class or, even less, as one élite, as in South Africa
or Kenya. In other areas, there has never been a
sizable number of Europeans, as in the British colonies on Africa's West Coast. In some cases, however, the descendants of the African slaves who had
returned from the Americas, where they had been imbued with western culture, played a somewhat similar

role to that of the western élite, as in the case of
Liberia and Sierra Leone.

In Ghana, because of its bad climate and the
prevalence of malaria, a European colony only developed just before and after independence.   Restricted
as it was to a few civil servants, teachers and
tradesmen, but a relatively large number of European
missionaries, it has never developed into an élite
group with a great sense of self-identification.
(The Roman Catholic missionaries, in general, were
not of British nationality.)   It has nevertheless--
and maybe even to a greater extent--made European
civilization the social target for Africans.   As
Busia remarked, the Europeans "have set standards
which have determined the goals and aspirations, particularly of the new élite of educated Africans to
whom the Europeans are a model."[32]

If, on the one hand, British indirect rule in
Africa has avoided as much as possible the employ-
ment of any local authority, which had not held a
recognized position of influence derived from indigenous custom or tradition, such as the Dutch had
in Indonesia, on the other hand, it left them room
for much greater initiative and freedom of action
within the framework of statutory regulations.
Therefore, it did not force a change in their dependency on traditional sources to that of dependency
on government support through education.   The aim of
British and Dutch indirect rule was the same: to use
the traditional authorities as agencies of change;
but, to succeed in this, it was necessary for those
traditional authorities themselves to suffer a radical change in the process.   This has now succeeded
better in Indonesia than in Ghana.

The political élite in Ghana, made up of the
Chiefs and Councillors, has only very lately taken
the path of Westernization through education and
therefore had been bypassed by a new western-educated
group.   On the other hand, of great importance in
Ghana has been the development of the bourgeoisie.
We have already spoken of the class of middlemen
which grew up during the period of the slave trade.

To this was added much later a kind of agricultural
bourgeoisie, based on the production of cocoa.[33]
This new bourgeoisie, which had often broken through
the tribal way of life, and which lived to a great
extent in the cities, often did its best to give its
children Western schooling. It is from this group
that developed the new western-educated élite which
was soon to take the country's destiny in hand.

The process of social change caused by the
growth of a European class, the development of a native bourgeoisie and, notably, the rise of a western-
educated native élite, was to be considerably accel-
erated by the emergence of a new social phenomenon
which we will discuss in our next chapter--that of
nationalism.

Footnotes to Chapter 3

1. For general reading, we reccmmend: Jacques
Boyon, Le Ghana, Naissance d'un Etat africain (Paris:
A. Colin, 1958; K. A. Busia, The Challenge of Africa
(London: Pall Mall Press, 1962); R. Cornevin, His-
toire de l'Afrique des Origines à nos jours (Paris:
Payot, 1956); J. D. Fage, An Introduction to the His-
tory of West Africa (Oxford: Oxford University Press,
1956); John Gunther, Inside Africa (London: Hamish
Hamilton, 1955); Hailey, op. cit.; George Padmore,
The Gold Coast Revolution--The Struggle of an Afri-
can People from Slavery to Freedom (London: Dennis
Dobson, 1953).

2. "We should aim at an even greater glory and
majesty than that which existed in the days of ancient
Ghana, the land of our forbears." Speech by Dr. Kwame
Nkrumah from his autobiography, Ghana (Edinburgh:
Thomas Nelson and Sons, Ltd., 1959), p. 153.

3. Cornevin, op. cit., p. 165.

4. Hailey, op. cit., p. 35.

5. Cornevin, op. cit., p. 165.

6.   "Head Chief" was the term originally used. The term "Paramount Chief" was introduced in 1925 by an order in Council of the Gold Coast Legislation.

7.   The term "stool" is probably of Dutch origin-- Dutch "stoel" meaning chair--indicating the sacred chair used by the paramount chief. The dismissal of a paramount chief was called "de-stooling," a prac- tice often used in the 18th century.

8.   Kaj. Birket-Smith, Geschichte der Kultur (Zurich: Urell Fussli Verlag, 1946). On p. 277, the author mentions: "bei den Aschanti laut z.b., das sich 'Blut,' Titel und festes Eigentum in der Frauen linie vererben, währen die Geister der väterlichen Ahnen, der Kult, die Totemzeichen und die bewechliche Habe der Mannes linie folgen."

9.   Cornevin, op. cit., p. 192.

10.   In fact, the V.O.I.C. was the first Dutch company to reach Ghana. As its Charter, however, stipulated that its territory lay between the Cape and the Straits of Magellan, and to allow other Dutch merchant interests to get into Ghana, the Dutch West Indies Company was founded. (Ibid., p. 210.)

11.   In 1642, the Portuguese and Dutch struck a deal whereby the Portuguese interests in Ghana were exchanged for Dutch interests in Brazil. (Ibid., p. 213.)

12.   It has served for many years as the residence of the British Governor General, and is still in use by the Ghanaian Government, who lodge their important visitors there.

13.   It obtained its Charter from Charles II in 1672. Later, it ran into trouble and was changed to the African Company of Merchants in 1750, and ob- tained a yearly Government subsidy as is mentioned in the Encyclopaedia Brittanica.

14.   Johan van Hulzen, Onze Westindische Geschie- denis (Den Haag: W. van Hoeve, 1946), p. 189.

15. Ibid., p. 279.

16. As mentioned before (note 11), the Dutch struck a deal with the Portuguese in 1642. In 1720, the German settlement was sold to the Dutch for 7,200 ducats and 12 slaves of which 6 were attached to golden chains. (Cornevin, op. cit., p. 213.) Likewise, the Danish sold their castle in 1850 to the British and the Dutch. Their possessions were sold to the British in 1872 in exchange for the withdrawal of British claims on Sumatra. (Boyon, op. cit., p. 12.)

17. Van Hulzen, op. cit., p. 193.

18. W. H. Macmillan, Africa Emergent (Harmondsworth: Penguin Books, 1948), p. 38.

19. In 1808, the shipping of slaves on British ships was forbidden. In 1833, Great Britain abolished slavery in all her possessions. (Van Hulzen, op. cit., pp. 319-320.)

20. Cornevin, op. cit., p. 290.

21. In 1896, King Prempeh and his royal family were deported to the Sechelles island from which they were only allowed to return in 1924.

22. Hailey, op. cit., p. 315.

23. Ibid., pp. 52-53.

24. Laurens van der Post, The Dark Eye in Africa (London: Hogarth Press, 1955), p. 91. The term "white man's burden" was first coined by Kipling.

25. In East and South Africa, under the influence of the large white settlements, a policy of "apartheid" was followed. This policy shares with that of assimilation the notion of the superiority of western culture. It considers that white supremacy can best be safeguarded by not letting the native share in it and in allowing him to develop his own cultural pattern.

26.   A. J. Hanna, European Rule in Africa (London: Cox and Wyman Ltd., 1961), p. 15.

27.   Ibid.

28.   From April 1, 1946 to March 31, 1960 Britain has made free grants available to her African dependencies, amounting to about £129,000,000 sterling. (Ibid., p. 16.)

29.   Hailey, op. cit., p. 1133.

30.   Ibid., p. 1134.

31.   Boyon, op. cit., p. 255.

32.   K. A. Busia, "The Present Situation and Aspirations of Elites in the Gold Coast," International Social Science Bulletin, VIII, No. 3 (1956), 427.

33.   According to a legend, the cocoa was introduced by Chief Tetteh Quarshie from Fernando-Po, around 1878. Probably because of the difficult climate the cocoa trade was never developed on a big scale by Europeans, but has remained a population product in the forest region.

CHAPTER 4 NATIONALISM AND THE POLITICAL ELITE BEFORE INDEPENDENCE IN INDONESIA

It has been said that nationalism is the biggest boomerang which western educational systems have hurled at the Asian and African colonial possessions. This might be an exaggerated statement and it certainly does not take into account the good aspects of nationalism which might bind a people together for better or worse. In talking about nationalism, therefore, it is necessary to make clear what is understood by the term.

To follow the development of nationalism, and the role it has played in giving birth to a new political élite, we intend to study in this and the next chapter the different organizations and movements which existed in Indonesia and Ghana in their pre-nationalist stages (the end of the nineteenth century and the beginning of the twentieth).[1] In Indonesia, the Sarekat Islam, Budi Utomo and the Indische Partij are typical examples of such movements, and we want to define which factors of a religious, socio-economic, cultural or purely political nature have helped to shape them. We also intend to analyze which factors of an international character have influenced the growth and development of nationalism as a political force of the first order, and thereby the orientation of the élite in its present form. We refer here especially to the influence of the two world wars, the birth of the United Nations, and the spread of such international concepts as socialism, communism and anti-colonialism.

Finally, the Japanese occupation has had important consequences for the building up of the various nationalistic forces and consequently for the attainment of independence.

THE NOTION OF NATIONALISM
IN COLONIAL COUNTRIES

A lot is being written about nationalism--that
uncontrolled source of energy which, as history has
shown, can be tapped for the promotion as well as
the downfall of peoples or nations. The outcome depends, in general, on the leadership group--the political élite--and the way in which it wants to play
on and use this emotional reservoir of a people.
There is no doubt that nationalistic feelings have
been one of the driving forces behind the process of
decolonization, the end of which we are witnessing
today, and that they will remain one of the most important tools for mobilizing a "national élan" which
could be used for the promotion of the welfare of
peoples in developing countries.

For our purposes, in this and the next chapter,
I would like to define nationalism in the following
terms: nationalism is the strongest emotional force
capable of aligning the mass of the people in a region behind a leadership group of that region. It
has set itself clearly political goals, aimed primarily at the realization or maintenance of independence for that region and consequently--or subse-
quently--the promotion of the welfare of the people
of that region.

Such a definition brings out different aspects
of nationalism. It underlines the fact that it is
an emotional force and therefore that it is very difficult to judge precisely its depth or strength at a
particular moment. In general, as we shall see,
nationalism, as a western idea, did not appear to
take a very strong hold in Asia and Africa before
the end of the nineteenth century, or even the beginning of the twentieth. This does not mean, however,
that nationalistic tendencies were not present in
one way or another before that time. For instance,
we note that with the arrival of the white man in
Indonesia in the seventeenth century, a great part
of the Indonesian nobility--which was Hindu--turned
to Islam, the religion of the people (see Chapter 2)

and thereby reinforced their position vis-à-vis the
Dutch invaders, a clearly nationalistic phenomenon
according to our definition.

This example reveals, however, another important aspect. Nationalism is a latent force which
does not come into the open unless it is evoked and
channelled by a leadership group. Such a leadership
group, if successful, can then count more and more
on the support of an increasing portion of the masses
and, in this way, the leadership may become a political élite. Nationalism has thus played a great role
in the emergence of the new political élite in Asia
and Africa.

However, the process is a gradual one. The
leadership group presents a platform; such a platform is attractive to the people and they will start
aligning themselves behind it. From then on, we
will see a continual interchange of ideas between
the élite and the masses. The leadership group wid-
ens or radicalizes its platforms; the masses approve
by remaining faithful, or disapprove by losing interest or turning to another new leadership group. All
these processes we have seen happening in Asia and
Africa, and they go on continuously, although it is
often extremely difficult to state in exact terms
the measure of interchange taking place between the
masses and the élite at any given period. Nevertheless, we can truthfully state that nationalism has
not only led to the emergence of a new political
élite, but that it has also had a great influence on
the role of that élite.

Finally, the goal of nationalism as stated in
our definition is primarily the attainment or maintenance of the independence of a region, and subsequently the promotion of the welfare of the people of that
region. Although its political character is thus
clearly given, this does not mean to say that all expressions of nationalism have had such a clear connotation from their outset. On the one hand, there is
a certain development which might take place in the
thinking of the leadership group; on the other hand,
it depends on the character and the orientation of

that group which might be initially, as was the case
in Indonesia, a strongly religious, colored group,
which later became a more social-conscious one (under the influence of socialism) and finally was a
western-educated political group. At the same time,
nationalism, as we have noted also in European countries occupied during the Second World War, can take
on the guise of a cultural and religious movement
for reform. Its political aims are not directly and
clearly presented, because circumstances do not per-
mit this, but they might nevertheless be considered
as fundamentally present, be it more or less consciously.

PRE-NATIONALISTIC FORCES: ISLAM, SAREKAT ISLAM, BUDI UTOMO, INDISCHE PARTIJ

In Indonesia, the presence of the Dutch started
to grow into an issue for the masses in the nineteenth century, because of the spread of western
ideals on the cultural and socio-economic level.
Slowly, these began to infiltrate the dessah, for instance through the forced cultivation system, and we
note in increasing reaction the growing influence of
Islam and its religious leaders, who became for the
population the upholders of the former indigenous
life and customs. The existing élite (Prijaji: see
Chapter 2) were driven to choosing either to align
themselves more closely with the Islamic leaders, or
to westernize themselves. In their choice, they
were influenced by three factors, of which the first
was the prestige attached to the West which had been
spread through its educational system. As was mentioned in Chapter 2, Wertheim believes that "the extension of the white man's power over the coloured
races in the 19th century was accompanied everywhere
by a marked rise in the social standing of the whites,
and high social regard for all outward characteristics, such as language, dress and skin colour, which
symbolized the white race." This was noticeable in
Indonesia, particularly in the cities, where with
the growth of a European community a certain western
way of life was introduced. A second factor was the

Dutch system of indirect rule, referred to earlier,
which made the Indonesian Prijaji class automatically the executors of colonial policy. The third was
that Islam, in the traditional and watered-down ver-
sion in which it presented itself, lost some of its
attraction for the upper classes.

Therefore, a growing attachment to western ideas
on the part of the Prijaji class may be noted, although this did not go so far as to make them become
Christians; this in contrast to the African élite,
among whom we see a growing number turning to Christianity.

At the same time, however, we note that Islam,
which until then was generally to be found in the
cities and on the coast, penetrated the interior.
"Islam gave the small man a sense of his individual
worth as a member of the Islamic community,"[2] and its
development could be described as a kind of pre-
nationalist movement directed against the penetration of western ideas. Within the Islamic community
certain reform movements developed, which were greatly influenced by Egypt or India, and which stressed
a return to the sources of Islam--the Koran--and the
development of a personal religion as, for instance,
in the "Mohammadyah" and "Ahmadyah" movements.[3]
Their aim, with the growth of education, was to prevent further westernization of the Prijaji and the
middle class, and it is these movements which have
played an important role up to the present time in
the development of Islamic cultural associations and
political movements.

The articulate leadership for such movements
was mainly drawn, apart from religious leaders, from
the Islamic middle class and traders, especially in
the city. They had a bourgeois outlook, were rather
moderate in their political convictions, but formed
at the same time a group which felt more and more
the pinch of Dutch economic policy, which gave little
scope for their commercial activities. Therefore,
they, more than the Prijaji class, were likely to
seek comfort in a religion which seemed very clearly
to separate the Indonesian from the European, and,

at the same time, were apt to support any movement
which allowed them to resist Dutch commercial and
economic pressure. A special section of this middle
class was made up of the Arabs and West Coast Suma-
trans, who had not suffered so much during the Dutch
economic regime in the nineteenth century, and who
had entrenched themselves rather well as the middlemen through which western and Indonesian products
were distributed to the population. Around 1900, however, they began to feel increasing competition from
the Chinese element which had become more active.

It was this group which, around 1904, started
an organization, "Jam Yat Khap," for mutual help and
assistance with a strong inclination towards Mohammed-
anism. They ran schools and brought teachers from
Arabia. The organization met with success in several
parts of Java and similar groups were later organized
in Sumatra.

More important, however, became another organization, probably inspired by the former, Sarekat
Islam.[4] Its organizer was a batik dealer from
Surakarta--Hadji Samanhoudi--who in his field felt
more and more the influence of the Chinese trader
and the European cotton industry. With the help of
Raden Mas Tirtoadisoerjo,[5] he organized the Sarekat
Dagang Islam--United Commercial Islam--in Surakarta,
in 1911. Membership grew very quickly, so quickly
in fact that it outgrew the commercial category for
which it had been created. If the intention had
been to resist, through mutual help, the growing
competition of the Chinese, its younger members soon
started to treat the Chinese as a dangerous racial
element, and to attack them. The Government intervened and Samanhoudi had to start all over again,
this time with the help of another Prijaji member,
Raden Amar Sayed Tjokroaminoto.[6]

In September 1912, the Sarekat Islam of Surkarta
was founded in his name and in that of eleven Solo
merchants and sultans' employees. Its aims were:
(a) assistance to members in difficulties through no
fault of their own; (b) advancement of the commercial
spirit among the indigenous population; (c) advance-

ment of the spiritual development and material interests of Indonesians, thereby assisting in raising
their standards, and (d) opposition to misunderstand-
ings about Islam while advancing the religious life
among Indonesian peoples in accordance with the laws
and customs of that religion.

Both the commercial aspect and the religious appeal of Sarekat Islam were more strongly emphasized
than in the preceding organization, and although it
had not existed for very many years before internal
strife broke out, it became the most powerful of all
organizations, existing until the independence of
Indonesia--as much to the surprise of its organizers
as to that of the Government. This must undoubtedly
be ascribed to its religious appeal. Tjokroaminoto
put it in this way: "The Sarekat Islam uses religion
like a rope, as a means to bind, and what is wanted--
all-out progress--is not hindered by that religion."[7]

Chapters were rapidly founded in all large cities, and in Djakarta, for instance, it soon claimed
more than 12,000 members. Nevertheless, its great
strength came more from the rural areas, in particular East Java. Because of its mass appeal, the
Sarekat Islam soon became the spokesman for the aspirations of the Indonesian people, although in the
beginning it was a very confused spokesman, as its
leaders had not counted on such success and had to
adapt themselves to their new role.

As to the attitude of the Government, although
there was much criticism among the European administration who feared the growing self-assertion of the
masses as shown through the Sarekat Islam, the organization was born at the height of the Ethical Policy
and Governor General Idenburg saw no reason to go
against this organization, although he refused it
legal recognition as far as its central body was concerned. His views are clearly set out in a letter
written to A. Kuyper less than a week before his re-
fusal to grant the organization legal status.

That which goes by that name [moral de-
generation] is nothing more than that

the native begins to reflect about himself and his environment. It is the beginning of his "awakening" and this does
not have to be a degeneration (and up to
now it is not such: I dare all to prove
the contrary), but it is the end of the
taillable et corvéable à merci. We must
be pleased by this even though it gives
us certain difficulties; we wanted it so--
at least so we said--and advanced it
through our education.[8]

As far as Sarekat Islam's attitude towards the
Government was concerned, at its first Congress in
1913 in Surabaya, Tjokro had stated the organization's position by saying: "We are loyal to the Government; we are satisfied under Dutch rule,"[9] although it is doubtful whether a growing majority of
its members thought likewise. It is interesting,
for instance, to note that, at another meeting later
in 1913 in Surakarta, it was decided to keep administrators as far as possible out of the organization,
and to restrict membership to natives.

While Sarekat Islam was a real mass movement,
strongly influenced by Islam and led by the bourgeois middle class, completely different were the
"Budi Utomo" and the "Indische Partij." Their existence shows another aspect of the changes taking
place.

They were, as von Niel clearly shows, an outcome
of and a reaction against that aspect of the Ethical
Policy which emphasized the importance of education
for the broad masses. The Budi Utomo (Beautiful Endeavour) was created in 1908, and it received legal
recognition the next year. It was dominated from
the beginning by the intellectual element from Java,
and its aim was the advancement of the Javanese
people and the rejuvenation of Javanese culture.

The original spark was ignited by a retired
doctor-djawa, Mas Wahidin Soediroesodo, who wanted
to establish a scholarship fund to aid promising
Javanese students. This idea was later enlarged,

and the Budi Utomo started among the young medical
students in Djakarta. Chapters were soon founded in
other schools such as the Veterinary, the Agricultural, and the administrators and teachers training colleges. The First Congress was held in 1908. It was
the more elderly and conservative elements who took
the reins, such as the first President, Raden A.
Tirikakoesoema, retired regent of Karanganjar; but
they were soon opposed by a more radical group, out
for direct political action, such as Dr. Tjipto
Mangoenkoesoema, and Soewardi Soerijningrat,[10] who
were convinced that the cultural approach would lead
to weakness and compromise.

A third group of middle-of-the-roaders was
formed by Raden Soetomo and Goenawan Mangoenkoesoema.[11]
They were not in agreement with the conservative section, which they felt only tried to secure their situation; nor were they in agreement with the radical
Tjipto-Soewardi wing, whose action they felt would be
suicidal for the organization. They stood for a raising of standards according to the Ethical Policy.
They found support among some of the high Javanese
nobility, such as the house of Paku Alam, but at the
same time, they found more of their adherents among
the lower Prijaji families and the lower civil servants who were more western in outlook than the higher Prijaji groups (see Chapter 2).

In 1911, they took over the Budi Utomo and
caused a three-way split. The conservative section
left, and created the Regentenbond (Regents Union)
in 1913, which aimed at greater recognition of the
traditional position of the Prijaji through more
local autonomy.

The radical group of Soewardi and Tjipto left
also and later with the Indo-European E. F. Douwes
Dekker[12] formed the Indische Partij (Indies Party).
This group, mostly under the influence of Douwes
Dekker, had clear political goals. He was the first
person in his newspaper, De Express, to come out for
an independent and united Indonesia. In fact, the
party was formed mostly of Indo-Europeans who were,
in the first place, interested in advancing their

social position and obtaining equality of treatment
in the civil service with the Indonesians.[13]   They
achieved this in 1918, although in 1913 the three
leaders were exiled, and the party never received
legal recognition.

THE INFLUENCE OF THE FIRST WORLD WAR

International events have contributed very
strongly to the forging of nationalism into a political weapon of the first magnitude. Among the most
important ones, we can count the two World Wars, the
growth of communications, the spread of international ideologies such as socialism and communism, and
the influence of the United Nations.

The First World War brought about, for all colonial countries, a certain severing of contacts with
the metropolitan powers. Communications became more
difficult, and this gave the colonial administrators
more independence to rule without too strict supervision from the metropolitan countries. The Netherlands, keeping a precarious neutrality, saw its contact effectively weakened by the British control of
neutral shipping--wireless contact with Java was
only established towards the end of the war. The
result was that, on the economic level, stimulation
was given to produce in the colonies goods which
were formerly imported. Numerous small industries
started to flourish, many of which died after the
war, because of a renewed liberal import policy,
thereby producing economic crises. On the political
level the creation of the Volksraad (peoples' council) was of some importance.[14]

In a sense, it would have been expected that
the First World War would have given a big stimulus
to one of the most important goals of the Ethical
Policy--the growth of an Indonesian "entrepreneurial"
middle class. This did not, in fact, happen. It
was mostly the Arabs and Chinese who profited from
the situation, and the Indonesian middle class, up
until independence, remained restricted mostly to
landholders, administrators and the intellectual

élite engaged in professions such as teaching and
medicine, in contrast with Ghana where we have seen
already that a producing (cocoa) and trading middle
class was developing.

It is more difficult to judge the psychological
effects of the First World War on the people in Indonesia. Had it shattered the superiority of the
white race? Did Wilson's Fourteen Points find a response in the colonial territories? Did the Russian
Revolution become a goal for indigenous societies?
In all likelihood, the greatest impact which the
First World War had on the colonized peoples must be
found in the changed attitudes and new ideals which
developed in Europe and the United States, and were
later exported to the colonized countries, either by
the white element directly, or through their educational system and universities.

In Indonesia, the reactions of the Indonesian
people are best seen by studying the development of
the Sarekat Islam during this period as their leaders reflected on what was going on among the Indonesian élite. The strength of Sarekat Islam was, as
we have already said, in the rural districts. Here,
in the dessah, it was the religious teacher who was
first won over to the idea, and he then generally
managed to create a local chapter. A lot of mysti-
cal and religious ritual was involved, such as the
taking of secret oaths, the selling of djimat--
tokens--for invulnerability, and so on. Important
in this was also the Javanese myth of the ratu adil--
the prince who would return to lead the people to
Paradise. Tjokroaminoto, Secretary of Sarekat Islam,
charismatic leader and most powerful orator, was
seen by many as the ratu adil. All this accounted
for the very quick growth of the organization. By
1918, the Sarekat Islam claimed nearly 3,000,000 members, but it should be added that most of the members were completely passive.

The leadership of Sarekat at this period could
be divided into: (a) the religious group, which was
very powerful on the local level but had little say
in the organization at the top; this changed later

on when intellectuals such as Hadji Agus Salem[15] organized this element against the more radical tendencies; (b) the original commercial group, in which we
continue to find Arab elements, but which soon declined as the organization turned away more and more
from its original commercial goals; and (c) the
western-educated elements--intellectual or semi-
intellectual--many of whom were dissatisfied with
the government structure of the time, such as the
above-mentioned Raden Goenawan in Djakarta, Abdoel
Moeis in Bandoeng, Semaoen in Semarang.[16]

In general, however, this élite wanted to pursue the aims of the Ethical Policy, and their leadership was not based so much on Indonesian thinking or
aspirations, as on western concepts which were con-
tained in the Ethical Policy and later in socialist
thinking.

Although the leadership could be considered--
from an educational standpoint--advanced and standing far above the masses, it did not comprise the
best-educated element in Indonesia, except for such
people as Salim. Economically, it came from the
middle income group, and socially it represented generally the lesser Prijaji group and--in the begin-
ning--some merchants.

Only when the organization became legally recognized in 1915 did it manage to obtain the sympathy
of some of the higher-placed Prijaji in the civil
service, such as Raden A. Wiranatakoesoemah, Regent
of Tjiandjur, and Achmad Djajadiningrat, Regent of
Seram.

Another and more fatal weakness of Sarekat
Islam was its lack of organization and finances. As
we have seen, the more the movement departed from
its original aims, the less support it received from
the merchants and commercial class. To support its
journal, the Utusan Hindia (Indies Courier), it had
to rely more and more upon advertisements from the
Chinese element, who in that way managed to stem completely the anti-Chinese forces present in the early
Sarekat Islam.

Most of the members in the villages paid their
membership fees once only. To remedy the situation,
the Sarekat Islam had to lean more and more on their
better-organized chapters in the cities, and seek
support also from trade union members. This, however,
led immediately to a shift in policy away from the
Islam appeal, to that of social and economic improve-
ment. In the end, it led to friction between the
Salim--religious--and Semaoen--communist--wings in
the Sarekat, and to its downfall.

What, then, was the policy of Sarekat Islam during this period, as voiced during its congresses?

We have already noted that, at its opening
Congress, Tjokro had stated: "We are satisfied with
Dutch rule." At its national Congress in 1916, he
repeated this in other terms, but expressed the hope
that the goal of self-determination should be
achieved in ten years. "Our motto should be: 'Together with the Government and in support of the Government to steer in the proper direction.'"[17] He
further stressed the need for more democratization
in local government and reforms in the dessah.
Semaoen, who was also present as representative of a
trade union, stressed the need for more radical
goals, but received little attention. However, at
the Congress a year later (October 1917), we hear a
more demanding tone. In a platform speech written
by Salim for this Congress, we read, among other
things: "The central Sarekat Islam denies the right
of any people or group to rule another people or
group of people," and: "In consideration of the
fact that the majority of the native people exist in
miserable living conditions, the C.S.I. will continuously oppose any domination by sinful capitalism."[18]

At the same Congress, Moeis launched an appeal
for Kemerdikaan--liberty--of the Indies.

A year later, in 1918, the tone became even
more radical, and Semaoen, who by now had entered
the inner circle, went so far as to brand the Ethical Policy as one of "divide and rule."

The leaders of the Ethical movement, including the Governors-General Idenburg and van Limburg Stirum, at heart supported the movement which was, in matter of fact, only proclaiming their own theses, including that of eventual self-government for the Indonesians. Wherever possible, they tried to pacify the feelings of Sarekat Islam. The opening of government jobs to all qualified persons, regardless of race, the removal of the head tax, the abolition of forced cultivation, the establishment of the People's Council, the expansion of education, are examples of this. However, a growing number of lower government officials, and other Europeans, did not agree with this policy. They feared that giving in would only lead to more exaggerated demands, and so there was a strong undercurrent working against Sarekat Islam. This in turn exasperated the Indonesian leaders.

Regarding the attitude of the Dutch administration, mention must also be made of the influence exercised by the Dutch adviser on Moslem affairs, Snouck Hurgronje.[19] During the nineteenth century the Dutch attitude towards Islam always had been one of the greatest apprehension, reinforced by upheavals which presented themselves as holy wars.[20] At the turn of the century Snouck pleaded, and won, the cause of a new policy towards Islam. His argument was that Islam as a religion was not a potential enemy; Islam as a political doctrine, shaped especially in the form of a pan-Islamic movement inspired by the outside, could however become one.[21] He therefore favored an attitude of tolerance towards Islamic religious life and opposed obstruction of the Mecca pilgrimage. In this way, he felt that Islamic religious leaders would be convinced that the Dutch colonial regime constituted no threat to Islamic religious life. On the other hand, if Islamic leaders engaged in political activities, the government should be on its guard and signs of incitement immediately suppressed.

His policy was first applied during the Atjeh wars, where it proved successful, and soon became the official policy of the government. It was for this reason that movements like the "Mohammadyah" or

"Ahmadyah" never encountered any difficulties from
the government. Sarekat Islam also had a religious
character and therefore fell, especially in the beginning, into the same category, but the more its
political character became apparent, the more it began to fall, in the eyes of many government officials,
into the second category of Islamic organizations
with political purposes against which action should
be taken.

The radicalization on the part of Sarekat Islam
finally led to local incidents, such as those in
Garut in July 1919, which brought to light the fact
that there was a revolutionary wing active in the
Sarekat Islam--the so-called Section B--which aimed
at independence by force. There is no doubt also
that certain sections of the European press used
this to flaunt Sarekat Islam as a revolutionary organization.

The result was keenly felt in the organization
itself. Most of the members had joined for the religious or associational aspect of the organization,
and did not want to subscribe to a revolutionary
movement. The bulk of the peasants fell away, many
turning to the Mohammadyah. The moderate intellectual element turned to the Budi Utomo, and the
Sarekat Islam had to carry on, reduced in numbers
and with its leadership split. Its role in Indonesian political life was over.

Historically speaking, it has been a mass movement, which had brought forward a leadership group--
few of whom, however, would later continue to play a
big role in the political evolution. It had not,
therefore, created a new political élite, but it had
certainly greatly influenced those who were to be
among the political élite of the future. What was
more, the end of Sarekat Islam also meant practically the end of the Ethical Policy. Being a group in-
doctrinated by, and largely willing to follow the
concepts of the Dutch Ethical Policy, its disappearance pulled the rug from under the feet of the European champions of the Ethical Policy.

As far as the fate of the above-mentioned Indonesian organizations during the 20's and 30's is concerned, one can make a few observations.

(a) Since the down-grading of Sarekat Islam in 1920,
    no organization ever managed to get a real mass
    following on a national level. Some, such as
    the Mohammadyah, flourished notably in the coun-
    try. Others, such as Budi Utomo, remained the
    resort of the intellectual element. Again,
    others, such as Sarekat Islam and the Communist
    Party, found their support in the cities among
    the organized workers.

(b) Many began to realize that, to be viable, they
    must find support among the youth. Both the
    Mohammadyah and the Budi Utomo, therefore,
    started youth groups. The first--the "Jong
    Islamiten Bond" (Young Islamic Union) was formed
    in 1925; the Budi Utomo formed the "Tri Koro
    Dharmo" (Three Noble Goals)--later to be called
    the "Jong Java" (Young Java) in 1918.

(c) It became clearer and clearer that the cities
    were the only places where it was possible to
    find a following which could be well organized
    and which was open to new ideas. This, undoubt-
    edly, is due to the process of disintegration of
    Indonesian customs, and to the fact that the pro-
    cesses of social and economic change were most
    felt in the cities. It would be interesting to
    devote a further study to the influence these
    cities wielded on the process of nationalization,
    both in Asia and Africa. Here, we must be satis-
    fied with taking note of this phenomenon. Even
    the Mohammadyah, which remained strongly country-
    based, found it had elements in the cities, and
    spread there through its school system.

(d) The new attitude of the government in not cooper-
    ating as before with those organizations, drove
    them in reaction towards a tendency of non-
    cooperation with the government. None of the
    leadership, nevertheless, turned against the
    authorities. They remained strongly influenced

by the old concepts of the Ethical Policy and,
notably, that of assimilation, in which they
started to run counter to new tendencies prevailing in government circles and among the young intellectual élite.

(e) Finally, we find among all these groups an opening up to socialist ideas; this was favored by
the economic recession after the war and the activities of socialist elements among the Dutch
in Indonesia.

NEW NATIONALISTIC FORCES: THE COMMUNIST
PARTY, THE STUDENT MOVEMENT,
PERHIMPUNAN INDONESIA

It is useful, at this point, to pay some attention to the development of the Communist Party in
Indonesia.

In general, one can say that the spread of communism in all colonial countries has been greatly
helped by those groups most opposed to it: the European bourgeoisie, the government official, and sometimes the Christian missionary. By reading into
every legally expressed aspiration towards more recognition for indigenous people a communist plot,
they have given communism an aureol which it has
never deserved, whether because communism best expressed the universal concepts of social justice and
equality in the beginning, or because it was the
driving force of nationalism and anti-colonialism
later on.

This we have also noted in Indonesia, where government reports and newspaper campaigns around the
twenties tried to exaggerate the communist movement
beyond all reality and, in this way, tried to dis-
credit all national movements and the whole concept
of the Ethical Policy. The "Partai Kommunis Indonesia" (P.K.I.) developed from a group of Dutch leftish socialists, who were active in organizing trade
unions in Semarang, a city where, because of industrialization and urbanization, the process of social

change was particularly acute. Its parent organization had been the Indies Social Democratic organization (I.S.D.V.) started by the Dutch Sneevliet in
1914, and which became more radical after 1917 when
the moderate socialists left, following a similar
break-away in the Netherlands. This group set out
to organize labor. One of the most influential trade
unions, and the one which became the backbone of the
communist element, was the "Vereniging van Spoor en
Tramweg personeel" (V.S.T.P.)--Union of Tram and
Railway Personnel--which was started in Semarang in
1908.

It found capable and dynamic leaders, such as
Semaoen, Raden Darsono,[22] Alimin, and later Tan
Malaka.[23] In May 1920, the I.S.D.V. changed its
name and became the P.K.I. (Communist Party of Indonesia). Darsono was the leader, with Sneevliet exiled and Semaoen in Moscow.

We have spoken already of the early efforts of
these leftish elements to infiltrate the Sarekat
Islam. They were successful in the beginning, thanks
to the support of the trade unions. Later, however,
in October 1921, Salim managed to oust the communist
labor wing at the 6th Congress of the Sarekat. They
then started their own section, the Sarekat Islam
Merah (Red Sarekat Islam), which was later to be
called the Sarekat Rakjat (People's Union), which
took in all the most radical elements of Sarekat
Islam. The strength of the Communist Party was
given in 1924 by Darsono as around 1,000 party members. Its activities from 1921 to 1927 were to organize some local strikes and the much-talked-about
revolt of 1926 in Bantam, West Java, and in 1927 in
the Menang Kabau, which led to its suppression. It
is clear that these revolts, although communist in-
stigated, were examples of uprisings where local
grievances were cleverly played upon.

Alimin, who was the leader, pushed the revolts
through at a meeting in Soerakarta late in 1925, as
he was apparently not able to hold the radical elements otherwise than by the pledge of an early revolution.[24] It seems, however, that neither the

Comintern nor the leaders in exile such as Tan Malaka,
were in agreement with the plans for an uprising.
Alimin, who later met Malaka abroad, received instructions from the latter on matters which were to be discussed with the Executive in Indonesia, instructions
which he did not carry out.[25]

It is interesting to note, in view of communist
claims later, that they were the leaders of the nationalist movement, that the communist leaders in
Indonesia considered nationalism as a contemptible
idea to be fought against. After the Garut incidents, and the government action against the revolutionary elements--section B--of the Sarekat Islam,
one of the leaders, Baars, wrote in Het Vrye Woord,
the P.K.I. organ, on November 20, 1920:

> Yes, it is we international communists,
> who alone have the right to condemn the
> actions of the C.S.I. [Central Sarekat
> Islam]. It is only our Party, none of
> the existing organisations, not even
> the government. They, all of them, are
> flirting with nationalism, and although
> they may at this moment hypocritically
> declare that they do not approve of the
> kind of nationalism of Section B, they
> are still only reaping the harvest which
> they themselves helped to sow. . . .
> This has been another striking illustra-
> tion of the fact that nationalism is de-
> cidedly no "eastern" product but, on the
> contrary, that it displays the same bar-
> baric features here as it does with
> Celtic Irish, or the Slavic Poles, or
> wherever else, for that matter. It is a
> purely negative ideology, and it is more
> securely anchored in hatred of other
> races and groups than in love for one's
> own race. . . . Nationalism is the
> ideology of unity of the [East] Indians,
> and we have already declared that the
> contradictions within native society are
> far too great and crass for any such
> unity.[26]

This seemed to rhyme with some of the conclusions of the Second Congress of the Communist International at Moscow, where it was stated that, although one should try to forge links between the
Western European Communist proletariat and the revolutionary peasant movement in the East . . . "It is,
however, necessary to wage a relentless struggle
against the endeavour to give a communist tinge to
those liberation movements in backward countries
which are not truly communist at all."[27]

The communist-led disturbances in 1926 and 1927
provoked firm action from the government. About
13,000 persons were arrested--about half of whom
were soon released; nearly 4,500 received prison sen-
tences, and about 1,300 were interned in New Guinea.
This meant the end of communist activities in Indonesia until the Second World War.

Van Niel[28] has done some interesting research
into the background of those interned, who were interrogated intensively while in detention (about
1,000 from Java). As to education he noted the following:

(a) the majority had finished their schooling in the
    period from 5 to 20 years prior to the uprising;

(b) of the total group, there were about 761 liter-
    ate, which is an amazingly high percentage if
    one compares it with the average degree of liter-
    acy. However, it is logical that it had to be
    the semi-educated or educated class, who alone
    could lead a revolutionary movement, and that it
    was this element which the Dutch government
    sought to deter first.

If one compares these figures with the over-all
educational figures, the following facts become evident: starting in 1914, and up until 1925, some
23,000 Indonesians had received diplomas from Dutch
native schools (H.I.S.) or European primary schools.
Of this number, 77 were among the communists who
were interned.

Moreover, at the end of 1926 when the revolt occurred, school enrolment was as follows:

406,000 Indonesians in Muslim religious schools;
917,000 Indonesians in Dessah schools;
313,000 Indonesians in Second Class native
        schools;
 79,000 Indonesians in Dutch language primary
        schools.

Against these figures, Van Niel rightly remarks: "It seems justifiable to conclude that the number of persons with education, who engaged in the communist movement, was exceedingly small, compared with the impact of that education."

Furthermore, as far as the function of the prisoners was concerned, only 601 out of the 1,000 gave information. These 601 listed 747 functions (some had more than one), the bulk being member of P.K.I. (249) or member of Sarekat Rajkat (216). Moreover, it was stated that, of the entire group, 57 were from the Prijaji class and 59 persons had made the pilgrimage (hadj) to Mecca.

It is clear that with these arrests, the backbone of the P.K.I. was broken, and so nothing more was heard of this party until the Second World War.

Of more importance from the point of view of our study is another élite which was slowly being trained at universities in the Netherlands, and later in Indonesia. After the First World War, the handful of Indonesians studying in Europe, especially in Leyden, had founded the "Indische Vereeniging" (Indies Society) which was meant to be a meeting-ground for Indonesian students, and which had strong socialist overtones. Under the influence of new members with new ideas who arrived after the war, the name was changed in 1922 to "Perhimpunan Indonesia" (Indonesian Organization). This was, however, more than a mere change of name; it presented a new orientation for a group which was becoming more and more politically conscious, as the declaration of principles accepted at that time shows.

> The future of the people of Indonesia
> is exclusively and solely vested in a
> form of government that is responsible
> to that people in the true sense of the
> word, because only such a form of gov-
> ernment is acceptable to the people.
> Every Indonesian should strive, in con-
> formity with his ability and capacities,
> for this goal, through his own power
> and endeavour, independent of the help
> of outsiders.[29]

What is new in this declaration is not the call
for a representative government, which had already
been voiced by others before, but for a delegation
of responsibility to each and everyone, not relying
on outsiders. It is clear also that there were Indonesians living in the West who had heard Wilson's
principle of self-determination.[30]

The mentor of the Perhimpunan was Dr. Raden
Soetomo. Among the names of the earlier members, we
find many who have played a great role during the
fight for independence, such as the Mangoenkoesoemas,
Raden Iwa Koesoema Soemantri, R. Sastroamuljano,
R. M. Sartono, all sons of the Prijaji class, and
Mohammed Hatta and Soetiman Wirjosandjojo, who came
from merchant families.

After 1924, the Perhimpunan Indonesia became
strongly influenced by socialist and communist thinking, due to the activities of Semaoen and Tan Malaka.
Dr. Soetomo had returned to Indonesia in 1923, where
he started similar clubs as the P.I., for example,
in Surabaia, Djakarta, Semarang and Bogor.

The best known certainly became the one started
in 1926 by Koesno Sasro Soekarno,[31] a young graduate
of the Engineering College in Bandoeng, the "Algemeene
Studie Club" (General Study Club). The Bandoeng group
was more radical than most of the others, and soon became a focal point for members of the Perhimpunan Indonesia, returning to their country.

The programme of the Club was brief: non-

cooperation with the government, and complete and immediate independence for Indonesia.

In 1927, the Club began to form a political party, the Perserikatan Nasional Indonesia (P.N.I.)--
the Indonesian National Union--which, one year later,
was to be changed into the Partai Nasional Indonesia--
the Indonesian National Party--with the same political goals as the General Study Club had had. Although it never acquired a mass following and its
leaders could be counted on the fingers of one hand,
it had great value as the symbol of the nationalistic aspiration for independence. Many of the leaders, moreover, were rather quickly put in prison or
exiled, as was the case of Tjipto Mangoenkoesoema,
who was accused of fomenting trouble among the Indonesian troops of the Netherlands Indian army, and
Iwa Koesoema Soemantri for his connections with communists on the East coast of Java, and later also
Sukarno himself. The leaders of the P.N.I. were
young men, imbued with western ideas and especially
with socialist and Marxist thinking which was understandable in view of their background and upbring-
ing. In general, they came from the lesser Prijaji
class, a group which often saw its promotion in the
civil service blocked by the higher classes, although
its members often had a better education; a group
who, moreover, had no vested interest in the economic
set-up as it existed in Indonesia, where nearly all
industry, trade and commerce were either in the
hands of the Dutch or the Chinese.

This, of course, laid this group open to socialist ideas. To this must be added an inborn desire
to turn to that side which was the most forceful in
expressing sympathy for the colonial underdog. This
again drove them to the socialist or communist side.

Finally, there is no doubt that, because of the
western education they had received, most of the members felt that they could do as good--if not better--
a job as any Dutchman could do. They did not want
guidance any more but wanted to lead themselves.
Indonesian society in those days offered small
chances for such a group.

This group was certainly responsible for forming one of the elements of the new political élite--
its revolutionary wing.

However, there is another element--in a sense
much larger and of equal importance--about which we
know relatively little. This was composed of those
Indonesians in the civil service who had also received a western education, and those active in the
professional field, the entrepreneurial class, teachers in non-government schools, and so on, who were
not organized. It is this group which we might call
a "functional élite," which kept Indonesian society
together, and was responsible for the changes which
were continually taking place. Its members also, in
all probability, had their ideas about an independent Indonesia, but they saw its development as one
which would take place more gradually. In effect,
they played a more important role, in that they were
going to be the men with experience, without which
no government can function, and whose example is followed by the masses with whom they are in daily contact. They were, however, not openly anti-governmen-
tal, and did not join political parties, organizations, etc., with political overtones, be it out of
fear of losing their jobs, or out of conviction.

It was only when Dutch authority was shaken, especially because of the Japanese occupation, that
they started to give their support to the Indonesian
political leaders and tipped the balance in favor of
the latter.

THE SECOND WORLD WAR AND
JAPANESE OCCUPATION

The Second World War and the Japanese occupation gave the Indonesian political élite its chance.
The Japanese authorities had realized right from the
beginning that the nationalist movements, which were
generally directed against the colonial governments,
might be made use of. Their general policy, determined by the Total War Research Institute, was that:

It must also be noted that the independence of the various people of East Asia
should be based on constructing East
Asia as independent countries, existing
within the new order of East Asia, and
that this conception differs from independence based on the idea of liberalism
and national self-determination.[32]

It is clear, therefore, that the Japanese were
willing to allow a certain amount of independence,
provided that the new countries were willing to follow Japanese leadership. The political élite realized full well the Japanese concept, but was quite
determined to pursue its objective of independence,
and run its own country by any means, including that
of serving in so-called Japanese "puppet" governments.

In the beginning, however, Japanese occupation
changed little in the situation. Japanese replaced
Dutch civil servants, and all political parties or
organizations were banned. The more the Japanese
war effort ran into difficulties, the more it had to
rely on the good will of its Asian brothers, and
therefore, to give in to national aspirations.

It is interesting to note Japanese policy towards Islam. The Japanese realized quickly that
Islam and Islamic organizations had real influence
in the countryside. They also counted on Islamic
leaders being less oriented and therefore falling
more easily for an Eastern co-prosperity policy.
Contrary, therefore, to the Dutch policy which tried
to make a sharp distinction between Islam as a religious group and Islam as a political movement, the
Japanese promoted Islamic leaders into semi-political
organizations. Also, "in their search for a reliable ally close to the millions of Indonesian peasants, the new rulers had shrewdly chosen the Kiyayi
and Ulama[33] as an entirely new element in the Indonesian political scene."[34] This brought about on
the one hand the politicization of Indonesian Islam
on the village level--something against which the
Dutch had always fought--and created on the other a
new political element aside from the Prijaji and
secular nationalist leaders.

An example of this policy was the creation in
1942 of the nationalist movement; the Putera (Pusat
Tenanga Rayak) center of the people's spiritual
power. This was led by the so-called Ampat Serangkay--
four-leaf clover--consisting of Sukarno, Hatta,
Dewantara and Mas Mansur, the latter of whom had been
one of the great leaders of the Mohammadyah.

Also in the creation of the Peta (Pembela Tanam
Air), a defense organization, a great number of
Kiyayi were taken in as officers.[35]

Later, in December 1944, the Islamic leaders
even obtained permission to create a religious army,
the Hizbullah-Allah's army.

In 1943, the Japanese appointed more and more
Indonesians as advisers to government departments.
Many of them came from the Prijaji class, who had
after all the most experience. At the same time a
central advisory council of 43 persons was introduced of which "the list reads like a Who's Who of
Javanese public life."[36] Important also was the
birth in that year of the Masjumi (Madjilis Sjuro
Muslimin Indonesia), consultative council of Indonesian Muslims, a political party which until today
has played a very important role in Indonesia's
political life.[37]

We therefore see a clear Japanese policy aimed
at keeping influence by playing the various élites--
Muslim, secular-nationalist and Prijaji--against
each other.

Further progress for the Indonesians was made
when, after the fall of Saipan--June 1944--which
spelled doom for Japan, the cabinet in Tokyo decided
to give independence to Java. This was not done immediately, but the Japanese army commander allowed a
renewed campaign for nationalism, and went further
in the Indonesianization of the civil service in
Java.

This was accompanied by a certain purge of Indonesians in government positions. The Dutch-trained
group was slowly replaced by a Japanese-trained élite.

On March 6, the Commander-in-Chief in Java decided to set up a Commission of Enquiry for the preparation of independence (B.P.K.I.). It was to consist of 60 members and be headed by Radjiman Wediodiningrad. In the committee we find, according to Anderson, 17 persons from the Prijaji class, 27 who could be considered as secular nationalists, and 7 who represented typically the Islam movements.[38]

The first meeting was held on May 28 and saw clashes between secular and Islamic nationalists about the role and place of Islam. However, the nationalists, being better trained, won the debate. It also set up a sub-committee to prepare the draft of a constitution.

However, the end of the war came more quickly than expected. The Japanese surrendered on August 14, but this was not made known in Java until August 21--the so-called "stolen week"--giving the Indonesians time to prepare themselves and, after much confusion and under special pressure from youth groups and the Indonesian resistance group of Sjahrir, independence was declared on August 17.[39]

The Japanese period was a very important one for the development of the Indonesian political élite. Its main consequences can be summed up as follows:

(1) It awarded political status to Islamic leaders and brought them into the political picture from which they were not soon to vanish;

(2) It gave the Indonesian secular nationalistic leaders their big chance. As they were better trained, through the sudden collapse of Japanese power, they got the chance to become the spokesmen for Indonesian political life;

(3) It diminished the influence of the old pro-Dutch Prijaji class who had to compete with the secular nationalist and political Islam leaders; and with younger elements trained by the Japanese in administrative and military matters.

Finally, the Japanese forestalled a return of Dutch administration by allowing the nationalist elements to grab power in the vacuum created by the Japanese surrender.

Footnotes to Chapter 4

1. For general reading on this subject, we recommend: H. Benda, The Crescent and the Rising Sun--Indonesian Islam under the Japanese Occupation (The Hague: W. van Hoeve, 1958); Willard H. Elsbree, Japan's Role in South East Asian Nationalistic Movements, 1940-1945 (Harvard: Harvard University Press, 1953); van Niel, op. cit.; Wertheim, op. cit.

2. C. Snouck Hurgronje, Verspreide Geschriften, Vol. IV, Part 2, p. 242, quoted in Wertheim, op. cit.

3. The Mohammadyah was founded in 1912 in Djocjakarta by Hadji Achmad Dachlan who had studied at the centers of reformist teaching in the Middle East. It received legal status from the government. Its success lay with its educational activity among young and old. In its schools we find incorporated as well a western style of education along with Muslim religious instruction. The Ahmadyah was a similar movement but of an Indian Muslim reformist nature. Both movements found their followers in the cities. As a counter-action, we see among the orthodox Islamic leaders the creation in 1926 of the Nahdatul Ulama which found its strength in the countryside. (Information taken from van Niel, op. cit., and Benda, op. cit.

4. Information on this organization is taken from van Niel, op. cit.

5. Raden Mas Tirtoadisoerjo was born of the Prijaji class, a son of an official in Central Java. After his education in an administrators' school, he entered government service only to leave quite soon after. After this, he was in journalism and founded Sarekat Dagang Islam in Buitenzorg (Bogor).

6. Raden Amar Sayed Tjokroaminoto was also a
Prijaji, who had followed the administrators' school,
entered government service only to leave quite soon
after. After this, he travelled with a travelling
Wayang show and gained a name because of his out-
spokenness.

7. P. H. Fromberg, Verspreide Geschriften
(Leyden: Verzameld door Chung Hwa Hui, Chineesche
Vereniging in Nederland, 1926), p. 545.

8. Quoted from van Niel, op. cit., p. 97.

9. Ibid., p. 94.

10. Soewardi was a high-class Prijaji, Tjipto
of a lower class, son of a Javanese school-teacher.

11. Goenawan was the brother of Dr. Tjipto but
of a different temperament. Raden Soetomo came from
a lesser Prijaji family. He later became a government doctor then went to Europe where he was the mentor of many Indonesian students.

12. Douwas Dekker was a journalist, an ideal-
ist but with an impressive egotism. He had fought
with the Boers in Africa and through his writing,
rallied the dissatisfied Indo-Europeans and Indonesians.

13. Although the Indo-Europeans were paid according to the European scale which was much higher
than the Indonesian scale, there was a certain discrimination in the civil service against them for
purely economic reasons. Sentiment was with them as
far as the Dutch were concerned, but Indonesians
were cheaper--an important factor for a government
service which had little money for expansion.

14. It opened its first session in May 1918
and it was made up of a mixture of elected and appointed members. Its role was thought to be an in-
strument in the advancement of the welfare of the
Indonesian people. It had no legislative authority
but could serve as a sounding board and also make
suggestions for new governmental measures.

15. Hadji Agus Salim was a Minang Kabauer--W.
Sumatra--of upper class family. He had worked a
long time in the Dutch government service in the con-
sulate in Jeddah and Indonesia. He had become a
leader of the reformist Islam movement and later,
having come into contact with Tjokroaminoto, he left
the government service and started working for the
Sarekat Islam.

16. Abdul Moeis had not succeeded in attending
the administrators' school (Stovia). He nevertheless worked for some time in government service--de-
partment of education--but later left as he was passed
over for promotion, and became a journalist. After
that he worked for a European paper Praenger Bode,
but later started his own magazine, Kaum Meda. He
was quickly promoted in the Sarekat movement and
soon became Vice-President. He played an important
role till the end. Semaoen came from a lesser Prijaji family. He became a pupil of the leftist socialist leader, Sneevliet, who took him into the
"Indisch sociaal democratische vereniging"--Indies
social democratic organization. He later entered
the Sarekat Islam and formed the radical wing. He
himself got more and more involved in communist
thinking.

17. Quoted in van Niel, op. cit., p. 127.

18. Ibid., p. 135.

19. Snouck Hurgronje had been appointed in
1889 advisor on Arabian and Native Affairs. He was
a Dutch Arabist and Islamologist who had lived for
some time in Arabia. He left Indonesia in 1906 but
as Professor in Leiden and consultant on native affairs to the Minister of the Colonies, he kept his
influence, especially in training the Dutch colonial
civil servants.

20. Benda, op. cit., cited the following examples of holy wars: the Banten war in the mid-18th
century, Tjirebo war (1802-06), Java War (1825-30),
the Padri war (1822-38) in the Minang Kabou area of
Sumatra, and the Atjeh war between 1872 and 1908.

21. The question might well be asked if, in
the light of subsequent developments, it was realistic to make such a separation between religion and
politics in Islam. According to Benda, "separation
of religion and politics, in other words, was at
best a temporary phenomenon of Islam in decline. In
an area of Islamic awakening, it could not survive
for long either in independent Muslim lands or in
Islamic areas ruled by non-Muslims." (Benda, op.
cit., p. 29).

It must be admitted, however, that Snouck's
policy in Atjeh brought results and that he specu-
lated not without grounds that the educational policy
of the government would create a great number of westernized Indonesian leaders who would have other attitudes towards the identification of Islamic religion
and politics.

22. Raden Darsano was another example of a
lesser Prijaji who had become dissatisfied with the
colonial government. As a soil expert he worked a
few years with the Department of Agriculture but
left later to become a free-lance journalist in
Semarang. He became strongly influenced by Marxist
literature and later came under the influence of
Sneevliet.

23. Ibrahim Dakut Tan Malaka, a Minang-kabauer,
was a European-educated school teacher. He had come
into contact with communist thinking in Europe and
started communist schools in Semarang. He was one
of the most brilliant doctrinarians of Indonesian
communism and has played an important role until after independence.

24. Since 1925, the PKI had started to enlist
the support of bandits and other uncontrollable elements which were always to be found in Indonesian
society.

25. Mentioned in a government document about
the activities of the communist policy in 1925/26.
Published in The Communist Uprisings of 1926-1927 in
Indonesia, Key Documents, Series Modern Indonesia
project (Ithaca: Cornell University Press, 1960),
Harry Benda and Ruth T. McVey, eds.

26. Quoted in ibid., p. 97.

27. Ibid., p. 98.

28. Van Niel, op. cit., pp. 235-236. He gives the following figures for education:

Out of 1,000	Total Attending	Graduates
College	0	0
Secondary School	24	1
Vocational Education (Secondary)	97	37
Primary only	640	396
Muslim religious school		45
Dessah School	40(?)	
Second-Class Native School	400 plus	250 plus
Dutch Native School	128	67
European Primary	32	10

29. Ibid., p. 225.

30. Annexed to the declaration went a statement that underlined that cooperation with the government would be impossible when Wilson's principle was not recognized.

31. Sukarno was a son of a western-educated school teacher who belonged to the lower Prijaji class. Attending secondary school in Surabaya, he came into contact with Sarekat Islam leaders. He stayed in the house of Tjokroaminoto and later married his daughter. In 1920, he entered the engineering college in Bandung where he got his degree in civil engineering in 1925. The General Study club which he founded was his first venture into politics, to be followed by many others which made him later the first President of the Republic of Indonesia.

32. Elsbree, op. cit., p. 29.

33. Kiyayi and Ulama are both religious Muslim leaders who derived their powers in the village from their knowledge of Islam and/or their Mecca pilgrimage.

34. Benda, op. cit., p. 135.

35. The senior Indonesian officer in the Peta was a Mohammadyah leader, Kasman Suiyodimedjo. The flag of the Peta showed the Islamic crescent super-imposed on Dai Nippon's rising sun.

36. Elsbree, op. cit., p. 86.

37. Its leadership was drawn from the Mohammad-yah and Nahdatul Ulama who formed the two pillars of the Masjumi.

38. Benedict R. O'G. Anderson, Some Aspects of Indonesian Politics under Japanese Occupation 1944-1945, Series Modern Indonesia project (Ithaca: Cornell University Press, 1961), p. 21.

39. An important role in the preparation of the independence declaration was played by the Navy's representative in Djakarta, Admiral Maeda. He brought different Indonesian groups together in his house and helped them against the Japanese army and police commanders. (See Anderson, op. cit.)

CHAPTER **5** NATIONALISM AND THE
POLITICAL ELITE BEFORE
INDEPENDENCE IN GHANA

In the definition of nationalism which we gave
in the last chapter, we stated that its primary aim
was the realization or maintenance of independence.
It is logical, therefore, that the attitude taken by
the colonial powers to channel or repress such movements had had its influence on the attitude of the
élite which incarnated and led the struggle for independence.

Ghana, as a British colony, offers a typical
example of the policy which was pragmatically worked
out to allow a country to accede to independence.
The policy adapted in Ghana has since been followed
with slight variations in the other British dependencies in Africa. In contrast with Indonesia, religious movements have not played such a big part in
the awakening of nationalist feelings. Pre-nation-
alistic forces were, nevertheless, present, such as
the "Aborigines Rights Protection Society" and the
"West African National Congress." Nationalistic
forces came to the fore with the birth of political
parties--first, the United Gold Coast Convention and
later the Convention People's Party. An analysis of
these two political parties and especially of the
leadership group gives a clear picture of the development and character of the nationalistic movement
which led to a peaceful transfer of power from
British into Ghanaian hands.[1]

BRITISH POLICY TOWARDS NATIONALISM

The way in which a sense of nationalism is in-
culcated and developed in a people depends upon many
factors, among which looms largely the colonial

policy of the metropolitan country, as we have seen
in Indonesia. Having reluctantly entered Ghana--see
Chapter 3--and realizing its relative importance after the abolition of the slave trade, the policy
followed by the British was one of cautiously giving
in to national aspirations. Several stages leading
to independence are to be noted as in many other colonial countries under British rule:

(a) Period of government by Governor and Colon-
    ial Office, the Governor holding all legis-
    lative and judicial power;

(b) Period of government by Governor and repre-
    sentatives. This happens when a system of
    franchise is introduced--in the beginning
    very restricted, later extended, ending
    with universal suffrage--and the Governor
    creates a legislative council. On this
    council we find in the beginning a few
    elected members and a majority of appointed
    ones. Slowly the balance shifts so that in
    the end there are only a few appointed ones
    --in general to ensure the interests of
    certain minority groups. At the same time,
    the Governor's powers are maintained by the
    right of veto in legislative matters.

(c) Period of restricted independence. In this
    period we see that the government depart-
    ments are being taken over more and more by
    the indigenous elements. An executive
    might be created in which key posts are
    held as long as possible by colonial ap-
    pointment--such as the Prime Minister, De-
    fence and Finance Ministers and the Attor-
    ney General.

(d) Period of home rule: the executive becomes
    official. The majority party elects the
    Prime Minister but the Governor still holds
    on to his power of veto.

(e) Full independence: when the Governor re-
    linquishes his power.

In such a process of decolonization, of which Ghana is an example, the nationalist movements have fulfilled the role of bulldozer or pressure groups which gradually pushed the colonial government over the doorsteps of these different phases.

PRE-NATIONALISTIC FORCES: THE ABORIGINES RIGHTS PROTECTION SOCIETY: THE WEST AFRICAN NATIONAL CONGRESS

In Ghana it is difficult to speak of nationalist movements until the thirties. Unlike Indonesia, where in the nineteenth century, Islam took on the aspect of a pre-nationalist movement, Christianity in Ghana has never played such a clear-cut role. This is understandable, in view of the fact that the colonizing power, whether Portuguese, Dutch or Danish in the beginning, or English later, were so-called Christian countries and the colonial administrator and missionaries generally came from the same cultural background. Nevertheless, it cannot be denied that Christianity has played a predominant role, through its educational institutions, in forming the leaders who would later lead the awakening of masses. President Nkrumah in a talk at a Pax Romana meeting in December 1957 rightly remarked:

> The person who introduced me mentioned the fact that I was responsible for the awakening of this great continent. I think this is not true. If we wish to view the situation correctly, we would say that the people who were responsible for this re-awakening are the Christian missionaries.[2]

In general, it is the Christian sects, such as the Kibanguists in the Congo, who have played the role of pre-nationalist movements in Africa.[3] They were often influenced by forces outside Africa such as the Black Zionist movement of Marcus Garvey in the United States from 1920 to 1925.[4] In the Ghana theatre their role was negligible.

The first organization which had a clearly pre-
nationalist character in Ghana was the "Aborigines
Rights Protection Society" (1897)[5] which was a kind
of ad hoc body of chiefs and educated Africans. Its
purpose was to serve as a link between the traditional rulers and the British Government, and its constitution bears similarities to that of the Sarekat
Islam (see Chapter 4), as:

> To foster in the rising generation a
> knowledge of their historical past, and
> to encourage the study of the laws, cus-
> toms and institutions of their country;
> to promote a sound national educational
> policy paying particular attention to
> agriculture, scientific and industrial
> training, and generally to facilitate
> the spread of industry and thrift in
> the whole country.[6]

Its immediate aim was to oppose certain legislation
and in this it was successful. It never had the
mass appeal which Sarekat Islam derived from its religious overtones, but it had, at least in the beginning, the loyal backing of all the traditional
chiefs which, at that time, automatically ensured
for it the support of the masses. Therefore, again
like Sarekat Islam, it was the organ through which
complaints could be passed from the masses to the
authorities. Its leaders were nearly all lawyers
and formed an educational élite in the country, with
such people as John Mensah Sarba, J. E. de Graft
Johnson and Jacob Wilson Sekyi.[7]

The influence of the society grew enormously between 1870 and 1920 and it became a kind of African
parliament. In the twenties the then Governor, Sir
Gordon Guggisberg, an ardent supporter of indirect
rule, was afraid of the influence the lawyers of the
society had on the native chiefs. He therefore was
looking for a way to weaken the influence of the
A.R.P.S. on the traditional chiefs and to bind the
latter closer to the colonial policy. He created
provincial councils in which the chiefs played a
predominant role. Later he added to this a joint

provincial council. The chiefs were delighted in
this way to play a role in the colonial policy especially as the Government had taken measures to see
to it that the chiefs in the council could not be
automatically destooled. In this way Guggisberg managed to draw the support of the chiefs toward the
government and to block the revolutionary spirit of
the lawyers of the A.R.P.S. With the support of the
chiefs gone, the prestige and the authority of the
society dwindled rapidly, as was the case with the
Sarekat Islam after its revolutionary tendencies became known.

     A society with a more nationalistic character
was the "West African National Congress," founded by
Casely Hayford[8] in 1920. It intended to promote the
economic, social and political aspirations of the
growing urban middle class and its field was not restricted to Ghana alone. Casely Hayford declared at
its opening conference in Accra, March 1920, that
"This conference has been brought about by the intelligentsia of British West Africa."[9] In a memorandum drawn up on this occasion we find demands for
self-government, elective franchise, no government
interference with regard to the appointment of
chiefs, the founding of a university and a restric-
tion on Syrian and other non-African immigrants.
Many of these demands were later recognized by the
government. Another special feature of the West
African Congress was that it was strongly influenced
by a movement which had its origins outside Africa--
the Pan African Movement of Dubois of the United
States, and Mr. W. Sylvester Williams of Trinidad.
The first Pan African Conference convened in London
in 1900 was a protest meeting against British colonial policy. The first Pan African Congress organized by Dubois took place in Paris with the aid of
the Senegalese Deputy and friend of Clemenceau--
Blaise Diagne. They petitioned the League of Nations that the former German colonies in Africa
should be placed under international control which
was partly realized by the institution of the mandate system. Pan African ideas were further developed in subsequent congresses: the second one, in
London and Brussels 1921; the third one in London

and Lisbon 1923; the fourth one in London in 1937.
It is in the school of these congresses that were
formed many of the present-day African leaders, such
as Casely Hayford and later Danquah, Nkrumah, Ken-
yatta. The ideas of Pan-Africanism can be summed up
as:

(1) to promote the unity and well-being of Afri-
    can people;

(2) to fight against racial discrimination;

(3) to promote the independence of African
    countries.

The West African Congress, therefore, appears
as a kind of regional branch in Africa itself of the
Pan African movement. The weakness of the congress
was, however, that it lacked mass appeal. It never
managed to get active backing from the chiefs, who
were supporting the government policy. Its membership remained restricted to the middle classes in
the towns, but it would be from these classes that
the new political élite would emerge.

As in Indonesia, where it was the higher Prijaji
class who, because of the indirect rule system, became the loyal supporters of colonial policy, so in
Ghana it was the chiefs who fulfilled this role. As
in Indonesia, where it was the lower Prijaji class
with western education who formed the milieu of the
future political élite, so in Ghana it was the western educated middle class who were going to play
this role. A particularly important role has been
played by the lawyers. This is understandable for
several reasons. First they were among the first
group who could speak the "magic" judicial language
which was needed to combat the foreign ruler.
Secondly, they in general enjoyed economic independence and were not as so many of the other élite
directly engaged in the public service as teachers
or civil servants. Thirdly, they had enough leisure
time to engage themselves in activities of a political nature.

THE BIRTH OF POLITICAL PARTIES:
THE UNITED GOLD COAST CONVENTION;
THE CONVENTION PEOPLE'S PARTY

After the First World War, we see an economic
upsurge in the country. Its timber and cocoa obtained high prices on the world market and a wise administration saw to it that finances were kept in a
sound state while investments were being made to
open the country geographically with railways and
roads, and intellectually with Achimota College.

In the thirties, however, Ghana like all producers of raw materials, felt badly the economic depression and with it, we see as in Indonesia, nationalist inspirations growing up among the middle class
and the youth. These were fed by outstanding African leaders, the Nigerian journalist Dr. Nnamdi
Azikiwe, editor of the _African Post_ in Accra,[10] and
Mr. Wallace Johnson, a native of Sierra Leone and
organizer of the West African Youth League. Although
they were both expelled, their ideas flourished, notably among the members of the youth conference organized by Dr. Danquah[11] and other middle class intellectuals in 1930. The activities of this group and
the consequences of World War II led the British Government to change the constitution (Burns Constitution, 1944) which was a further step on the road to
independence. However, this did not satisfy many of
the African leaders and Danquah decided to start a
political movement. "The United Gold Coast Convention" (U.G.C.C.) founded in 1947 at Saltpond aimed
at ensuring "that by all legitimate and constitutional means the direction and control of the government
should pass into the hands of the people and their
chiefs in the shortest possible time."[12]

Among the leaders of this movement, we find lawyers such as the above-mentioned Dr. J. W. de Graft
Johnson and younger "eager beavers" like Akufo Addo
and Ako Adjei[13]--people who, like the members of the
Perhimpunan in Indonesia, received a western education and were convinced that they could do as good a
job in running the country as any Englishman. The

chairman of the U.G.C.C. was Mr. George Grant, a
rich African, with parliamentary experience as a
former member of the Legislative Council.

If the "head" was good, the "body" was absent.
The U.G.C.C. first tried to get mass support by win-
ning over the chiefs--in this they failed. What was
worse, none of the leaders had the organizational
capacity or personality to go out to the people and
win them to their cause. This was going to be the
task of Dr. Kwame Nkrumah who Danquah called from
England at the end of 1947 to become Secretary of
the organization. Nkrumah lacked neither organizational ability, political experience, personality
nor ambition, and soon launched a drive for membership which, as the Watson Report mentions, "endeav-
oured to enlist under its banner everyone who had a
public or private grievance against the government,
and to seize upon every complaint great or small,
which might inflame a population avid for excitement."[14]

The Government helped the U.G.C.C. by imprisoning six of its leaders, among whom were Danquah and
Nkrumah, after the riots of February 1948 for which
the U.G.C.C. was not responsible at all.[15] This
made them popular heroes. To appease the situation,
the British Government later ordered a new constitution to be drawn up by the Africans themselves. A
committee of 40 was appointed in December 1948 under
the chairmanship of a member of the Gold Coast Supreme Court--Mr. Justice Coussey. The members comprised chiefs and middle class people as well as
political leaders such as Danquah, Grant and Akufo
Addo, but excluded the more radical elements such as
Nkrumah. Since they had not been consulted, these
latter elements felt free to criticize this constitution from the moment it was drafted. This led to a
rift in the U.G.C.C. which was later widened when
the conservative wing tried to oust Nkrumah from the
Secretaryship. Nkrumah, who had the support of the
youth--whom he had organized in the Committee of
Youth Organization (CYO)--and the masses, did not
hesitate to launch a new party, the "Convention
People's Party" (CPP) on June 19, 1949. It was a

much more radical party, as can be seen from the
first of its five points of action. "To fight re-
lentlessly by all constitutional means for the
achievement of 'Self-Government Now' for the chiefs
and people of the Gold Coast."[16]

Nkrumah, with a group of young enthusiastic
lieutenants such as Mr. Gbedemah, Mr. Botsio, Mr.
Edusei, Mr. Welbeck, Mr. Baako, and Mr. Iddrussa[17]
started to tour the country and soon managed to
bring the majority of the masses over from the UGCC
to the CPP. The CPP called a "Ghana Representative
Assembly" in November 1949 where they attacked the
Coussey Report and drew up a memorandum which con-
tained their own ideas as far as a new constitution
was concerned. From that moment, the fight with the
government was on. In January 1950, Nkrumah launched
a campaign of "positive action" based on the Gandhi
principles of non-violence and non-cooperation. This
positive action was an idea developed in the fifth
Pan African Congress held in Manchester in 1945. The
government retorted by imprisoning the leaders, con-
fiscating their publications, etc.--measures which in
the eyes of the people made the CPP appear as the
only valid nationalist movement and Nkrumah as its
most popular leader.

At the beginning of 1951 when the Coussey Commission had published its report, the Government took
the important step of deciding to hold general elections, which took place between February 5th and 8th.
To be able to hold the elections, the British Government insisted that they should be contested along
party lines. This forced all parties to come into
the open with programs which distinguished them from
each other. Those participating were:

    (a) the CPP which at that time could be de-
        scribed as leftist in orientation and ap-
        pealing especially to the masses for "self-
        government now";

    (b) the National Democratic Party (NDP) which
        appealed to a conservative section and
        wanted the British to develop the economy
        further before independence was sought;

    (c) the UGCC representing the moderate African
        leaders and professional class;

    (d) the People's Democratic Party which was a
        typical communal party appealing for the
        Ashanti vote.

The result of the election was an overwhelming
victory for the CPP which won 34 of the 38 municipal
and rural seats, notwithstanding the fact that many
leaders, among whom was Nkrumah, were imprisoned.
Gbedemah and Botsio were the organizers of the CPP
victory. The UGCC won two seats and the indepen-
dents another two. The road was open for the CPP to
enter the government and lead the Gold Coast to in-
dependence--a task which was completed six years
later in 1957.

There are three reasons which can be advanced
for the success of the CPP over other political parties. In the first place, the CPP was the only
group which was led by full-time politicians--people
who did nothing else but work for the party. This
was in contrast to the other parties which were run
by chiefs and professional element, notably the lawyers. In view of the fact that in general the CPP
officers were not well-to-do people, they were in a
more natural position to fight for radical reforms
and not afraid to bear the consequence of this in
terms of imprisonment. The leaders of other groups
were by background more conservative and hesitant to
bring upon themselves the wrath of the government.
The history of the decolonization process shows, however, that the more radical elements, in a process
of growing nationalism, can count on the most support.
And as the Daily Telegraph rightly reported,

      What has been happening in the Gold
      Coast national movement during the period
      since February 1948 has been a process
      of splitting along lines of economic and
      social interest. Every movement for na-
      tional independence in a colonial coun-
      try contains, of course, these two ele-
      ments: the element of revolt against

poverty and exploitation, the demand
for political independence and the demand for improved economic standards
and social justice. What is interesting about the Gold Coast is not that
this cleavage should have occurred but
that the CPP representing the left wing
of the national movement should have
emerged so quickly as the dominating
force.[18]

Secondly, the CPP was out for the vote of the masses,
the laborer and petty trader in the cities, and the
farmer in the country. Because of their professional
partymen, they were better able to go around the
country and explain their ideas in simple terms.
Moreover, they were much better organizers and the
CPP had, right from the beginning, a well-organized
youth section and had made a well-directed effort to
win over the women--a group which has always played
an important role in Ghana.

The other parties whose leaders were well-to-do
professional men, or chiefs, thought that they would
not have to go out for the vote of the masses as
their natural prestige and professional qualifications gave them sufficient status. They had hoped
notably that the countryside where the mass vote was
would follow the chiefs who were in general anti-CPP.
The miscalculation was that they had not sufficiently realized how much the prestige of the traditional
chief had dwindled since, through the British system
of indirect rule, he had become a kind of civil servant and the possibility of destooling him had been
severely limited by legislation.

Thirdly, there is no doubt that the victory of
the CPP was mainly due to the personality of Dr.
Nkrumah. Although intellectually on a par with the
best of the leaders of the other parties--he holds
a M.A. and M.Sc. from the University of Pennsylvania
and studied at the London School of Economics--his
simple background (his father was a goldsmith and
his mother a petty trader) made him understand much
better the aspirations of the common man. A tireless

worker, clever politician, and a powerful orator, he
became the charismatic leader around whom the people
could rally. All nationalistic movements at one
time have thrown up such people who are to a large
extent responsible for the success of the movement,
and who at the same time are made great by the movement. Nkrumah follows this pattern, in the path of
a Gandhi, and later a Nehru in India, a Sukarno in
Indonesia, a Mao Tse Tung in China, and a Nasser in
Egypt. In times of crisis a people look for a person rather than an institution or a party to lead
them, and in our modern times with improved communications, newspapers, radio and television, the image
of the national leader becomes so much easier to fix
on each and every citizen. Nor is this a process
which we see only in countries fighting for their independence, but it is also to be seen in times of
crisis in countries where democracies have been a
living reality for many centuries, in a Roosevelt
and a Churchill during the war and an Adenauer or
de Gaulle in more recent days.

CHANGES IN THE POLITICAL ELITE

The change in leadership which the victory of
the CPP brought about can be clearly seen if one
analyzes the social and economic position of the members of the old legislative council and the new assembly formed after the elections. In the old council
of 28 members we found (apart from the eight Europeans) six chiefs, six lawyers, five merchants, two
doctors and one school teacher. In the new and enlarged assembly of 84 members,[19] apart from the European element, we find on the one hand fifteen chiefs,
five lawyers, twelve merchants and traders, twelve
teachers, one doctor, five pharmacists, two journalists, and on the other six trade union leaders and
party officials, seven employees of the native administration, four farmers, as well as a carpenter,
an engine driver, a letter writer, a stenographer, a
house agent and a postal clerk. Many of these have
not even completed their elementary school education.

If the political élite which came forward in

the early stages of nationalism consisted of a mixture of traditional chiefs and western-trained intellectuals, notably lawyers, from well-to-do middle
class families, the new political élite as embodied
in the leadership of the CPP was from a more humble
background, but nevertheless, in general, also
western-trained and educated. This is clear if we
look at the party officials of the CPP in 1951.
Apart from Mr. Nkrumah, we find that the acting
Chairman, Mr. K. Z. Gbedemah; the General Secretary,
Mr. Kojo Botsio; and the Treasurer, Mr. Denkle Dzewu
have had university training.[20] Also in the first
Cabinet which was formed after the CPP victory we
find among the CPP Ministers (six of the eight Africans) apart from Nkrumah, Gbedemah and Botsio, three
others--Mr. A. Casely Hayford, Mr. Hutton Mills and
Dr. Ansah Koi, all of whom had received university
education.[21] Furthermore, with the exception of Dr.
Nkrumah himself, all these leaders of the CPP in the
early days came from good middle class families and,
in this, distinguished themselves little from the
leadership group of the UGCC and other parties.
Apart from this old guard we note, however, a second
group of younger people who were to become more important and whose background and education was not
on the same level, such as Mr. Krobo Edusei, Mr.
Kofi Baako and Mr. Kofi Tettegah.[22] It is this
group which has done much to radicalize the party,
but it is also these people who helped to win a mass
following for the CPP, such as the farmers in Ashanti
for Edusei, from among the youth for Baako and from
among the workers for Tettegah.

     Apart from this political élite coming up
through the political parties, there was in Ghana
another élite made up of civil servants, professional people and well-to-do merchants, which served as
a functional élite and which helped greatly in making the transition of the country from Gold Coast
colony to independent Ghana a peaceful process without too many abrupt changes in the socio-economic
and cultural life. Again, as in Indonesia, we know
little of this élite as it never manifested itself
on the political plane. In Indonesia the new political élite has come forward from the political parties

which carried nationalism as their banner--notably
the PNI.   In Ghana we see the same process going on
with the CPP fulfilling this role.   In Indonesia
this political élite formed a relatively small group
as was the case in Ghana.   In both cases, the group
has come forward from lower middle class milieux and
has received a western-style education; most of its
members held university degrees or had been at university.   In addition, we find that in both countries, the colonial policy of indirect rule managed
to win for the government the loyal collaboration of
the old political élite (the Prijaji class in Indonesia and the chiefs in Ghana) which until independence had generally been loyal to the official government policy and, because of this, came increasingly into opposition with the new western-educated
élite.   Their prestige dwindled because, for one
thing, they were not always so well educated but
even more because through their position as a kind
of civil servant, they came to be identified with
the colonial government.   When this government with-
drew its support--in Indonesia this happened because
of the Japanese occupation, in Ghana because of the
Governor's attitude after the elections of 1951 when
Sir Adrian Clark tried to work loyally with the CPP
and its leader Nkrumah--they found their political
influence greatly diminished.   If the processes have
been similar to a certain extent there are, nevertheless, differences which should not be overlooked.
Although the new political élite in both countries
had been western-educated, differences still existed
because of the different religio-cultural background.
An Asian, whether he comes from a Hindu, Buddhist or
Islamic cultural background, might, in the process
of his western education, lose the faith of his
fathers.   Nevertheless, he does not become so westernized in his thinking, behavior, or cultural outlook, that he becomes one hundred percent western.
Kipling's "East is East and West is West and never
the twain shall meet" holds in this respect all its
significance.   The only exception which might possibly be made is the Philippines where Christianization by the Spanish rulers and the long and far-
reaching educational influence of the United States
have produced a different type of Asian.   The African,

however, notably in those parts where Islam has not
exerted any strong influence, as in Ghana, was much
more inclined to become a complete western in the
cultural sense of the word. If for the Asian the
West signifies superiority with regard to material
aspects of its civilization, for the African it signifies superiority in nearly all cultural aspects,
and the realization that Africa also has a cultural
past is a very recent phenomenon and is still not
taken quite seriously by many of the young students
of today. This difference has also had its consequences in their political outlook. To this should
be added that the Indonesian political élite obtained
its independence as a result of the Japanese occupation, and managed to maintain it, thanks to the influence of the United Nations and, notably, the United States against the Dutch policy in the years
1945-49. In Ghana, the process has been much more
peaceful with much less outside interference.

    It is therefore understandable that the politi-
cal élite in Indonesia was, on the eve of independence, generally much less pro-Dutch inclined than
the Ghanaian political élite was pro-English. Having been present at both ceremonies marking the de
facto independence--in Indonesia in December 1949
and in Ghana in March 1957--the difference was clear
to see for everybody. In Indonesia, the ceremonies
were distinguished by a certain bitterness on the
part of the Dutch and a cautious optimism on the
part of the Indonesians, who could not quite believe
they had finally gained their cause. In Ghana, they
were marked by an explosion of joy on the part of
the Ghanaians and a deep satisfaction on the part of
the British who had, in the years of transition,
learned to trust Nkrumah and the CPP. The difference in the treatment of the Dutch in Indonesia and
the British in Ghana after independence has further
illustrated this point.

    There is another difference which should not be
neglected. If the functional élite in both countries was largely trained under a western colonial
system, that of Indonesia was also partly trained
under a Japanese and anti-western regime, that in

Ghana completely under a British regime.

Notwithstanding all these differences the main
fact remains that both countries entered upon independence with the typical western system of parliamentary democracy based on a party system. The
leaders of the parties were in general western-
educated persons. In Ghana, following the British
system, there appeared a two-party system after in-
dependence--the CPP and the United Party; Indonesia,
again in analogy with the Netherlands, had a multitude of parties, P.N.I., Masjumi, P.S.I., P.K.I.,
etc. Developments after independence, however, led
in both cases to strong presidential regimes as we
will see in the next chapter.

Footnotes to Chapter 5

1. For general reading on this subject we recommend: Sir Gordon Guggisberg, The Gold Coast. A Review of Current Events 1920-1926, and the Perspec-
tives for 1927-1928 (London: Bureau of Current Affairs, 1927); Padmore, op. cit.

2. Africa, a Christian Continent, Pax Romana
Publication (Fribourg, 1958), p. 3.

3. For details see Thomas Hodgkin, Nationalism
in Colonial Africa (3rd ed.; London: Frédéric Müller,
1960), Part II, Chapter II.

4. Marcus Aurelius Garvey was an extraordinary
person. He launched a "back to Africa" movement and
got widespread support through his journal, The
Circle. He stood for racial separation, but the
black man should be as prejudiced against the white
as the latter were against the former in the United
States. He established a kind of parliament, gave
out titles like Duke of the Nile, Earl of Congo,
Baron Zambesi, founded an African Orthodox Church,
founded a shipping company to bring Africans back to
Liberia. His movement gained world-wide attention
in the years 1920-1925 when the movement collapsed
because of mismanagement of funds.

5. Information on this and other organizations in Ghana are taken from Padmore, op. cit.

6. Ibid., p. 37.

7. Mensah Sarba was the son of the first African to serve on the Legislative Council. A barrister and authority on Fanti laws and customs. De Graft Johnson and Wilson Sekyi were lawyers. Notably the latter was for a long time the driving force of the A.R.P.S.

8. Joseph Casely Hayford MBE was a distinguished African scholar and lawyer and member of the Aborigines Rights Protection Society. He was strongly influenced by Pan African ideas. Padmore stated of him that "he reflected all the virtues and political limitations of mid-Victorian liberalism." (See Padmore, op. cit., p. 46.)

9. Ibid., p. 48.

10. Dr. Azikiwe played a great role later in the independence movement in Nigeria (especially Eastern Nigeria) and is at present its first President.

11. Mr. Joseph Kwame Kyerchwi Boakye Danquah, born in a chieftain's family of Kibi, received a western education at the University of London where he became a lawyer in the Inner Temple. After his return, he founded the Times of West Africa and started the Gold Coast Youth Conference. In 1947, he started the United Gold Coast Convention and called Nkrumah from London to become its secretary. He later became an opponent of Nkrumah. In 1957 he formed his party, the United Party, which was the official opposition group. He has recently been imprisoned by Nkrumah on sedition charges. (Information obtained during interviews in Accra with Mr. Nkrumah.)

12. Padmore, op. cit., p. 60.

13. Ako Adjei, son of a Ghana cocoa farmer,

studied in Lincoln University and Columbia and later
at the London School of Economics. He was President
of the West Africa Students' Union. He was offered
the job of Secretary of the UGCC but declined, convincing Danquah that Nkrumah would be a better man.
He stayed with the UGCC until 1952 when he joined
the CPP. He has held the portfolio of Minister of
Trade and Industry, Interior and Foreign Affairs,
but fell into disgrace in 1962. (Information obtained during interview with Mr. Kofi Baako, Accra.)

14. Watson report, appendix 12, Colonial No.
231. Cited by Padmore, op. cit., p. 62.

15. These riots started in Accra on February 28
when British troops fired on a group of ex-servicemen
who were demonstrating. It followed in the wake of a
nation-wide boycott of European and Syrian shops ordered by an Accra chief, Nij Kwabena Bonne.

16. Padmore, op. cit., p. 72.

17. All these comrades-in-arms of the first
hour held important positions in the party and government after independence. Some, such as Gbedemah
and Botsio, have now fallen into disgrace or have
had to leave the country.

18. Daily Telegraph, February 14, 1951. Cited
by Padmore, op. cit., p. 128.

19. The membership in this assembly was made
up of:

        (a) three senior British civil servants,
            so-called ex-officio members nominated
            by the Governor;
        (b) six special members, of which only two
            had voting rights, elected by the
            chambers of commerce and mines;
        (c) eighteen territorial members elected
            by the chieftainship councils of the
            colony, Ashanti and southern Togoland;
        (d) nineteen members representing the
            Northern Territories;
        (e) thirty-three rural members;

(f) five representatives of the municipali-
     ties--Accra 2, Cape Coast, Secondi,
     Takoradi and Kumasi one each. (Infor-
     mation taken from Padmore, op. cit.)

20. Mr. K. A. Gbedemah, son of a medical dis-
penser in the Nigerian Government service, did his
secondary studies at Adisadel College, Cape Coast.
He got his B.Sc. later at Achimota College. Mr.
Kojo Botsio, a Fanti, son of a civil servant, did
his secondary school studies at Adisadel College and
later taught at St. Augustine's College, Cape Coast.
He studied later at Fourah Bay (Sierra Leone), Bras-
more College, Oxford, and the London University Institute of Education. (Information obtained from
interview with Mr. Kofi Baako, Accra.)

21. Mr. A. Casely Hayford, son of the founder
of the West African National Congress, received
secondary education at Mfanesipin and later went to
Dulwich College, London, and Clara College, Cambridge, and the Inner Temple. Dr. Ansah Koi did
secondary school studies in Sierra Leone and later
studied medicine in University College Medical School
in England.

22. Mr. Krobo Edusei, an Ashanti, received
primary education at Government Boy's School in
Kumasi. After school he became a debt collector,
journalist and drug seller. In 1947, he founded
with others the Ashanti Youth Association and joined
the CPP in 1949. He later became Chief Whip and
Ministerial Secretary at the Ministry of Justice;
still later Propaganda Secretary, the Minister of
the Interior and Minister of Commerce. A capable,
tough man with a strong personal following, he is
one of the few who fell into disgrace in 1961, was
later rehabilitated and taken back into the government.
     Mr. Kofi Baako received a secondary school
education at St. Augustine's College in Ghana. Later he worked in the Survey Department and in 1947
was editor of the Cape Coast Daily Mail. He was
very active in the Committee for Youth Organization
of the UGCC but went over to the CPP when Nkrumah

started the party. Mr. Baako is one of the most
faithful followers of Mr. Nkrumah. He was secretary
of the party, political secretary to the Prime Minister, Government Whip, Minister of Information and
Minister of Defence, and is the only person of the
original group around Nkrumah who has not fallen into disgrace so far. He is also the person who tried
to develop in later years the ideology of Nkrumahism.
        Mr. John Kofi Tettegah received his early
education at the Roman Catholic school in Jaditon
and later at the Secretarial College in Accra. He
later worked as a stenographer in several British
firms and soon became active in the trade union movement. A member of the CPP, he became Secretary of
the Mercantile Workers Federation and later, in 1959,
General Secretary of the Trade Union Council. He
has also been active in the Pan African movement and
brought the trade unions to close support of CPP
policy. (Information obtained in interview with Mr.
Edusei and Mr. Baako, Accra.)

PART **III**

THE ROLE OF THE NEW ELITE

CHAPTER **6** THE NEW ELITE
AND
POLITICAL INSTITUTIONS

As we have seen in the previous chapter, both
Indonesia and Ghana adopted, as independent states,
some form of parliamentary democracy, a process
which has been repeated by nearly all states of Asia
or Africa on their attainment of independence. It
is an amazing phenomenon that with local variations
most young nations adopted constitutions modelled on
those of older democracies and introduced a machinery in the way of political parties, electoral procedures, parliamentary institutions and a civil service, designed to put their principles into effect.

However, in the process of doing this, they encountered enormous difficulties of government which
added to their basic problems of an economic and
social nature. The great question was: Could any
machinery destined to carry out a political revolution be transformed quickly enough into a governing
apparatus, able to carry out the necessary social
revolution which had to follow, and that through
democratic processes? Just as the introduction of a
democratic parliamentary system after independence
was the result of a certain option of the new political élite, so future development depended largely on
the character of the political élite, the role it
was willing to play and the ideas it had on how to
go about it.

In this and the next two chapters, therefore,
we shall take a look at the attitude of the élite
towards the political institutions, the social institutions and the new dimension in world politics--
the international dimension.

THE SOCIAL BACKGROUND

The political élite in power after independence, both in Indonesia and Ghana, was western educated. Soemardi, who studied the social origin of the Indonesian political élite, concludes: "In general, it can be said that political power passed into the hands of Indonesians who had been able to enjoy secondary and university education in the pre-war period."[1] He studied the composition of all sixteen cabinets existing from the moment of independence until July 1955, including a total figure of 146 cabinet members, 243 members of parliament and 61 top level civil servants.

He shows in two tables (see Appendix I) the importance of education for those who sought membership in the political élite. Of 146 cabinet members, 68 percent had been to university and 32 percent held secondary school degrees. For the 234 members of parliament, the cyphers are respectively 27 and 64 percent, and for 61 top civil servants, 87 percent and 13 percent. Moreover, a good many of them had done their studies abroad--27 percent of the cabinet ministers, 7 percent of the parliamentarians, and not less than 50 percent of the high-ranking civil servants.

In view of the relatively small number of people who had received secondary or university education it is clear that it was this small group who formed the majority of the political élite in Indonesia during the first years after independence, and that those with university education abroad had a particularly good chance at belonging to this élite. In a sense, even more revealing is another table of Soemardi's (see Appendix II) which shows the non-political occupations of Indonesian political decision-makers.

The table shows clearly that the new political élite has come forward from the civil service or the professional classes where we find the sons of the lower and higher Prijaji class and therefore the

middle or upper middle classes of Indonesian society.
It is also interesting to note the rather high percentage of non-governmental teachers and journalists,
but we must not forget that among both groups nationalistic feelings in general ranked highly.

Finally, in regard to the age group, Soemardi
discovered that at the time of their appointment the
greatest number fell into the 30-50 age groups (see
Appendix III).

We therefore might conclude that the political
élite of Indonesia was overwhelmingly made up of relatively young people from the middle class who had
received western education in secondary schools
and/or university, often abroad. It was the higher
and lower middle class--Prijaji class and professional milieu--which had sent their children to universities and from which came the new political élite.
That the democratization of the universities in Indonesia has not advanced very much since independence
and that it is the middle classes which send their
sons to university are shown by a recent study (1961)
made by a group from the World University Service in
Indonesia.[2]

It showed that at the university of Indonesia in
Djakarta the social background of the students was:

> 46.4% - sons of professors, professional milieux,
> officers, contractors and high-ranking
> civil servants;

> 41.5% - sons of secondary school teachers,
> middle class businessmen, middle-ranking
> civil servants and pensioners;

> 12.1% - sons of elementary school teachers,
> lower-ranking civil servants, non-
> commissioned officers and peasants.

Although similar tables are not available for
Ghana, we have every reason to believe--and the analysis of the leaders of the CPP (see Chapter 5) indicates this--that the situation in Ghana was similar,

with this difference, that nearly all university education was undertaken abroad (Sierra Leone, the United Kingdom, the United States) as a real university
was only started after independence; and that many
of the CPP élite came from the lower middle class or
peasant milieu (see Chapter 7).

THE ELITE AND THE POLITICAL PARTIES

Without the existence of political parties, the
functioning of a parliamentary democracy is not
thinkable. The fact that the political élite striving for independence was dominated by a western-
educated group is certainly the most important single
factor in explaining the appearance of a party system and the setting-up of a parliamentary democracy
after independence.

In Indonesia after the declaration of independence in August 1945, President Sukarno wanted to
create one national party.[3] This however was soon
opposed by leaders such as Mohammed Hatta and Sutan
Sjahrir and, in November 1945, the green light was
given for the formation of parties. Very soon they
became numerous. The most important were:[4]

(a)   Masjumi (Madjilis Sjuro Muslimin Indonesia--
      Council of Indonesian Muslim Associations)
      founded in 1943 (see Chapter 4). It tried to
      group all the former Muslim organizations such
      as the Mohammadyah, Partai Sarekat Islam Indo-
      nesia and Nahdatul Ulama. In total, it grouped
      around eleven Muslim religious, social and edu-
      cational organizations and was therefore quite
      heterogeneous. One of its leaders, Sjafruddin,
      once called it "an elephant with beri-beri."
      Among its leaders we found different tendencies.
      There was the old-time Islam nationalist such
      as Dr. Sukiman Wirjosandjojo and Samsuddin; the
      religious socialist like Tjokroaminoto, Hadji
      Agus Salim (from the old Sarekat) and Mohammed
      Natsir, Mohammed Roem, Sjafruddin Prawiranegara
      and Yusuf Wibisono; and orthodox Muslims such
      as Kiai Hadji Wachid Hasjim and Kiai Ahmed Hassan.

The policy as defined by its religious wing was
that of religious socialism "in harmony with
the constitution and still open to individual-
ism, individual initiative and individual responsibility."[5] The intellectual brain trust
of the party was formed by the liberal Muslims
of the Mohammadyah, such as Dr. Sukiman, Natsir,
Mohammed Roem and Wibisono. They stood opposed
to the conservative Muslim section led by
Kartiwinata--who split off very soon and led
the PSII--and Wachin Hasjim who later split off
with the Nahdatul Ulama. The Masjumi drew its
members from the Muslim world but especially
from the commercial middle class and the peasants. The brain trust, however, was also divided,as we shall see later.

(b)   The Partai Sarekat Islam Indonesia (PSII--The
       Indonesian Islamic Association Party), founded
       July 1947, was a splinter group of the Masjumi.
       It was a right-wing orthodox group opposed to
       contacts with the Dutch and led by mass leaders
       such as Tjokrosujoso and Kartiwinata who were
       opposed to the Sukiman, Natsir intellectual
       wing.

(c)   Partai National Indonesia (PNI--The Indonesian
       National Party) carried the name of Sukarno's
       pre-war party and the one started in August
       1945, and it considered itself a direct continu-
       ation of it. Its strength lay with the Prijaji
       class and the civil service and it commanded a
       good following among the peasants. It was un-
       derstood to be the party closest to Sukarno and
       had a great following in the city. Its program
       was rather vague, stressing national unity,
       socialism and collectivist economy. Again, in
       this party, one could recognize different ten-
       dencies. There were the pre-war nationalist
       leaders--mostly lawyers--such as Mr. Sartono,
       Ali Sastroamidjojo and Isqaq Tjokrohadisurjo.
       They were rather conservative in outlook and
       pro-Western, and stood intellectually close to
       the Natsir-Masjumi group. A second section was
       formed by young intellectuals who had come up

during the revolution, such as the union leader
Wilopo, Lukman Hakim and Notowidigdo who, ideo-
logically speaking, stood close to Sjahrir's
PSI. A third group was made up of radical
nationalists, strongly influenced by the Japanese and anti-Western period, such as Sidik
Djojosukarto and Manai Sophian. The PNI, like
the Masjumi, soon saw a right-wing split. This
was the Persatuan Indonesia Raja.

(d)   Persatuan Indonesia Raja (PIR--Greater Indo-
      nesian Union) founded December 1948. Here the
      old upper class Prijaji were to be found. They
      considered the Masjumi too religious, and the
      PNI too Western in cultural outlook. They want-
      ed to be a typical Indonesian party of the aris-
      tocracy with a paternal authority over the
      peasants. Leaders were Wongsonegoro and
      Tadjuddin Noor.

(e)   Partai Socialis Indonesia (PSI--Indonesian So-
      cialist Party) founded in December 1945, a mer-
      ger of Partai Socialist Indonesia of Amir Sjari-
      fuddin and Partai Radjak Socialist of Sjahrir.
      This was a typical party for the intellectual
      élite. Sjarifuddin broke off later as he was
      very leftist and merged with the Communist party
      during the Madiun rebellion in September 1948.
      The party stood for an economic development
      plan and against extreme nationalism and anti-
      foreign sentiments. It proclaimed a positive
      neutralism and a mild socialism with an Indo-
      nesian flavor. It was against authoritarianism.
      The party was led by great thinkers such as
      Sjahrir, Djohan Sjahroezah, Subadio Sastro-
      Satomo and Dr. Sumitro Djojohadikusuma. The
      ideas developed in this party carried great in-
      fluence with the intellectual wing of other
      parties and among army officials. However, it
      never managed to obtain a real mass backing.

(f)   Partai Komunis Indonesia (PKI--Indonesian Com-
      munist Party). We have already mentioned (see
      Chapter 4) its activities before the war.
      After independence, it was revived but its

leadership was weak.[6] The party was led by
people such as Alimin, Sardjono and young Musso
who returned from Moscow in 1948. Following
the Stalinist line of struggle against the Mar-
shall Plan and against American influence, they
were opposed to the Renville Agreement in 1947.
Musso organized a revolution in September 1948
which was crushed and several of the party leaders were killed. This rebellion put the Communist party in the "dog-house" as far as the
nationalist leaders were concerned. After 1951,
we see a new development with leaders such as
Alimin--under Chinese influence--Aidil Lukman
and Njoto Sudisman. They found renewed strength
in the trade unions (SOBSI), were very anti-
Western and later played the pro-Sukarno line
for tactical reasons.

(g)   Partai Murba (P.M. Proletarian Party), founded
      in 1948. It was a leftist party with marxist
      tendencies and led by typical mass leaders,
      such as Tan Malaka, Adam Malik, Sutan Demanis.
      It was very nationalistic and held an attrac-
      tion for leftist intellectuals and labor
      groups.

(h)   The Parkindo (Protestant) and Partai Katolic
      (Catholic) parties were permanent minorities
      whose existence was a typical reflection of
      the Dutch situation where the Protestant and
      Catholic parties have always played an impor-
      tant role. Their influence has been much
      greater than the number of Christians would
      make plausible, as in both groups we find a
      great number of highly-educated people and out-
      standing leaders such as Dr. Leimena and Mr.
      Tambunan for the Parkindo, and Dr. J. Kasimo
      for the Partai Katolik.

These were the main parties on which, after independence, the Republic of Indonesia was founded.
After a short period of Federal Government from December 1949 to 1950,[7] the Republic of Indonesia became a unitarian state, a republic with power centered in the President, cabinet and lower house of

237 members. Mohammed Natsir formed a cabinet in
September 1950. The division in parliament at that
time was such that the Masjumi, the Persatuan Indonesia Raja, Partai Socialis Indonesia with the Christian parties and some others, holding between them
154 of the 237 seats, formed the government while
the Partai National Indonesia, Partai Komunis Indonesia and some smaller groupings formed the opposition.[8] The main difficulties which the government
had to face in the beginning were: the problem of
internal security, the labor problem (Sobsi and KPI
organized frequent strikes which crippled the economy
and hampered exports), the development of agriculture, the attraction of foreign capital and the
orientation of foreign policy including, notably,
the question of West Irian.[9]

Four cabinets have struggled with these problems.
The first federal cabinet, led by Mohammed Hatta,
lasted from December 19, 1949, to September 6, 1950;
the first cabinet of the Republic of Indonesia,
Mohammed Natsir's Cabinet, from September 6, 1950, to
March 20, 1951; Mr. Sukinan's cabinet from April 26,
1951, to February 23, 1952; and Mr. Wilopo's cabinet
from March 30, 1952, to June 2, 1953.

The first cabinet was a coalition of Masjumi,
PNI, Christian and Federalist parties. The PSI, as
the big party, stayed out. The second cabinet was
again a coalition which did not take in all major
parties: Masjumi, PSI--in; PNI and PKI--out. The
third cabinet was based on PNI and Masjumi with the
PSI excluded. Finally, Wilopo's cabinet was an attempt to have all the big parties--PNI, PSI and
Masjumi in the cabinet with the exception of the
Communist. It is clear that, given the problems
the country had to face, only a cabinet which was
able to count on the three big democratic parties,
Masjumi, PNI and PSI, with the communist in opposition, could enable the government to follow the
strong policy which was needed by the country. The
downfall of the Wilopo cabinet because of internal
strife in the different parties was the danger sign
for the democratic development of the government in
Indonesia. It gave the extra-parliamentary forces

in the form of the President and the army another
chance to increase their influence, and meant the
slow disintegration of the democratic parliamentary
regime in that country.

The reason for this process of disintegration
is to be found in the split among the political
élite, and particularly in a growing diversion between the intellectual element, who were more responsible, less radical, had a broader outlook but
had not much mass support; and the mass leaders, who
were often less educated, more radical, often representing extreme segments but with a real mass following. The kind of parties which were found in Indonesia were, with the exception of the Communist party,
"caucus" parties with no strong united aim and where
party discipline was slack or non-existent. Moreover, it should not be forgotten that party life was
played essentially in the capital (Djakarta). Here
at clubs and cocktail party combinations were made,
intrigues prepared, cabinets built or demolished
often with scant attention paid to the needs or
thinking of the people in the country. "Political
parties at this time," remarked Ruslan Abdulgani in
1952, "are still concentrating mainly on parliamentary and cabinet struggles, paying scant attention
to efforts in society."[10]

In view of the fact that no elections had been
held, the division among the parties was made rather
arbitrarily and inter-party strife was too great to
make quick arrangements for elections. They were
only to come later when the pressure of the army became too great and accusations were made that the
political parties did not represent the country, so
that a political impasse occurred which could only
be solved by elections. In this period, however,
many of the parties were completely unaware how
great their strength was. Party membership was
often interpreted on the strength of the party in
Djakarta, and in some other big cities, where recruitment was fairly easy and people were often
ready to join a party for material reasons--espe-
cially if it was in the government and a good job
could be assured. Mr. Yusuf Wibisono wrote in 1951

of the Masjumi: "Based on the number of its branches,
the membership of Masjumi is estimated at 13 million
but only 600,000 are registered with the Secretary
of the party's Executive Council and only 400,000
have been given membership cards."[11]

Finally, we should not forget the temptations
of power to which politicians were open after independence. Especially in colonial countries where
the indigenous élite had seen the relative wealth in
which the Europeans lived, they felt that big houses,
cars, cocktail parties, trips abroad, were the necessary status symbols of a political élite. To this
should be added that, in Asia and Africa particularly, family ties are much stronger and the family comprises a much greater number of people and that it
was understood and normal that a member of the family who had reached a high position would care for
the whole family--which might number from five to
twenty-five persons.[12]

If corruption is a phenomenon we find in all
states, its occurrence is particularly marked in the
young countries where attempts by business and commercial firms to bribe government officials often
take on fantastic proportions.

In Indonesia, moreover, it was often considered
normal that a Minister or high official of a party
would see to it that the financial resources of the
party were not too low. The Chief Inspector of Commerce of East Java readily admitted, for instance,
that he had received more than 200,000 rupiah in
bribes for the benefit of the PNI campaign treasury,[13]
and at the PNI Congress in Surabaya at the beginning
of 1953, ministers were urged to strengthen the party
and help overcome its financial difficulties.

In such a situation, where the political élite
lived in a kind of vacuum in Djakarta and showed
signs of wealth and prosperity, it is easy to imagine the struggle for power which went on and the
relative facility of discrediting such a group in
the eyes of the people (who did not immediately see
the economic advantages of independence) by skillful
propaganda put out by mass leaders.

However, taking all this into account, we must
not forget that in the first years after independence,
corruption was not too widespread, and the political
élite--against all odds--showed a great sense of responsibility. In certain fields steady progress was
made. However, a split slowly appeared among the intellectual élite and the mass leaders in the different parties.

According to Feith, the division could schemati-
cally be described as follows:

Political groups led by intellec- tuals	(... (Socialist (sympathizers (democratic (attitude	(Partai Socialis Indonesia (Masjumi: Wing Natsir, Roem (PNI: Wilopo group ((Christian parties
	(Conservatist (more inclined (to strong man (regime	(Masjumi: Wing Dr. Sukiman (PNI: Ali, Sartono group (PIR
Political groups led by mass leaders	(Conservative (Radicals	(Minor nationalist parties (PRN and SKI (Nahdatul Ulama (PSII (Masjumi Isa Ansharey Wing
	(Opposition (leftist (radicals	(PNI Sidik group (Partai Murba
	(Extreme left	(PKI

While in 1950 a certain consensus existed among
the intellectuals whose ideas (especially of the PSI)
were generally accepted, gradually we see differences
appearing in regard to economic policy. While in the
first few cabinets problems were dealt with on a day-
to-day basis, the Wilopo cabinet went in for long-
range planning. Such planning caused a split between
those with a socialist and those with a more liberal
view. The domination of the Natsir-Roem wing in the
Masjumi led, moreover, to the breaking away of the

more orthodox religious group, the Nahdatul Ulama,
which seriously weakened the Masjumi. A similar
split on economic theories was to be seen in the PSI
between the Wilopo and the Ali Sastroamidjojo, Sartono group. This split was further increased by the
attitude of each towards the President, since the
PSI, Natsir, Wilopo, Christian parties were against
the President's attitude in often trying to assume
more power than the constitution allowed him, and
the Sukiman, Ali, PIR were in favor of it. Once
this split had occurred the mass leaders got their
chance. Generally less educated, they often represented special interest groups. Trained during the
Japanese period and the revolution, they were not so
convinced of the usefulness of a parliamentary democracy, and so gave the extra-parliamentary forces
their chance. If we look at the different cabinets
in Indonesia from 1949 to 1957, we can make the following division:

1. Hatta cabinet   ) Transition) Parliamentary
         1949-1950) cabinet from) democratic sys-
                          federal   ) tem led by the
                          structure to) western-
                          unitarian   ) educated in-
                          state. No) tellectual
                          great inter-) élite
                          nal unity.)

2. Natsir cabinet   ) Unity inside)
         1950-1951) the cabinet)
   Sukiman cabinet   ) based on in-)
         1951-1952) tellectual)
   Wilopo cabinet   ) conceptions)
         1952-1953) which trans-)
                          gressed   )
                          party lines)

3. Ali Sastroamidjojo) No unity in-) Interim period.
         1953-1955) side the   ) Influence of
   Harahap cabinet   ) cabinet. In-) parliament dim-
         1955-1956) tellectual) inished. Extra-
   Ali Sastroamidjojo) wings are   ) parliamentary
         1956-1957) split. Mass) forces grow.
                          leaders play) Mass leaders play
                          more and   ) dominant role.
                          more a role)

4. Dr. Djuanda cabinet) Business   ) Extra-parlia-
            1957-1959) cabinet led) mentary forces.
                       by intellec-) President and
                       tuals   ) Army dominate
) guided democ-
) racy.

     A special group among the Indonesian intellec-
tuals is the technocrats of whom Dr. Djuanda is a
typical example. Highly competent but without any
political connections, he has been a member of practically all cabinets since independence. It was on
such a person that Sukarno called to put his ideas
of guided democracy into action.

                THE ELITE AND THE OPPOSITION

     If a democratic state wants to function well ac-
cording to our western system, it needs the institution of what is generally called a "loyal opposition,"
a party or parties which can freely express their opposition to government policy, which might try to
win a majority to their view and which, if they
should be successful, are in a position to accept
power and assume responsibility for government. It
was rather naive for the western governments to believe that with the introduction of parties, and the
installation of a parliament, the "loyal opposition"
would come forward automatically and the game would
be played on both sides according to the rules.

     There were a lot of factors to prevent the func-
tioning of a loyal opposition in Ghana or Indonesia.
In both countries the colonial powers had not accepted the opposition of the indigenous élite to their
governing as they accepted the opposition at home.
The opposition leaders in general passed more time
on the prison bench than on a possible opposition
bench, as both Sukarno or Nkrumah can witness.
Therefore, the example given by the former colonial
powers was not very convincing. To this, it must be
added that nationalistic feelings in countries such
as Ghana or Indonesia were primarily directed against
the colonial powers. The sense of unity which was

cultivated during the fight for independence often
received a serious setback the moment independence
was achieved and centrifugal forces came into play
immediately. In Ghana on March 5, 1957, three days
before independence, I was able to assist at a meeting of the Ashanti council of chiefs who were hotly
debating a motion as to whether they should send a
delegation to Accra to celebrate independence or to
ask for British protection against independence.
Also, one of the first actions of Mr. Nkrumah after
independence was to send troops to EWE country to
prevent a sedition there.

In Indonesia, independence was first given in
the form of a federal government which, however,
quickly disintegrated and after six months became a
unitarian republic. However, here also the government had to take immediate measures against seditious movements such as those in West Java (Darul
Islam), Amboina, Makassar, etc. Under such circumstances, it is understandable that opposition groups
are quickly regarded as seditious groups. This
might explain why in Ghana, Nkrumah moved rather
quickly to stifle the opposition party under the
pretence that it was harmful for the unity of the
country.

The basic problem, however, is that the idea of
a loyal opposition is alien to the character of the
Ghanian or Indonesian people and could not be developed overnight.

In Ghana, as in most parts of Africa, the system of debate is the "palaver." Having watched African student groups debate, I have always been struck
by the way an issue is debated. In the beginning,
everybody seems to have his own opinion on the subject, opinions which are often fundamentally opposed.
It ends, however, practically always, by a decision
being taken unanimously. It seems to be considered
unfair that someone should break the unity by oppos-
ing it. If one feels that the time is not yet ripe
for most people to agree, then the meeting is post-
poned or debate prolonged. In such a context the
role of an opposition party is quite different from

that which we know in Europe. It can, so to speak,
prevent any decision being made by not sharing in a
unanimous decision, after it has had sufficient time
to explain its point of view (a kind of filibustering
by threatening to vote against the motion), and it
encourages the tendency on the side of the governing
party, too, to break this stalemate by seeing to it
that such opposition people are no longer present.
The reply of an African teacher in Accra whom I once
questioned on what he thought of President Nkrumah's
attitude in jailing the opposition leader and his
former comrade-in-arms, Mr. Danquah, was quite revealing. His answer boiled down to: Mr. Danquah
did not play the game; he can speak his mind in parliament but should not always vote against the motion; what else could the President do but put him in
jail or exile him and get on with the job.

     In Indonesia we find a system similar to the
African "palaver." Two terms are very significant:
one is the Musjawarah, which is consultation without
voting, and the other is Musfakat, which means consultation which ends in a vote with unanimous consent. President Sukarno's idea of a guided democracy
is very much based on those two concepts. After the
troublesome period when sedition had broken out
everywhere, Dr. Djuanda, the new cabinet leader,
called for instance a "Musjawarah Nasional"--national
conference--September 10 to 16, 1957, where all regional leaders were present and the President, Mr.
Sukarno, and the Vice-President, Mr. Mohammed Hatta,
made a joint appearance to plead for unity. Sukarno
in introducing his system of guided democracy called
for a system "in harmony with the soul of the Indonesian people," a system in which "all members of
the family sit at the table--at the eating table and
at the working table."[14] Sukarno wanted a Gotong
Rojong (mutual cooperation) cabinet of all parties
and a National Advisory Council, led by Sukarno,
which would comprise, apart from party people, functional groups, representatives of regions and the
army. The cabinet would be under such a system, become the image of parliament and the national advisory council of Indonesian society. It is clear,
however, that in such a Gotong Rojong democracy

there is no place for a loyal opposition and it is
difficult to see how, at the same table, different
groups such as the Communist or the Moslim Masjumi
would eat and work peacefully together.

THE ELITE AND LOCAL GOVERNMENT

Democracy can only work if there is an association of the people with the government on all levels.
A parliamentary system which only operated at the
center but in which there is no experience of democratic functioning on the local level can have little
reality for those going through the motions of cast-
ing a ballot.

In Indonesia, with its geographical extension
and its diversity of peoples and economic resources,
the need for some form of local government was particularly great. It was also the only way to prevent sedition movements gaining ground. On the
other hand, the central government had to foresee
the need of a central authority. In looking at the
situation from 1950 to 1956, one must admit that the
system of local government had something of a colonial flavor, in the sense that it attempted to pre-
serve central authority in the local governments.
From 1957 to 1959 we see an effort made to achieve a
much greater degree of true local government, a tendency which is strongly reversed again after 1959.[15]
The setup of local administration in Indonesia is
pyramidical. On top is the Ministry of Home Affairs;
underneath is that of the provinces; the provinces
are divided into residencies; they in their turn
into Kabupatens (pre-war regencies), Kabupatens in
Kewedanaan (districts) and Ketjamantan (sub-districts).
At the base we find the dessah (village).

This setup is administered by Governors (for
provinces), Residents (for residencies), Bupatis
(Kabupaten), Wedanas (Kewedanaan) and Tjamats
(Ketjamatan).

Such a system looked towards an effective form
of central government and was largely taken over

from the former Dutch administration. The big problem for local government was whether these administrators (called the Pamong Pradja) would all be appointed from above, or elected from below.

Law 22 of the Republic of Indonesia in 1947
laid down that, in the establishment of each local
government region, there should be a representative
council (Dewan Pewakitan Rakjat Daerah--DPRD) and an
executive council (Dewan Pemerintah Daerah--DPD).
The head of the daerah was supposed to be nominated
by the Home Ministry from a list presented by the
DPRD. However, because of the difficult situation--
the war with the Dutch--this plan in general was not
followed. After independence a new law was worked
out which came into effect in 1957 (Law I 1957). It
catered to three types of self-governing regions--
ordinary regions (daerah swatantra), special regions
(daerah instimewa) and municipalities (kotopradja).
Within each region room was made for three levels of
local government (Level I, Level II, Level III,
roughly corresponding with the Javanese provinces,
kabupatens and dessah).

An important fact was that the heads of the
local governments were to be elected by the council
and later ratified--by the President for Level I,
the Home Ministry for Levels II and III.

> Membership of representative coun-
> cils has reflected the narrowness of
> Indonesia's political élite. Even at
> the Kabupaten level, council members
> could hardly be regarded as represen-
> tatives of the rural community which
> formed the great mass of constituents,
> and on the provincial level, the con-
> nection was still more tenuous. By
> far the greatest single occupational
> group to be found on councils has
> been formed by civil servants.[16]

Legge studied eight second-level councils in
Java and four in Sumatra and found that one-third
and one-half of the members were civil servants.

The transitional representative council of the province in East Java, which came into being in 1956,
could count 23 out of 69 members as civil servants.
The others were small traders, religious leaders,
labor leaders and industrial workers. This, however, is not so surprising, especially at the beginning, as the civil servants were the group which had
experience of government and came generally from the
Prijaji class--a group which carried prestige. It
would take years for local councils to find their
feet and the necessary experience and for the population to take an active interest in these councils
and to see to it that different categories of the
population would be represented on it through democratic processes.

The establishment of the local councils gave a
big boost to the parties. The system of proportional representation was established both for the representative council and for the executive.[17] This, of
course, did not make for strong government. It was
in a sense, however, again a reflection of the
Musjawarah and Musfakat principle which one wanted
to apply to these councils. It had, as we explained
above, its negative sides, as often decisions were
deferred, but "the foreign observer is likely to be
puzzled by the number of decisions for which no vote
is recorded but which are said to have been made by
automation."[18] Parties had to try and be nation-
wide to be able to have seats on regional councils.
It forced the parties to seek the grass-roots level
and those who did not find it were swept away. On
the other hand, and even more important, it allowed
local leaders to climb the political ladder through
the municipal or Kabupaten level to the provincial
or national level.[19] In this way, local politics
would have become a training ground for national
politics and a new political élite would have arisen
as is normal in all democratic countries. This democratic role of producing a new political élite, however, has never been fully played in Indonesia. The
first regional elections were held in Java in 1957.
The result showed a surprising increase in strength
of the PKI in Central and East Java. In Central
Java, it became the strongest party, beating the PNI.

In East Java it closely followed the Nahdatul Ulama;
in West Java it came second after the Masjumi. By
that time, however, the national situation was changing and there followed a period of national disunity
which led to Sukarno's emergence as strong man. The
process of political sophistication which the local
councils could have fulfilled was strongly curtailed
by the introduction of guided democracy. Presidential Edict number 6 of September 1959 suspended the
provisions of Law 1/57 and reverted to the principle
of appointment of regional heads rather than the holding of elections. With this, the old system of a
strong central government was reintroduced. The
DPRD's could remain in function but could not elect
the DPD any more.

    With regard to appointments, the growing influ-
ence of the army could be noted,[20] especially on
first-level councils. On the second-level councils
"where a tradition of Pamong Pradja appointments existed, these were preferred if local feeling was in
favor of it."[21] Finally in September 1960, Edict
6/59 disbanded the existing DPRD's to replace them
in analogy with what happened on the national level
with gotong rojong assemblies (50 percent party representatives and 50 percent representatives of functional groups, both categories to be appointed).

    This meant the definite end of the schooling in
democratic procedures which the elective councils
could have fulfilled. At the same time, it reduced
the incentive for party life in the regions and the
change in the political élite through a democratic
process.

    The Indonesian experience is not a particularly
good one in the sense of an experience in democratic
functioning on the local level. The same holds true
for Ghana, although for completely different reasons.

    We have noted that, under British rule, some
local--provincial--councils of chiefs existed topped
by a joint council (see Chapter 5), and that city
councils were also in operation. After the CPP had
scored a victory in national elections, the first

Nkrumah cabinet undertook new changes and established:
(a) district councils over a wide rural area; (b) urban and local councils.

Both types of councils were composed of representative members (two-thirds elected by universal
adult suffrage) and traditional members (one-third
appointed by traditional authorities). The councils
fell under the Ministry of Local Government.

This setup was a very wise one. It allowed on
the one hand for the widest possible opportunity for
the majority of the people to contribute to the process of government; it took into account the traditions existing in Ghana; and it opened up the possibility for chiefs to play a new role in the modern
state. The elections for these local councils took
place in April 1952. Most unfortunately for the development of democratic processes, the opposition
party decided to boycott them. The CPP, therefore,
had the field wide open for itself. The suppression
of the opposition party a few years later prevented
a possible return of party differences through the
system of local government.

In conclusion, we can say that the case of Indonesia and Ghana both show that the system of indirect rule did not take sufficient notice of the
changes in economic, social and cultural life, and
were too slow in adapting themselves to it through
the establishment of local government based on democratic processes. Both countries, therefore, obtained independence without a firm foundation and experience in local government. The efforts made to
introduce it after independence failed and thereby
weakened considerably the chances of democracy in
these countries. Moreover, the absence of such systems prevented a change and extension of the political élite through democratic processes. The example
of India where, because of the system of direct rule,
some form of local government has been introduced
since 1880, shows that democracy has a better chance
of surviving if people have become familiar with democratic procedures and assumptions and have learned to
operate them on a local level before applying them on
a national scale.

THE ELITE AND THE PRESIDENCY

The challenge to the parliamentary democracies
established in the developing countries comes in general from two sources: on the one hand the extra-
parliamentary force to be found in the army; on the
other, the one represented by the presidency. Since
it was the revolutionary forces which led to independence, it was logical that the tendency existed to
nominate as head of state the kind of person who, on
the one hand, embodied best the struggle for independence and, on the other, was the type of leader who
would command the most authority in the several regions which the new states encompassed. If such a
person could be found, he was generally a mass leader
with great authority.

However, it was often not easy for such a person to play the role expected of a president in a
parliamentary democracy of the western European type
--that of a national symbol, a figurehead standing
above the parties, a guardian of the constitution.
In the case of both Indonesia and Ghana, it is clear
that the personality of the president contributed in
a singular way to the breakdown of parliamentary
democracy.

We have already described the influence which
President Sukarno has exercised in Indonesia before
and during the war period. Founder of the PNI and
one of the triumvirate whom the Japanese entrusted
to bring home rule to Java, it was logical that he
should have been elected president at the declaration of independence in 1945. The constitution of
that time gave him considerable powers, comparable
to those of an American president.

> The structure of government as defined
> in the 1945 constitution, whereby the
> president was accorded virtually un-
> restricted powers, was radically changed
> when provision was made for the working
> committee (of the Indonesian Central
> National Committee--KNIP) to function
> as a legislative body participating in

decisions on the general orientation of
state policy and with the introduction
of the system by which the Ministers
were answerable to the working committee.[22]

When in 1949 the Dutch recognized the Republic
of Indonesia, a constitution was drawn up for a federal state (1949) to be changed in 1950 to a new constitution for a unitarian state. However, in both
constitutions, presidential power was diminished and
he became more of a president in the western European fashion. In both the 1949 and 1950 constitutions, it was stipulated in Article I that the sovereignty of the people would be exercised by two
bodies, i.e., the government and parliament. It was
further clear that the government was understood to
mean the president, with one, several or all of the
ministers. The president was head of the state
(article 45). Further attributions he had were:
the formation of ministries (article 50); the right
of dissolution of the Chamber (article 84); the
granting of decorations (article 87); the pardon of
crimes (article 10); the declaration of war (article
128), and the proclamation of a state of emergency
(article 129). However, in all these cases, the
word "president" means "government" (President and
ministers).

It is clear, however, that President Sukarno
never agreed, at heart, with this constitution, and
has consistently tried to push his own ideas across
and to restore the constitution of 1945. He finally
succeeded after the split in the intellectual élite,
and with the help of the army on the one hand and
the communist party on the other--both out themselves to increase their own power.

Sukarno's viewpoint is best revealed in his own
words, taken from a speech he delivered at the 30th
anniversary of the Indonesian national party in
Bandung (July 3, 1957).[23]

Sukarno is the typical example of a natural
mass leader. A powerful speaker, sly politician and
man of action, rather than contemplative, he was

POLITICAL INSTITUTIONS 163

convinced that "the only power which can throw off
Dutch imperialism in Indonesia is revolutionary action by the masses."   The fundamentals of the PNI
which he founded in 1927 were "a just and prosperous
society; the conditions of attaining it . . . via
the golden bridge; and the only means by which the
golden bridge could be won . . . revolutionary mass
action."[24]

He admits, however, that such mass action was
never organized before the Japanese handed over the
government, "a mass action by all of Indonesia's
Marihaens[25] who are tens of millions strong. And
this, brothers and sisters, happened after August
17, 1945, when all of Indonesians Marihaens--yes,
those who were young men and women, who were workers, who were peasants--rose and acted."

Interesting also is Sukarno's opinion of Dutch
colonialism.

> The Dutch imperialism which operated
> in Indonesia was primarily of the kind
> that Hilverdinck called "finance capi-
> tal"--money to invest in Indonesia in
> the form of factories, in the form of
> estates, in order to squeeze out, to
> dig up, to scratch up all kinds of
> riches there are in Indonesia.

This was the reason, according to him, why little
attention was paid to education, "and therefore, the
people of Indonesia were not taught. . . . The imperialism of capital investment suppressed the needs
and the skills of the people."

It is clear that Sukarno never saw the implications of the system of indirect rule and its consequences for Western-style education of the subjugated
people. This comes to light even more clearly when
he compares Dutch colonialism with British colonialism, as applied in India.

> This had the character of a mercantile
> imperialism--a trade imperialism, in

order to sell British-made goods in
India. It was because of this, brothers and sisters, that in 1927, 1928
and 1929, I said: "British imperialism provided education for the people
of India quite early." Schools were
established in India, even colleges
and universities were set up in India,
just in order to maintain some purchas-
ing power among the Indian people. And
therefore the Indian people were not
made too poor.

Parliamentary democracy is considered by Sukarno
to be unsuitable for Indonesia. It established political democracy, but not an economic democracy. It
is, moreover, a liberal system brought about by "the
growth of a bourgeoisie in Europe over several de-
cades. . . . Let us not imagine that we can establish a just and prosperous society--equality, social-
ism--by pursuing a policy of liberalism in the form
of parliamentary democracy . . . because parliamentary democracy grew out of the philosophy of political liberalism, and liberalism is the enemy of socialism." Therefore, Sukarno believes that "we cannot create a just and prosperous society by parliamentary democracy alone. This is why I said in my
lectures: 'let us not aim only at political democracy; we must also create economic democracy!'"

Sukarno was the man who introduced the idea of
the "Pantja Sila"--the five basic principles. These
were: belief in one God; belief in humanity; the
unity of Indonesia; the sovereignty of the people;
and social justice.

The philosophy behind this assertion was once
expressed by Mohammed Hatta in the following words:

The principle of belief in one God
guides our national ideals towards doing
our utmost for the people and the community, whereas the principle of humanity, its logical continuation, involves
carrying this guiding principle into

actual living practice. The principle of nationality affirms the character of Indonesia as a national
state with its own ideology, whereas
the principle of people's sovereignty
calls for just government, exercised
with a sense of responsibility, in
order to achieve the social justice
which is incorporated as the fifth
principle.[26]

Sukarno expresses himself, however, somewhat
differently in explaining later his idea of the
Pantja Sila.

> Did I not say in the book: The Birth
> of Pantja Sila, that Pantja Sila could
> be compressed into three, into Tri-
> Sila, namely belief in God, socio-
> nationalism and socio-democracy? Did
> I not say this Tri-Sila could be com-
> pressed further to become one, Eka
> Sila, namely, Gotong Rojong?

Here we meet one of Sukarno's basic ideas--a
Gotong Rojong cabinet, which would include all four
of the major political parties of Indonesia (PNI,
Masjumi, Nahdatul Ulama, PKI) and a National Council,
which would reflect the tendencies existing in Indonesia and which would serve as a bridge between Parliament and the people--"a national council which is,
in the first place, composed of outstanding men of
the functional groups of society; this national council is the channel for the wishes of the community,
and is also drawn from the community."

Sukarno's theme was that the revolution had not
ended, that it was going on still, and that, therefore, one had to think and rethink, shape and reshape.
To achieve political and economic democracy was not
possible by the system of parliamentary democracy.

> Through parliamentary democracy alone,
> we cannot achieve politico-economic
> democracy. This is the reason, brothers

> and sisters, why after thinking and
> rethinking, I have arrived at the
> point at which we must reshape; shape
> and reshape. This, brothers and sis-
> ters, is the core of my intention in
> setting up the national council which,
> God willing, I shall establish on the
> twelfth of this month.

The idea of establishing a state in which not
only political but also social justice would be done,
and that this state should have specific Indonesian
characteristics, was generally agreed upon by the
intellectual wing of the political élite as, for instance, was expressed by the Vice-President, Mohammed Hatta: "Whatever its other sources, Indonesian
democracy should also evolve from indigenous Indonesian democracy."[27]   Among them, also, were many
elements derived from the indigenous democracy preva-
lent in the Indonesian village, such as the general
meeting, mutual consultation, Gotong Rojong or mutual assistance. But, "the good points of our village democracy cannot all be applied indiscriminately
on the level of the State," as "it would be impossible to reach such unanimous decisions in a parliament with all its different parties and political
antagonism. In this matter, whether one likes it or
not, one has to accept the system of Western democracy whereby decisions are taken by a majority of
votes."

These intellectuals saw the faults of their political parties clearly. "Political parties which,
in reality, are a means of organising public opinion
so that the people may learn to feel responsibility
as citizens of the state and members of society,
have been made an end in themselves, the state being
their tool." However, they felt that because of
this, one could not condemn the democratic system as
such. "In point of fact, our national revolution,
having continued for several years, ought to be
checked." People had to be trained in democracy,
and since the general elections had finally taken
place, and a genuine parliament representing the
will of the people was in existence, this should

have been possible. "Now that we have a parliament
today, based on the will of the people as expressed
in the general elections, so that now we have a foundation for parliamentary democratic government at
the present time, is it possible to go back from
here?"

        That was the big question for Indonesia, to
which the western-educated wing of the political
élite said no, but the mass leaders and the president said yes. From the moment the electoral élite
lost its hold on the big parties, which happened
with the fall of the Wilopo cabinet, the extra-
parliamentary forces embodied in the president and
the army became too strong and a new way was chosen--
that of guided democracy--which has shown itself to
be another term for the "strong man" regime, where,
however, the "strong man" has a Janus head, represented by the president on the one hand, and the
army on the other.

        The situation in Ghana is developing along simi-
lar lines. Kwame Nkrumah is another example of a
typical mass leader who had no great respect for the
middle class intellectuals who were the early leaders of the independence movement. In his autobiography, he related what he himself thought of the
leaders of the U.G.C.C. who asked him to become
their secretary in 1947.

                This assessment of the situation forced
                me to the conclusion that it was quite
                useless to associate myself with a
                movement backed almost entirely by re-
                actionaries--middle class lawyers and
                merchants, for my revolutionary back-
                ground and ideas would make it impossi-
                ble for me to work with them.

Therefore, he continued, "I was very sure of the policy that I would pursue and was fully prepared to
come to loggerheads with the executive of the
U.G.C.C."[28] This he did, as we have seen. Like
Sukarno, he believed in mass organization and revolution through the masses. "A middle class élite,

without the battering-ram of the illiterate masses,[29]
can never hope to smash the forces of colonialism."[29]
However, Nkrumah realized that "mass movements are
well and good, but they cannot act with purpose unless they are led and guided by a vanguard political
party."[30]   Therefore, he built up the CPP into a
large well-organized party which steamrolled over
all others existing.   Independence Day saw the CPP
as the party and Nkrumah as its leader with a popularity which came near to that of a Gandhi or Nehru
in India.   It is difficult to explain why a man who
had shown such skill and moderation in the years before independence, that the Manchester Guardian in a
leader on the 17th of July 1953 should write:
"great credit is due to both Dr. Kwame Nkrumah and
his colleagues and the governor and the other members of the colonial service, for the wise and sin-
cere way in which they have handled a situation
which might have been made intolerable by rancour or
ill faith or even vanity on either side" would turn
into a dictator with little regard for his opponents;
a man who, in 1955, said at a party meeting (June
12):   "I have always expressed both in public and
private that we need a strong and well-organized
opposition party in the country and the assembly,"[31]
and who subsequently pushed through a preventative
detention bill in 1958 providing for imprisonment
without trial for a period of up to five years, and
then in 1958 proceeded to put in jail forty-three
members of the United Party.

        All this did not seem necessary; the opposition,
insofar as it existed, was not of great importance.
This was not like Indonesia, where there was an army
difficult to control and avid for power, and where
the economic situation was deteriorating day by day.

        Nkrumah, like Sukarno, believes that democracy
should not be of the purely western type, but should
take into account African conditions.   "Ghana society
is by its own form and tradition fundamentally democratic in character."   Now, Ghana has inherited a
parliamentary system of the western type.   "This, by
its very nature, is a very difficult and cumbersome
system to apply to our traditional pattern of govern-

ment." Therefore, "I have no doubt that in time, we
in Africa will evolve forms of government rather different from the traditional western pattern, but not
less democratic in their protection of the individual
and his inalienable rights."[32]

The problem is the same one as that posed in
Indonesia after the political revolution for independence, namely, a need for a social revolution to ensure a higher standard of living for the people. To
achieve this "demands every effort from the people,
a total mobilization of brain and manpower resources,"
and the belief is that "capitalism is too complicated
a system for a newly-independent nation; hence the
need for a socialist society."[33] But also we should
not forget that "a system based on social justice
and a democratic constitution may need backing up by
measures of an emergency nature."[34]

Three years after independence, Ghana became a
republic with Nkrumah as its first president. The
constitution laid down that the president would be
the leader of the majority in parliament, so that
the president and the assembly could work as one
body. The election of the president was linked to
the election of members of the national assembly,
and if the national assembly and president should
disagree, the issue had to be decided by a general
election.

In this way, Nkrumah received more power than a
president in Western Europe. He could be at the same
time, party leader, leader of the majority in parliament, and president. If Ghana is to follow the path
of democracy in the years to come, it will depend on
one person--namely Mr. Nkrumah, the president.

THE ELITE AND THE ARMY

One of the greatest problems which the new
élite had to face when installing a democratic regime of the western parliamentary type was that such
a form of government, a republic based on elected
representatives, had no genuine local traditions

behind it. The complicated processes of a parliamentary system, with legislative bodies, parliament and
the other paraphernalia, were not always understood
by the masses and sometimes not even by the leaders.

One problem, for instance, is that of authority
in a democracy. The will of the majority was not always understood and the idea of a "loyal opposition"
was completely foreign to the Indonesian or Ghanaian
peoples. Therefore, in all the young nations of
Asia and Africa we have been able to see occasional
or chronic rebellion, the seizure of power in a non-
constitutional manner, the dismissal of parliamentary bodies or cabinets by governors or presidents
who override majority action. All this has shown us
that the principle of democratic obedience is still
not understood. In Indonesia the problem became
acute on the issue of the supremacy of the civil
over the military authority. We have known this
problem in many of the old established democracies
and we must not forget either that Latin America offers us a clear example, that where democratic institutions function badly over a long period, the
military power might present a permanent threat.
Every nation which has had to call its population to
arms in order to fight for its independence faces,
after the victory is won, the problem of how to establish civil authority over army leaders whose
power always grows during wartime, and how to diminish the number of people carrying weapons and to get
them to resettle into civilian life.

In Indonesia where, during the guerilla period
against the Dutch, a host of guerilla groups operated
apart from the official army, this was a particularly
difficult problem; to make the army leaders obey democratic processes was a practically insurmountable one.
The early years of Indonesian independence, therefore,
were abundant with cases where the army intervened in
the political field. A typical example is the incident which occurred in October 1952. In the army,
after independence, three elements were found:

1. Former K.N.I.L.-- Royal Dutch Indies Army--
    which formed the best trained element but

which had not participated in the fight for
independence;

2.   P.E.T.A.--<u>Pembela Tanah Air</u>--which had been
     Japanese-trained;

3.   T.R.I.--<u>Tentarah Republic Indonesia</u>--which
     contained, apart from an educated element,
     all sorts of groups which clung around a
     leader (<u>Bapakism</u>).

The army had capable leaders in the persons of
Colonel A. M. Nasution, Army Chief of Staff; Major
General T. B. Simatupang, Army Forces Chief of Staff;
and Ali Budiardjo, Secretary-General of the Ministry
of Defence; and Sultan Hamengko Buwono, Minister of
Defence.

In 1952 they wanted to rationalize the army; to
retire about 60,000 irregular soldiers and 30,000
policemen. Such a rationalization would particularly affect the P.E.T.A. and was used by certain political parties such as the PNI to introduce a motion
against the Minister of Defence and the Army Chiefs.
The motion was carried but as a reaction the army
organized demonstrations on October 17th and sent a
delegation to the president to ask him to dismiss
parliament.

Feith reports that "it may be regarded as established that Colonel Nasution was engaged for several
months before October 17 in working out plans for a
military coup."[35] Observers agree that the aim of
the army was to give Sukarno greater power, all the
while making him more dependent on army support.
This aim, which has been pursued continually by
Nasution up until the present, failed in 1952 as at
that time Sukarno did not want to go along with it.
The coup, therefore, did not come off and several
officers were replaced.[36]

The intervention of the army, however, had one
good effect. It showed that there was a need to
hold general elections, which inter-party strife had
until then prevented. The elections were needed at

this point in order to dismiss the army claim that
the provisional parliament did not really represent
the people. The intervention also had one bad effect. The balance of the extra-parliamentary forces,
which were represented on the one hand by President
Sukarno and on the other by the army, was tilted in
favor of the president. Before, these two forces
had kept each other in check allowing parliament to
try to do its work as long as it was united and led
by a consensus of opinion among the intellectual
élite.

However, the more the party system seemed un-
able to solve the urgent socio-economic problems
which Indonesia was facing, and the more the regions
outside Java felt they were being neglected by the
central government, the more the army felt it had
the responsibility to intervene directly. A typical
example, for instance, was the arrest on the order
of the Assistant Chief of Staff, Colonel Lubis, of
the Foreign Minister, Ruslan Abdulgani on August 13,
1956, just before his intended departure for the
Suez Conference in London. The reason given was
that Abdulgani was involved in a bribery affair.[37]
The viewpoint of the military leaders is clearly revealed in an article by Colonel Lubis of June 1955.
After he had forced the fall of the first cabinet of
Ali Sastroamidjojo, he said: "strictly and juridi-
cally speaking, I have committed insubordination.
But what do you want? . . . I decided to act according to the dictates of my conscience. . . . Islam
teaches me that I must obey my leaders, but also I
must do good works for the general welfare."[38]

It is easy to blame the army leaders for their
undemocratic authoritarian attitude but one must not
forget that (a) they considered themselves, often
rightly, as the pioneers of national independence;
(b) in practically no country is the army a good
training ground for democratic processes and only
where democracy is ingrained in a population is the
army willing to keep its proper role of guaranteeing
security inside and outside; (c) in Indonesia security had never reigned in the whole archipelago. Not
only was there active opposition from guerilla groups

of the Darul Islam in West Java,[39] but also the more
the situation deteriorated from an economic point of
view the more regional army leaders broke away from
the central government, such as Colonel Simbolon in
North Sumatra--December 22, 1956; Lt. Col. Ahmed
Husein in Central Sumatra--December 20, 1956; Colonel
Barlian in South Sumatra--March 9, 1957; and Lt. Col.
Ventje Sumual in East Indonesia--March 2, 1957.

At the end of 1956 and beginning of 1957, it
looked as if the Republic of Indonesia was falling
apart. A counter-government was set up in Central
Sumatra. The insurrection failed as the leaders did
not get the hoped-for support of eminent political
leaders such as the Vice-President, Mohammed Hatta
and the leaders of the PSI, Sutan Sjahrir. Also,
they had miscalculated the popularity in which President Sukarno was still held by the masses of people
in Indonesia and above all, they had not expected
the capable and efficient counter-measures taken by
the Chief of Staff, Colonel Nasution. If the integrity of the republic was saved, it meant nevertheless the end of a parliamentary democracy in Indonesia. The main failure, however, lies with the
political élite which had lost its original unity.
The struggle between the western-educated élite and
the leaders of the masses in the different parties,
which we have explained above, led the government to
stagnation and presented the possibility to the extra-
parliamentary forces, the president and the army, of
installing a so-called "guided democracy."

While the army leaders could be considered an
élite group which wielded much power, certain observations can be made about them. It was not a group
which was united by training or social background.
We find among them the former non-commissioned officers of the Royal Dutch Indies army, well trained in
the leading of troops but without too much general
education; the leaders trained during the Japanese
period in the Hizbullah--a kind of shock brigade;
and the educated elements of the TRI--Tentarah Repub-
lik Indonesia. It was this last group which in general had had at least secondary education and many
of them came forward out of the Tentarah Peladjah

Indonesia--the student brigade. Two separate groups
were the Indonesian Navy and the Military Police;
better disciplined, better commanded (in general by
educated people from the Prijaji class), they formed
the hard core which was mostly western influenced
and was the most faithful to government policy.[40]
Many of the top army leaders, such as Simatupang,
Ali Boedjardo, Gatot Subroto, were politically close
to the PSI. Most were staunchly anti-communist and
the growing influence of the communist party--which
the army had fought already during the Madium affair,
often gave them an excuse to intervene in the political field. The army leaders as an élite group can
be classed in the category of mass leaders. In
close contact with their troops, often, especially
in the regions outside Java, having to play the role
of a civil leader, they were much nearer to the
masses than the western-educated élite who concentrated in Djakarta and played at politics. This
role of mass leader was reinforced in later years
when the army started youth movements, controlled
newspapers, ran firms and plantations, etc.

        Ghana was not plagued with the same trouble.
The transfer towards independence took place peacefully. The army was restricted to relatively few
troops, well trained and under British command.
Moreover, President Nkrumah had the political insight to leave command of the forces in British
hands.[41] In view of the tradition in the British
army, he thereby ensured that as long as the forces
were commanded by British troops they would never
present a threat to government. I was able to observe this particularly clearly in the autumn of
1960 when I met some British officers in the Congo
commanding the Ghanaian troops who were in there
under U.N. command. Although they were highly critical of the policy pursued by President Nkrumah towards the Congo, the idea of going against his orders or laying down their command never entered
their heads.[42] Colonel Mobutu, who at that time was
the strong man in the Congo, rightly remarked in an
interview I had with him:

Nkrumah a un anglais qui dirige son
armée; il est donc sur qu'il sera
obéi, meme si son général n'est pas
d'accord. Moi, je suis le commandant
des forces congolaises, mais mon
problème est que mes officiers et
soldats ne m'obéissent pas, meme
s'ils sont en général d'accord avec
moi.

Footnotes to Chapter 6

1.   Soemardi Soeloeman, "Some Aspects of the
Social Origin of Indonesian Political Decision-
Makers," Transactions of the 3rd World Congress of
Sociology (London, 1956), p. 338.

2.   Economic Factors Affecting Access to the
University, World University Service, Studies on
the University Scene in 35 Countries (Geneva, 1961),
p. 120.

3.   This was the Partai National Indonesia, a
continuation of the pre-war party. Because of the
differences between Hatta and Sukarno, it only sur-
vived from August 22nd to 31st. Sukarno wanted it
to be the national party, grouping all shades of
opinion; Hatta was opposed to it.

4.   Information about the parties is taken from
the publication, Asian Nationalism and the West, a
symposium based on documents and reports of the 11th
Conference of the Institute of Pacific Relations,
New York, 1953, by W. T. Holland, George McT. Kahin,
Philippe Devillers, Th. Sileoek, Ungku Azir; and
Herbert Feith, The Wilopo Cabinet 1952-1953, a Turn-
ing Point in Post Revolutionary Indonesia (Ithaca:
Cornell University Press, 1957).

5.   It was expressed like that in a pamphlet of
Sjafruddin Prawiranegara, published in 1948, Politiek
dan Revolusi Kita (Politics and Our Revolution).

6. Some of the Communists who had been in Holland took a very curious attitude. They were in favor of an agreement with the Dutch, and against independence. They saw in Sukarno a kind of fascist-like Quisling--an attitude which was widespread among the Dutch people after the war.

7. The Republic of the United States of Indonesia came into being on 27th December 1949. It comprised sixteen states with a President, a Senate (two members per state) and a lower house. The first cabinet was led by Mohammed Hatta and comprised 11 Republicans and 5 Federalists. Soon, however, the United States of Indonesia fell apart.
        On 10th February 1950 the Pasoedan (West Java) gave up its independent status and incorporated itself into the Republic. On 7th March 1950 the same thing happened in East and Central Java and Madoera. On 22nd April, West Borneo followed suit. On 21st April President Sukawati of East Indonesia proposed a merger, in a unitarian state, with the Republic of Indonesia. This was accepted, and the unitarian state was formed on 19th May 1950 as the Republic of Indonesia. (Information taken from Asian Nationalism and the West.)

8.   Parliamentary Division during
        the NATSIR Cabinet 1950/51
            Total membership 237

Government parties		Opposition parties	
Masjumi	50	PNI	41
Persatuan Indonesia Rajah	18	PKI	8
Partai Socialist		Front Buruh	7
Indonesia	16	Partai Buruh	
Fraksi Democrat	11	Indonesia	5
Parindra	9	PKR	5
Partai Katolic	8	Partai Socialis	2
Partai National		Partai Murba	3
Indonesia Merdeka	6	Partai Buruh	7
Partai Sarekat Islam		Barisan Tanih	
Indonesia	5	Indonesia	5
Partai Kristen	4		
Non-party members	27		
	154		83

9. The Hague Agreement which gave Indonesia
its independence did not bring a solution to that
part of the former Dutch East Indies called West
Irian or New Guinea. The agreement stipulated that
the status quo of Irian would continue for one year
after independence. After that, two conferences
were held in the Hague from June 21 to August 1950.
No agreement could be reached. The Irian question
has continued to be a point of strife between the
two governments, and has caused great bitterness to
both parties. A solution was finally found under
the aegis of the United Nations in 1962.

10. Ruslan Abdulgani, cited by Feith, op. cit.,
p. 30.

11. Ibid.

12. A typical example was the case I came
across in Lagos (Nigeria). A Nigerian Jesuit priest,
who had done his studies in biology in the United
Kingdom, had been nominated to a secondary school in
Lagos. Very soon, seven members of his family arrived from the Eastern province, demanding that he
should take care of them. His explanation that, as
a Jesuit, he received no money was of no avail, and
the Bishop had to intervene personally.

13. Reported in Java Trade, October 31, 1956.

14. Sukarno in a speech on February 21, 1957.
Published in an article by Justus M. van der Kroef,
"Guided Democracy in Indonesia," Far Eastern Survey
(August, 1957), p. 115.

15. Much use has been made of the study of
J. D. Legge, Central Authority and Regional Autonomy
in Indonesia: A Study in Local Administration, 1950-60
(Ithaca: Cornell University Press, 1961).

16. Ibid., p. 134.

17. In the period of transition, before elections had been held, the party composition in the
executive D.P.D. was calculated on the basis of

proportional representation to the party distribution in the D.P.R.D. and reflected the actual party
distribution in the D.P.R.D. (Ministerial regulation
17 of 1956). Later, when Law I came into operation,
parties could put forward lists of candidates, and
thereby inter-party agreements became possible in
the composition of the D.P.D.

18. Legge, op. cit., pp. 141-142.

19. Legge mentions, for instance, that in the
Kabupaten Malang (East Java), during the elections
of 1955 and 1956, all but three members of the old
temporary D.P.R.D. were elected to Parliament, the
constituent Assembly, or the Provincial D.D.R.
Ibid., p. 145 fn.

20. In Greater Djakarta, Council nominees, including a former Minister of Home Affairs who had
the support of the big parties, were passed over in
favor of a military appointment. In West Java, the
D.P.R.D. nominees, including both the existing Governor and Kepala Daerah, were both rejected, again
in favor of a soldier. (See ibid., p. 219 fn.)

21. Ibid., pp. 220-221.

22. A. K. Pringgodigdo, The Office of President
in Indonesia as Defined in Three Constitutions in
Theory and Practice, Series Modern Indonesia Project
(Ithaca: Cornell University Press, 1957), pp. 17-18.

23. Sukarno told the United States expert,
Professor Mct Kahim, in February 1959 that he thought
this address was most important as an expression of
his political philosophy, as Mct Kahim writes in a
foreword to a translation of this speech, Marhaen
and Proletarian, Modern Indonesian Project, Translation Series (Ithaca: Cornell University Press, 1960).
The address was given in Bandung, July 1957.

24. These and the following quotations are
taken from his address, Marhaen and Proletarian.

25. The golden bridge is, in Sukarno's view, Indonesian independence.

26. "Marhaen" is Sukarno's expression for all the people who are destitute as a result of the Dutch colonial period.

27. Taken from the address by Mohammed Hatta, upon receiving the degree of Doctor Honoris Causa from Gadjah Mada University at Djakarta, November 27, 1956: Past and Future, Nov. 27, 1956, Modern Indonesian Project, Translation Series (Ithaca: Cornell University Press, 1960).

28. This and the following quotations are taken from Hatta's address at Gadjah Mada University.

29. Nkrumah, Ghana, p. 51.

30. Ibid., p. 177.

31. Ibid., p. vii, Introduction.

32. Kwame Nkrumah, I Speak of Freedom (Accra: Heinemann, 1961), p. 42.

33. Speech for the Indian Council of World Affairs, quoted in ibid., p. 158.

34. Nkrumah, Ghana, p. vii, Introduction.

35. Ibid., p. viii.

36. Feith, op. cit., p. 128.

37. For instance, in Central Java, Lieutenant-Colonel Suwanoto was replaced by Lieutenant-Colonel Sudirman. In East Indonesia, Colonel Gatot Subroto was replaced by Colonel Warouw; in South Sumatra, Colonel Kosasih was replaced by Colonel Bambeng Utojo.

38. Justus M. van der Kroef reports in "Instability in Indonesia," Far Eastern Survey (April, 1957), pp. 49-62, that Mr. Abdulgani was implicated

in a bribery affair by Lie Hok Thay, Director of the
National Printing plant for a sum of 11,000,000
rupees. On April 19, 1957, Abdulgani was condemned
by the Supreme Court for having violated foreign exchange regulations.

39. Published in the <u>Nieuwsgier</u>, Djakarta,
June 2, 1955.

40. The Darul Islam was a fanatical Muslim
group which wanted to create an Islamic State. It
had great support in West Java, and rebelled against
the New Republic from Independence day.

41. The officers of the Indonesian Navy came
out of the Dutch Merchant Marine, or had been
trained in the Netherlands with the Royal Dutch Navy.

42. In 1961, the British commanders of the
army, air force and navy were replaced by Ghanaians;
nevertheless, a British mission continues to serve
with the Ghanaian forces.

43. A specific example was the incident which
took place around the Ambassador of Ghana, Mr. Welbeck. Having been caught inciting revolutionary action in favor of Mr. Lumumba, he was declared <u>persona
non grata</u> by the Congolese Government. He did not
want to leave and had to be protected by Ghanian
troops and police, under British command. Several
important British officers, who were highly critical
of Ghanaian policy in private conversation, nevertheless carried out this maneuver, not without great
risk to themselves personally.

CHAPTER **7** THE NEW ELITE
AND SOCIAL
INSTITUTIONS

In the running of a country, political institutions play an important role, but if they are designed to carry out ideas generated by society they
are not always the fountainheads of thought. In our
democracies, we note that the intellectuals often
provide an arsenal of ideas which are spread throughout society, discussed in countless groups in view
to become a common good. Programs for national welfare and public policy sometimes find their progeny
in a trade union or a social department of a university. Discussions about political problems in the
press can help just as much to foster the solution
to such problems as their treatment in a commission
of Parliament.

The arsenal of a democracy is not only made up
of free elections, a Parliament and a Cabinet, but
also of institutions such as an autonomous university, an independent trade union movement, a free
press and a competent, free-from-party-politics
civil service. Moreover, it is in these social institutions that we often find a new leadership which
rises up to form part of the political élite. They
are often, so to speak, the nurturing ground for the
political élite.

In this chapter, therefore, we intend to treat
the attitude of the élite towards institutions such
as the university, the trade unions, the press and
civil service.

THE UNIVERSITY AND THE ELITE

The fact that the new élite is mostly made up
of people who received a western education is understandable in view of the enormous prestige which is
attached to education in countries where up to 80
percent of the population is illiterate. The student at the university and even in secondary school
is already considered a leader whose opinions and
actions are considered very important. In general,
the student himself is the first of the family to
receive any schooling. This is shown by a study I
undertook in Ghana in 1962 among the students of the
Catholic Higher Seminary in Gold Coast, Ghana (see
Appendix 4) and from data taken from application
details given by students at the University of Ghana
in 1962 (see Appendix 5). Of the 46 students at the
Higher Seminary in Cape Coast, Ghana, only 4 came
from families where the fathers had had a secondary
school education, 14 where the fathers had been at a
primary school, while 22 where the fathers had had
no formal education. As far as the mothers were concerned, 36 were illiterate. As could be expected,
given the agricultural character of Ghana, most of
the seminarians came from farming families--25.

Remarkable also was the fact that when questioned as to what job they considered to be the most
useful for their country, 20 out of the 46 gave
first priority to the teaching profession, 2 to membership in Parliament, 3 to social welfare work, one
to politics, 6 to medicine, and 14 to the priesthood.
The importance attached to education, therefore,
comes to light unmistakably.

This is also proved by the results of a sample
of the applications received for admittance to the
University of Ghana in 1962 (see table in Appendix
5). Out of 749 applications for the B.A. General
Degrees, the B.Sc. General Degree, the Certificate
of Education and study of Law, I took a sample of 74
applicants (25 B.A.'s, 20 B.Sc.'s, 20 Certificates
of Education and 10 law students). As with the seminarians, we notice a predominance of farmers among

the parents of the students (with the exception of
those wishing to study law), and the large number--
41 out of 75--who wished to go into the teaching
profession. The importance attached to the teaching profession can be seen everywhere, even with the
Ghanaian students abroad. An enquiry made among a
group of Ghanaian students studying in London shows
that, although they are from upper-middle class
milieux, the majority feel that teaching is the most
important profession. The sample I took was that of
9 Ghanaian students who met regularly at the student
hostel belonging to the Overseas Chaplaincy in London (see Appendix 6). Six of the nine considered
teaching the most important job, although only three
were preparing themselves for a teacher's role. It
will be remembered also that all the students (men)
except two expressed a desire that their wives
should have had some education. We can conclude
therefore that education is rated very highly among
students in Ghana, and that a majority sees the
teaching profession as one of the most useful in pro-
moting the welfare of the country.

        In view of the importance of education, and par-
ticularly of university education for the new élite
in countries such as Indonesia and Ghana, it is useful to give some consideration to the kind of education they received. No doubt the Indonesian, whether
he studied in the Netherlands or in Indonesia before
the war, got a typically Dutch, western-style of education and the Ghanaian, whether he studied in Ghana,
Sierra Leone or the United Kingdom, a British western-
style of education. It is here in the universities,
that the student--apart from his professional training as a lawyer, physician or teacher--learned the
notions of individual responsibility, democratic
processes of government and social justice, so typical of western civilizations. It is here, also,
that he would hear about the struggle for political
independence of the Dutch nation, of the French revolution, of the American independence movement, and
draw his conclusions for his own country. As long
as he studied in a western country, however, he
would have received an education which made him understand democracy, the party system and the

processes involved in a western parliamentary democracy. Small wonder, therefore, that he wanted to
apply such notions to his own country once independence was achieved.

There were, however, other institutions of high-
er education, such as the "International Students'
Institute in Japan,"[1] and the "National Foundation
Training Institute," established by the Japanese in
Java, where emphasis was placed on spiritual education, greater East Asian history, military administration, the Japanese language, etc. There was also
"The University of the Toilers of the East,"
(K.U.T.V.U.) established in Moscow in 1919, and the
"Sun Yat-Sen" University in the same city, both run
by the Comintern. The first catered to South East
Asian and African students; the second especially
for Chinese; but, as a former lecturer in KUTVU remarks, if the Sun-Yat-Sen saw thousands of Chinese
pass through yearly, in KUTVU, the number of Africans
remained restricted to a dozen.[2]

It was these institutions which created an élite
differently orientated, and if more students from
Indonesia or Ghana had gone to this type of university, the development of democracy after independence day might have followed a different path, as
it did in China after the war.

The great advantage, therefore, of the western
educational system has been that it has given a unified western outlook to the new élite of the young
countries. This has not only promoted cohesion
among the élite in each country, but equally has
helped them to achieve a certain understanding on
the international plane. The difficulties for democratic development start the moment unity among the
élite is broken, either because other groups with a
different educational background--the Army or the
Trade Union leaders--come forward, or because the
educated élite is being trained in different schools
of thought, as is happening today with an Algerian
élite formed partly in Western Europe, partly in
Eastern Europe and Russia, and partly in the Middle
East.

Although the universities see to it that the
student gets a certain intellectual training, they
often offer little in the way of character building
and leadership formation. It is the student organizations, political parties or other social organizations of which he becomes a member, which often have
a much more decisive influence. This is particularly true of the Indonesian or Ghanaian student, who
is studying overseas and therefore is generally cut
off for a number of years from his family background,
but it also holds true to large extent for those who
do their studies in their home countries, since the
secondary schools are generally boarding schools and
the universities are often of a residential type.
This does not mean that there have not been certain
universities or professors which have not had a last-
ing influence on the students' thinking. The London
School of Economics, under Professor Laski's influence, for instance, has had a very great effect on
political leaders in many Asian and African countries.[3] The same can be said for Harvard University
when Mr. Ralph Bunche was a professor in the United
States of America, and for the Sorbonne in Paris.

Nevertheless, the importance of student associations has often been under-estimated in the West--
probably because of the still-lingering idea that
student groups can never be taken seriously.

We have previously pointed out the importance
of the Perhimpunan Indonesia, which gathered together
the Indonesian students in the Netherlands, and similar clubs later formed in Indonesia, out of which
the Partai National Indonesia, with Sukarno as leader, emerged. The same can be said for the West African Students' Union in England, in which Nkrumah,
Botsio and other Ghanaian leaders played a role.
R. Bastide made a study--for UNESCO--among the African students in France, and he draws the following
conclusions:

> We see that an élite is not only the
> product of University training, but of
> its own vital experiences. . . . In
> this sense, the potential élite is

> developing, first and foremost, in the
> student associations, in holiday camps,
> in African parishes, whether Catholic
> or Protestant, in territorial or phil-
> anthropic student hostels, and in the
> course of visits made by students to
> Africa during their holidays, so as
> not to lose touch with the realities
> of life in their own countries.[4]

From my own experience, having worked ten years
in an international student organization, I can only
endorse this view. It is in the student milieu that
the leadership qualities are developed. It is here,
and in contact with other organizations or leaders,
that notions are learned as to how to run a meeting,
as well as how to publish a newspaper, and how to
deal with other people of different convictions. It
is here again that political ideas about social or
economic development, as well as the students' sense
of responsibility--or irresponsibility--towards his
people and his country are developed. If the new
élite in Indonesia and Ghana was conservative or pro-
gressive, pro-Western or anti-Western, religiously
inclined or Marxist-orientated, much of this was due
to the atmosphere and thinking which reigned in the
organization to which he belonged, the kind of European with whom he had been in contact, the kind of
family which had received him into their homes--or
did not want to receive him into their homes.

In Indonesia, both President Sukarno and the
former Vice-President, Mr. Mohammed Hatta, received
their first training in student groups. If one reads
the autobiography of the President of Ghana, one re-
ceives again the clear impression that it was in the
student organization that he developed his talents,
for instance, in speech-making to student groups.

> This began soon after Aggrey died,
> when a few of us got together and
> formed the Aggrey Students' Society
> in his memory. The society acted as
> a forum for speech-making and mem-
> bers used to prepare lectures and

deliver them to the other members of
the society. Eventually this became
a debating society.[5]

Later, in the United States of America, at Lincoln
University, he became a member of the Phi Beta Sigma
Fraternity. "It was a great fraternity to belong
to, [and I] . . . took part in the Freshman oratori-
cal contest, where I gained second place and won a
gold medal."[6] Later on, "while at the University of
Pennsylvania I helped to set up an African Studies
section there. It was there also that I began to or-
ganise the African Students Association of America
and Canada."[7] Of this, he became and remained President during his time in the United States of America.
With other now prominent leaders in Ghana, such as
Ako Adjei and Jones Quartey, he also started a paper,
The African Interpreter. Later again, in England,
he was very active in the West African Students'
Union, especially in one group of which he became
the Chairman and which was a vanguard group, called
the Circle.

The case of a Nkrumah or a Sukarno is not excep-
tional. In view of the important role which student
groups played during the revolutionary period of decolonization, it was logical that the student leaders who had shown their gifts in the local, and
later regional or national student groups were soon
projected as leaders in the independence movements,
and have become outstanding members of the political
élite today. It is a tribute to the leftish movements in Europe--socialist and communist--that they
have discovered this early and thereby have been
able to influence this élite considerably.

THE TRADE UNIONS AND THE ELITE

In general, the trade unions have played a considerable role in the nationalist movements of the
young nations. The first ones often came into being
at the same time as the precursors of the nationalist movements. In Indonesia, for instance, the first
indigenous trade union, the Vereeniging van Spoor en

Tramweg Personeel in Nederlands-Indie (V.S.T.P.)--
the Union of Railway and Tramway Personnel in the
Netherlands East Indies--was started in 1908, the
same year as the Budi Utomo was founded (see Chapter 4).

The history of the Indonesian Trade Unions can
be divided into four periods:

(a) 1908-1927: the Trade Unions during this time be-
    came the battleground for two parties, the Com-
    munist party and the Sarekat Islam, as we have
    already indicated in Chapter 4;

(b) 1927-1945: in this period, political parties
    were suppressed and the colonial government kept
    a careful watch on all other organizations. The
    trade unions, therefore, had to be very careful
    not to engage themselves too much in politics.
    Nevertheless, the parties existing, such as the
    Sarekat Islam and later the Partai Nasional Indo-
    nesia, were in competition for the favor of the
    trade unions. During the Japanese period, trade
    unions were forbidden;

(c) 1945-1949: at this time, once again we see a
    prodigious development of the trade unions, in
    which the communists, in the persons of Mr. Iwa
    Kusuma Sumantri, and Mr. Njono,[8] and the social-
    ist party, in particular, battled for power;

(d) after 1949, when we see a great number of trade
    unions develop, each one coached--so to speak--
    by a political party. The most important ones
    are:[9]

    The Sentraal Organisasi Buruh Seluru Indonesia
    (SOBSI)--the All-Indonesian Central Organisation
    of Labour. Founded 29th November, 1946, declared
    membership of 2,500,000, the SOBSI is practically
    run by the Communist Party, the P.K.I.

    The Kongres Buruh Seluruh Indonesia (KBSI)--All-
    Indonesia Congress of Labour, founded 12th May,
    1953, declared membership, 750,000. This trade

union is strongly influenced by the Socialist
Party, the P.S.I.

The Sarekat Buruh Islam Indonesia (SBII)--Union
of Indonesian Islamic Workers. Founded 27th
November, 1948, declared membership about 275,000,
this trade union is part of the Masjumi Party.

The Kesatuan Buruh Kerakjatan Indonesia (KBKI)--
the Democratic Workers Union of Indonesia, founded 12th December, 1952, membership about 100,000.
This trade union is closely linked to the National Party, the P.N.I.

Other less important trade unions linked with
political parties are: the Himpunan Serikat Serikat
Buruh Indonesia (HISSBI) founded in 1952 and linked
to the Partai Buruh (Labour Party); the Sentral Or-
ganisasi Buruh Republic Indonesia (SOBRI) founded in
1957 and linked to the Partai Murba (the Trotskyite
party).

As is clear from all this,

> throughout its whole history, the Indone-
> sian trade union movement revealed its
> political character. The Unions cherished
> political ideals, were engaged in politi-
> cal activities and maintained close rela-
> tions with political parties. . . . Polit-
> ical leaders and political parties involved
> the Unions in their business and Government;
> both the Colonial régime and the Republic
> government dealt with them as political
> bodies, although in different ways.[10]

This intermingling of trade unions with political parties and consequently the political character
of the trade union movements, which we note in most
young nations, can be explained for the following
four reasons. In the first place, the restricted
number of the political élite in those countries is
one reason. For leading a political party or a
trade union, one needs a person with a certain degree of education, with organizational talents and

leadership capacities. Such people are rare in countries where the overwhelming majority of the population is illiterate and where colonial regimes allowed
little place for the development of organizational or
leadership talents. Therefore, we often see an interchange of leadership between political parties and
trade unions. In some cases, people come up in trade
unions and then go into political parties, such as
an Alimin or a Wilopo in Indonesia, a Sekou Touré in
Guinea, or a Tom Mboya in Kenya.[11] Or political
leaders start playing a role in the trade unions,
such as Mr. Jusuf Wibisono, the Masjumi leader, or
Mr. Ahem Erningpradja of the PNI, who have both become respectively Presidents, of the SBII and the
KBKI Trade Unions.

In the second place, this close relationship
can be explained by the fact that, for a political
party, it is very important to obtain the backing of
a trade union. The trade unions are mass organizations "par excellence." Through them political ideas
can be infiltrated among people who it would otherwise be difficult to interest in political parties,
and through them again, a mass vote can be gathered
at the moment of elections. The Communist parties
were the first to see the advantage of such a connection and they have constantly applied this principle
with considerable success. In Indonesia, the PKI
was founded by the leaders of the VSTP, as we have
seen before. Socialist parties, also, have always
tried to put this principle into practice, but also
parties with a religious orientation such as the
Catholic or Protestant parties in the Netherlands,
as well as the Moslem parties in Indonesia.

Thirdly, during the fight for independence, historical reasons explain to a large extent the strong
links between the trade unions and the political parties. Industries, commerce and plantations in colonial countries were in general in the hands of foreign
elements. The policy of the colonial authorities was
often such that they tended to protect foreign interest and were against trade union claims for better
working conditions, higher pay and shorter working
hours. This distrust was further augmented by the

opinion on the part of the colonial governments that
the trade unions were necessarily communist in outlook, and therefore to be suppressed. The true
trade union leaders consequently became convinced
very quickly that the primary aim of the union had
to be to oust the colonial government. Once this
political aim was accepted, the unions very quickly
came to feel the need for political theories and
practice; this drove them straight into the arms of
the political leaders.

In many of the constitutions of the trade unions
in Indonesia, we find political platforms, such as
the defence and upholding of the Indonesian Republic
(KBKI), the abrogation of the Round Table Conference
Agreements between Indonesia and the Netherlands
(SOBSI), the struggle for the defence of Indonesian
Independence (SOBRI).[12]

Fourthly, the attitude of the governments of
the young countries often encouraged certain political tendencies on the part of the trade unions. In
Indonesia, in the provisional parliament set up by
the Government, a number of seats were reserved for
trade union leaders. President Nkrumah's opinion
was that trade unions in Africa are "expected to
play an active role in the struggle against colonialism."[13]

At the same time, however, it has been Nkrumah's
policy to make the Ghana Trade Union Congress part
and parcel of the CPP.

> There can be no split loyalties. No-
> body has the right to call himself a
> true labour fighter if he is not also
> an honest and loyal member of the Con-
> vention People's Party because, funda-
> mentally, the Convention People's Party
> is the political expression of the
> Ghana Trade Union Movement.[14]

The trade union leaders are, generally speaking,
mass leaders. If, before independence, they have
often played important roles, their importance has

grown after independence during the period in which
social revolution has been taking place. In the developing countries, two sorts of trade union leaders
exist: (a) those influenced by socialist or communist ideas; (b) those influenced by religious motives
like the leaders of Christian or Muslim trade unions.

Among the first group, we find those who come
out for democratic socialism such as that propagated
in Indonesia by the P.S.I., the P.N.I. or the Partai
Buruh, and those who accept the interpretation and
elaboration of socialism by Lenin, such as that
propagated by the P.K.I.

Among the second category we also find strong
socialist trends, for instance, with regard to the
nationalization of industry. However, one important
difference is that the second category in general re-
jects the class struggle as a guiding theme, following thus the "solidarity principle" of the religious
trade unions in Europe. For instance, the SBII in
Indonesia "advocates mutual understanding and cooperation between all people, between labour and
capital, between union and management, for the benefit of both, and in the interests of the community
as a whole."[15] Trade unions as mass organizations
have generally adopted the Leninist concept of "democratic centralism" in the developing countries.
This system which presents the outward appearance of
democracy (voting, discussions, reports, criticisms)
is, in fact, an authoritarian principle which leaves
all authority to some top people and ensures rigid
organizational discipline from top to bottom. In
Indonesia, nearly all trade unions adhere to this
idea of democratic centralism, although sometimes
the term "guided democracy" or "democracy with leadership" is used. The same holds true for Ghana.

It is understandable that trade union leaders
who are used to this system, consciously or uncon-
sciously, try to transpose this also on the political plans of government. As their powers were great,
due to the mixture of trade unions with political
parties, we find here one of the reasons which divided the western-educated intellectual élite in

Indonesia from the mass leaders who set the downfall
of parliamentary democracy in motion, as described
above.

The political influence of the trade union leaders and the absence of a native managerial class in
the developing countries go a long way towards explaining why the young countries have opted for a
socialist form of state. Their political influence,
with that of the army, is one of the major reasons
why most countries have left the road of parliamentary democracy. In this respect, some trade unions,
especially those under communist influence, have
often helped to create a situation whereby the frustrated feelings of a population and the failure of
political parties to ensure social betterment may
make totalitarianism appear as an attractive alterna-
tive in the eyes of a large section of the population.

THE PRESS AND THE ELITE

It is difficult to overestimate the influence
of the press on a population avid to leave the category of illiteracy. For a class which is uneducated,
but able to read, the newspapers are like the Bible.
In discussions, one often hears the assertion that
this or that was in a newspaper, and is therefore
true, used as a conclusive argument. With this goes
a great prestige for the journalists's profession
and, as we have seen in the previous chapter, a fair
number of the political élite in Indonesia, for instance, have been journalists at one time or another.

In our western democracies, freedom of the
press has become a sacred principle and during the
colonial era one could note that although colonial
governments were quick to suppress political or
other organizations, they were much more hesitant
about suppressing publications. An added reason for
this attitude might have been that, in view of the
great percentage of illiteracy, the influence of the
press was in general restricted to a small segment
of the population in the cities. It is understand-

able, therefore, that many of the young revolutionary
leaders went into the journalistic profession, which
was one of the few outlets open to them. People like
Sukarno or Sharir in Indonesia, Nkrumah or Kofi Baako
in Ghana, Azikiwe in Nigeria, Johnson in Sierra
Leone, Leopold Senghor in Dakar, all have been active in journalism at some time.

Publications are, however, costly to run and
one notes therefore, the appearance in colonial countries of two types of newspapers: those directly
linked to a political party--e.g., Indonesia Pedoman
and Indonesia Raya linked to the PSI; Abadi with the
natsir wing of Masjumi, and in Ghana, the Evening
News, organ of the CPP, or the Ashanti Pioneer, opposition paper--or, so-called independent papers which
were supported by business circles, and therefore,
generally under the influence of a foreign element,
European or Chinese. In Ghana, as in most parts of
English-speaking West Africa, moreover, we find a
situation whereby several papers were set up by the
Daily Mirror group of Great Britain. After independence, the influence of these papers was seen to
diminish considerably.

What, now, has been the influence of the press?
During the colonial period, it has helped to promote
nationalist feelings among the educated middle-class
elements. After independence, as long as the principle of a free press was maintained, it often formed
a mighty weapon to denounce unfavorable trends in
government; however, on the other hand, some papers
had difficulty at times in overcoming an attitude of
criticism, which, before independence, was understandable, but which was not always constructive after
the new states came into being.

However, the population reached through the
press--although expanding rapidly--is still small;
Feith estimated that, in 1951, the total circulation
of all newspapers in Indonesia was 515,700,[16] which
means that the number of the public reading the newspapers can be estimated as between 1,000,000 and
1,500,000 (out of a total population of 90,000,000).

In 1957, the most important newspapers in existence were those listed in Appendix 7.[17] Of the 33
papers with a circulation beyond one city only, we
find that four are party organs, 16 are in favor of
one party or of the President in their editorial
orientation, and 13 are independent, of which 5 are
newspapers catering especially for the Chinese group.

In Ghana, the press has been much less developed.
The most important newspapers were: the Ghanaian
Times; the Daily Graphic; the Evening News; the
Ashanti Pioneer. Freedom of the press, however, did
not last very long and at the moment, all newspapers
are pro-CPP with the Evening News remaining the official party paper, and the Daily Graphic trying to
maintain a certain independence.

The newspaper-reading public can be considered
the group which is the most political conscious, and
it is clear, therefore, that all parties have had to
make great efforts to ensure the alliance of this
public to their way of thinking. It is for the same
reason that some governments such as the one in
Ghana felt that the press had to be orientated by
the government and that opposition papers could not
be allowed.

The Ghana newspapers take an important part in
the torrent of adulation for Mr. Nkrumah, which has
been sweeping Ghana in the last few years. Phrases
like: "Kwame Nkrumah: the founder of the nation";
"Our great leader, Kwame Nkrumah"; "On to victory behind our Father and Leader, Kwame Nkrumah" are to be
seen in print daily, and one famous columnist,
"Rambler," of the Evening News, and leader in the
Nkrumah cult, ended his fulmination against some engineering errors in the city, by referring to it as
a state of affairs "shocking in this modern city of
Accra, in the year of our independence, in the year
of our great Kwame Nkrumah, not to mention the year
of Our Lord 1958."

The interest among the students in the Ghanaian
press is decreasing daily; as one student put it to
me, cynically: "Students are supposed to read a lot,

but certainly not our national press, which is the
most underdeveloped of any in Africa today."

In Indonesia, too, there seems a tendency,
alongside the development of guided democracy, for
the government to "guide" the press more and more.
Often, newspaper editions are seized with hardly any
explanation given. Therefore, it looks as if the
role of the press in freely orientating a growing
public in the affairs of the state is severely hampered. By the same token, there is diminishing interest among the educated middle-class in the press,
and a lowering of the prestige of the journalist's
profession. In this regard, it is typical that none
of our Ghanaian students interrogated as to their
future careers mentioned journalism.

THE CIVIL SERVICE AND THE ELITE

As we mentioned in Chapters 2 and 3, among the
civil servants we find a "functional élite" which
has played a very important role during the colonial
regime, but which did not manifest itself openly.

Once independence was achieved, the role of
those civil servants became even more important.
The reorganization of the state, the rapid development of education, social services, the drawing up
of economic three- or five-year plans, and their
implications--all this has come to rest on the shoul-
ders of the civil servants.

If it is for the political organs of the state
to decide on what the government wants to do, it is
up to the civil servants to carry out this policy.

There were, of course, great difficulties to
overcome; in most new countries, the civil service
was set up under a colonial regime and the original
organization of government has often followed a pattern designed for a colony, which is not suitable
for a modern democratic state. Moreover, the training of top level civil servants is not a task to be
accomplished overnight, and many governments were

practically forced, if they wanted to maintain a certain level of efficiency, to maintain a large force
of officials from overseas. This maintenance was
possible in Ghana, where the change-over was peaceful
and the governments of Nkrumah followed a sensible
policy.

In 1925, the number of Africans who held a so-
called "European" appointment was 27. The Africanization scheme introduced by Sir Gordon Guggisberg
aimed at augmenting this number by 1946, to 231. In
actual fact, however, this failed, and in 1946 only
89 Africans held "European" appointments. By 1952,
when Nkrumah formed his first Cabinet, the number of
senior African officers had risen to 520, among whom
15 occupied super-scale posts. By the end of 1956,
the number of senior Africans had risen to three
times that number, and those holding the top position to six times the number of 1952. Nevertheless,
on independence day, not less than 30 percent of the
civil service posts were held by foreigners.[18]

In Indonesia, in view of the open hostility
which had existed between the Dutch and the Indonesian government, it was psychologically impossible to
retain a large contingent of Dutch civil servants
after independence. Therefore, there was a serious
lack of trained civil servants. In 1952, the total
number of experienced civil servants was estimated
at 7,111, while the number of unskilled civil servants was estimated at 571,243.[19]

The normal career of the student from a young
country is either the civil service or the teaching
profession, as might be illustrated by the table in
Appendix 8 concerning a number of Catholic students
who hold university degrees in Ghana.[20] Of a group
of 74 men and 11 women, all Catholics who represented
the overwhelming part of Catholic graduates in the
period 1955-1958, 43 were in the civil service and
36 in teaching professions.

As far as Indonesia is concerned, we have already given an indication in the table in Appendix 1
as to the educational background of 61 top civil

servants in that country. It is clear, therefore,
that those in public service including the civil service and those in the teaching profession, are becoming more and more the bulwark of the western-educated
élite.

This natural trend can, however, be reversed
the moment the civil service is no longer a politically neutral institute, loyally serving the government regardless of its political complexion. The
relationship between the civil servant and the politician in the young countries is no different from
that in all other countries.

Although there may be difference in educational
and cultural background--the senior civil servant belonging to the western-educated élite, and the politician often being a mass leader and a man of lesser
education--the relationship is essentially that of
two groups following separate professions, who are
looking at the same problem through different eyes.
On the other hand, in view of the character and background of the civil service people, it might be that
a great number have a particular sympathy for one
party which best represents their opinions.

In Indonesia, since many of the civil servants
come from the <u>Prijaji</u> class, it was a well-known fact
that many civil servants were pro-PNI--in which the
<u>Prijaji</u> class has always played an important role.
Also, the PSI, as the only party led by western-
educated intellectuals, was favored by them.

On the other hand, in Ghana it is noticeable
that with the new trend in government, a certain
restlessness exists among the civil servants. Although, as we have seen, nearly half the students,
after obtaining a degree, go into the civil service,
as we have noted an overwhelming majority of the
present students prefer the teaching professions
above the civil service--41 to 7. This is a clear
indication of the uneasiness prevailing.

In general, in view of their educational background, one can say that civil servants, both as

officials and as private citizens have been favoring
the setting up of a parliamentary democracy, and are
for the safeguarding of democratic principles.
Their collaboration with a government based on political parties was best as long as the western-educated
élite was in the majority. Relationships will become
increasingly difficult when the mass leaders become
more and more the dominating element of the power
élite.

As someone with considerable experience in the
field of civil service, and a close adviser of Mr.
Nkrumah for many years, once wrote:

> Experience in the new states so far
> shows that there is a fair chance of
> creating and maintaining a well-
> qualified and effective civil service,
> capable of serving a "democratic welfare-
> oriented state." Time, however, will be
> needed for a completely national service
> to be developed, and in that process,
> much will depend on the government's
> attitude towards the service, and of its
> determination not to sacrifice standards
> on the altar of nationalisation.[21]

Footnotes to Chapter 7

1. Elsbree, op. cit., p. 106, declares that,
during the war, the following numbers of students
were brought there:

Burma	47	Sumatra	16	Burma	9
Philippines	51	Ceram	3	Thailand	12
Java	47	Malaya	11	French Indo-China	7

2. George Padmore, Pan Africanism or Communism
(London: Dennis Dobson, 1956).

3. I discovered, for instance, in discussions
with Ministers of the first Cabinet in Singapore after independence, that they had nearly all attended

the London School of Economics, and that their ideas were taken straight from the socialist teachings of Professor Laski.

4.   R. Bastide, "African Students in France," International Social Science Bulletin, VII, No. 3 (1956), 492.

5.   Nkrumah, Ghana, p. 16.

6.   Ibid., p. 25.

7.   Ibid., p. 35.

8.   Iwa Kusuma Sumantri was a brilliant lawyer who had studied in the Netherlands and in Moscow. On his return, he was active in trade union work in Medan. In 1930, he was arrested and then set free when war broke out. In the first Cabinet of the Republic, he became Minister of Social Affairs.
     Mr. Njono was, at this time, leader of the trade union Congress in Djakarta. He is now the Secretary General of the biggest trade union, the SOBSI.

9.   Iskandar Tedjasukmana, a former Minister of Labour, estimated the number of national unions in 1958 at 150, plus several hundreds of local unions. Information about the unions is taken from his publication, The Political Character of the Indonesian Trade Union Movement (Ithaca: Cornell University Press, 1958).

10.   Ibid., p. 23.

11.   This process is, however, not restricted to the young nations, as the examples of Mr. Aneurin Bevan in England, and other leaders of the Labour parties on the continent, show.

12.   Tedjasukmana, op. cit., p. 44.

13.   Nkrumah, I Speak of Freedom, p. 88.

14.   Ibid., p. 188.

15.   Tedjasukmana, op. cit., p. 60.

16.   Feith, op. cit., p. 23.

17.   Material for this table is taken from the Wason collection at the library of the Modern Indonesian Project at Cornell University.

18.   The figures are taken from Mr. Nkrumah's address on the motion for approval of the Government's Revised Constitution, held on 12th November, 1956, in the Parliament.

19.   From Kementarian Penerangan (Ministry of Information publication), Djakarta, 1957. Mentioned in Feith, op. cit.

20.   This sample was taken during the preparation of the first meeting of Catholic intellectuals in Ghana in 1961. The groups of 74 men and 11 women represent the overwhelming majority of Catholic students, who had received a degree in the period 1955-1959.

21.   Taken from an unpublished address given by Commander Jackson at an international conference in Rhodes, September, 1959.

CHAPTER **8** THE NEW ELITE
AND INTERNATIONAL
CONCEPTS

A particular characteristic of the new élite is
that it has taken its ideas from the West (either
western Europe and the U.S. or Russia) and that it
has been strongly influenced by the international
situation, marked as that is by the existence of the
cold war and the presence of the first world parlia-
ment--the United Nations. In this chapter we want
to try and see how far this élite has been influenced
by the concepts of two world systems--that of Communism and that of Christianity, the latter particularly in its Roman Catholic context, and what its attitude is towards the United Nations and concepts such
as Pan-Asianism, Pan-Africanism and the so-called
neutral bloc.

COMMUNISM AND THE NEW ELITE

Since Russia is not a colonial power in the traditional sense of the word, it has managed to introduce itself into many countries as the champion of
the colonialized people; however, its success in influencing the élite with Marxist-Leninist principles
has been, generally speaking, rather poor. Apart
from China, it has not managed so far to convince
the majority of the élite in developing countries of
the validity of its theses. The reasons for this
are two-fold.

In the first place, the former policy of the
Kremlin was to try and introduce communism into colonial areas mainly through the efforts of the Communist parties of the metropolitan countries. These
parties, however, are often tainted with the same
colonial outlook as prevailed generally in the metro-

politan countries. An example, for instance, was
the attitude of Dutch Communist leaders who after
the war influenced the rebirth of the Indonesian Communist parties and who took an anti-Sukarno attitude
as they regarded him more as the Quisling of the war
period than the nationalist leader of before the war.
The Madiun revolt of the communists against the Indonesian Republic during the colonial war, which was
also an outcome of this, discredited the Communist
party in the eyes of the nationalists for many years
to come. The same thing holds true for the Communist
party in France which, while in the Government in
1945, supported the sending of troops to Vietnam.
The ambiguous attitude of the French Communist party
during the Algerian crisis is another example.

The mistakes made with regard to Asia were repeated for Africa; and an expert on this subject
such as George Padmore, who himself lectured for
some time in Moscow, could state that

> to a large extent, the failure to make
> a greater impact upon popular negro
> opinion has been due to the tactical
> mistakes and psychological blunders
> which the Communist parties of the
> western world--America, Britain,
> France and South Africa--have made in
> their approach to the darker peoples.[1]

A second weakness was that Communism was not
able to penetrate the educational institutions, both
in the colonial countries themselves or in western
Europe where most of the students were studying, and
that it never succeeded in drawing great numbers of
students to the universities in Russia. We have mentioned already the existence of the Sun Yat Sen University for Chinese students and the KUTVU University for people from S.E. Asia or Africa. However,
as we have already seen, this latter institution
never drew great numbers of students. The best and
most logical way of influencing the up-and-coming
élite in those countries was therefore missed.

To this should be added that before the war

Asian and African students came in general from
rather prosperous middle-class families. Consequently, they had a bourgeois middle-class outlook and
were no easy prey for Marxist-Leninist thinking.
This situation has changed, however, since the war
when more students from lower middle-class families
have entered the western European universities and
the success of the Communists in attracting them has
grown considerably, although "in fact most of them
shed their Marxist garments on returning home and
revert to what they have always been at heart--bour-
geois nationalists."[2]

A third difficulty for communism has been its
growing loss of a universal orientation and appeal
because of differences in the Communist bloc itself.
The split between Moscow and Belgrade has given Tito
his chance to become the prophet of a neutral kind
of "socialism" for developing areas. The rapidly
growing split between Moscow and Peking will have
even greater consequences. Peking represents a much
greater revolutionary élan and represents the non-
white population, two factors which are bound to
assure it a hearing in developing countries; however, it is economically still too weak to be considered by the young countries as a big force to
draw upon. The growing rivalry between the Belgrade,
Moscow and Peking brands of communism, however, is
felt clearly, not only in the Communist parties and
international Communist organizations, but also in
their aid programs, as I could clearly see during a
visit to Guinea.

Since the end of the Second World War, the Communists have followed a new approach which has met
with more success. The new policy consisted of working through "front organizations" of an international
character, and their main efforts were directed particularly at three categories of people: (a) trade
union leaders, (b) youth leaders, and (c) students.
The projection--so to speak--of the Communist image,
but under the apparently neutral sponsorship of an
international organization, was left to the World
Federation of Trade Unions (WFTU) and the World Federation of Democratic Youth (WFDY), both founded in

1945, and the International Union of Students (IUS)
founded in 1946.[3] Well organized, under capable
leaders and with the necessary financial backing,
these three organizations have done much to organize
Communist trade unions, youth groups and students,
or to infiltrate the already existing ones. As we
have seen in our previous chapter, in Indonesia they
have managed to capture the biggest trade union
(SOBSI). In Ghana, success has been less spectacular. In the beginning the CPP did not tolerate any
Communist influence and, for instance, two CPP members with Communist leanings--Mr. Anthony Wood and
Mr. Tureson Ocran--were ousted from the party, after
they had attended a meeting of the World Federation
of Trade Unions in Vienna in 1954.

It was through such organizations, which did
not bear an overt Communist stamp, that contact was
sought with individuals or groups, both in the developing countries and in western Europe. By inviting
them to international meetings, they were brought
into contact with Communist groups and Communist
ideas. Those who showed interest were often then
given scholarships or internships in Communist countries. The importance the Communists attach to this
kind of work might be shown by the organization of
World Youth Festivals sponsored by the International
Union of Students and the World Federation of Democratic Youth.[4] At the one held in Moscow in 1957,
35,000 young people participated, and the costs were
estimated at $10,000,000.

In this way, it must be admitted that among
young people a certain amount of good will was created
for the Communist cause, particularly among those
from developing countries, as the struggle against
"colonialism and imperialism" was generally one of
the main themes of all meetings and gatherings and
one which had the instinctive sympathy of the youth
of those countries.

Groups or organizations affiliated to these international organizations have often become recruit-
ing grounds for Communist parties and trade unions.
Moreover, through these groups, large quantities of

propaganda material or books could be sent out and
distributed.

If it is true, therefore, that the Communists
have failed to win over to any considerable extent
the old western-educated élite, greater progress has
been made with the second generation, and notably
the mass leaders, or trade union leaders.

Today, the élite in Asia and Africa is not very
much interested in Marxism-Leninism as an ideology,
to which at most they pay some lip service. What
many are looking for are instruments which allow
them to rule the country with a mere handful of
people. Europe has only two examples to offer--
Communist or fascist dictatorship. As Fascism has
been much discredited since World War II, the Communists have a good chance of selling their technique
to those mass leaders who want to keep all power in
relatively few hands. We see examples of this both
in Indonesia and Ghana.

It is clear that after each journey through the
Communist world, Sukarno learned something about
these techniques. For instance, he learned the advantage of having one single party.

> In countries with only one party, shap-
> ing and reshaping, thinking and rethink-
> ing, can proceed easily. For instance
> in the Soviet Union, brothers and sis-
> ters, if it be necessary to reshape, it
> is very easy; once that single party
> managed to change its opinion, it starts
> the reshaping. . . . So, look at the
> Government in the Soviet Union, brothers
> and sisters: it is elected from and by
> the Presidium, the Presidium is elected
> by the Supreme Soviet; the Supreme
> Soviet is elected by the people. Don't
> you feel that or, let's say, here the
> cabinet--is an extension of the commun-
> ity? . . . For that reason things are
> extremely easy, brothers and sisters.
> To put something into effect, the

> Government takes action and is fol-
> lowed by the whole people.[5]

Sukarno's whole concept of a <u>Gotong Rojong</u> cabinet,
a Supreme Advisory Council, a national planning
council, all based on a national front which would
be the only party, is clearly based on the Leninist
concept of democratic centralism. All this has not
yet been achieved, but it is interesting to note
that the Communist forces so far are helping Sukarno
on this road, realizing that they can capitalize
more on a form of dictatorship run by a little
clique of technocrats and mass leaders than on a
democratic system led by the western-educated intellectuals.

In Ghana we note a similar development, which
has taken place much more quickly. Because of the
overwhelming popularity of the CPP on independence
day, it was relatively easy to suppress the practical existence of other parties. Since then we see
the development of a monolithic state. One party,
one trade union, one youth movement--the Young Pioneers. Nkrumah himself stated that the Convention
People's Party is Ghana, and Ghana is the Convention
People's Party.[6] To this we might add that the CPP
is Nkrumah and Nkrumah is the CPP. Nkrumah himself
has read the works of Marx and Lenin but he is certainly not a Marxist. It is, however, again the
Soviet methods which are attracting the leaders in
power and many of the leaders of the Young Pioneers
or the trade unions have made extensive visits to
the Communist world.

To sum up, we might state that Marxism-Leninism
as an ideology has so far had little grasp on the
élite in the young countries, but that Communist
methods and techniques on how to run a country with
a small élite and through a monolithic system of
government in which the method of democratic centralism is employed, are attracting increasing attention,
especially among the mass leaders.

CHRISTIANITY AND THE NEW ELITE

We have already mentioned that both the Christian and Muslim religions have had a great influence on the pre-nationalist movements (Chapters 4 and 5). The activity of the Christian churches during the colonial period has rested on two pillars--education and health services. There is no doubt that the Christian churches, both in Asia and Africa, have been the pioneers of education, but we should add, of western education. Although the Roman Catholic church from its early beginnings has always held to the thesis that Christianity cannot be identified with western or any particular culture, but that it should take in all that is valuable from all cultures, the factual situation has been that during the eighteenth, nineteenth and beginning of twentieth centuries, this identification of Christianity with western culture was understandable in the eyes of the colonized. The missionaries, willingly or unwillingly, knowingly or unknowingly, have contributed to this.

The idea that western civilization was superior dated from the days of colonialism and was shared by the overwhelming mass of missionaries. The style of the Catholic churches and objects of holy art shows that even today. But in other manifestations this also came to the fore. In Africa I noted, for instance, that where Irish missionaries had been active, the feast of Saint Patrick was considered by most Africans as one of the greatest religious feasts of the year. Such an identification has done harm to the church in Asia after independence. Christian communities, especially in Asia, run the risk of becoming small ghettos of groups which are not only religiously speaking different, but also culturally speaking different from the rest of society. In Black Africa this danger has never been so great. Christianity did not face here long-standing cultures like those of the Chinese or Hindu world and, up to the present day, we do not see such an upsurge of traditional cultures as in Asia (the so-called "negritude" remains the privilege of a

small, specially French-educated group of African
intellectuals).

The great importance attached to western education by the churches has, however, had important consequences for the formation of the élites. In Black
Africa outside the Muslim regions it is hard to find
a leader who has not passed through a Christian
school or a Catholic minor seminary.[7] In Asia the
influence of the Christian communities has, for the
same reason, often been out of all proportion to
their numbers.[8]

We have already noted the popularity and prestige attached to the teaching profession in developing countries. If one would study the background of
a great number of the élite one would note that the
majority at one time or other have been in the teaching profession, and a large number of them have
taught in Christian schools--whether they themselves
were Christian or not. Examples of this in Africa
are, again, the presidents of Ghana, Tanganyika,
Congo (Leopoldville or Brazzaville) and Senegal, and
the Prime Ministers of Nigeria and Dahomey.

All this has led to a situation whereby a great
number of the élite are either Christian, whether
practicing or not, or have been in close contact
with Christian thinking during some phase of their
educational development.

But if the Catholic Church managed to create a
church élite, she has been late in trying to train
an élite of laymen and women in the Christian sense.
In this she stands behind the Protestant churches.
The Catholic church gave more attention to education
at the lower level--primary schools--and only recently more attention to secondary and higher education.[9]
The Protestant churches, however, were more interested in forming a small, well-educated élite through
some high-level secondary schools, or at the uni-
versity--such as the University of Sierra Leone, the
oldest in Black Africa and started by Protestant
missionaries. To this should be added that although
we do not include clerical people in our concept of

power élite, with regard to education, prestige and
influence on the masses, they form nevertheless a
typical élite group. We have already pointed to the
influence of the Muslim religious leaders (see Chapter 3), but also the Protestant pastor or Catholic
priest carries great weight, notably in Africa. The
Roman Catholic Church saw earlier than the western
political leaders the necessity of the association
or Africanization of its leaders in those countries.
Thus it has singularly enhanced its prestige in
those areas and the editorialist of Le Monde could
rightly write: "We must therefore not be amazed to
note that religious decolonization has preceded
political decolonization."

INTERNATIONAL POLITICS AND
THE NEW ELITE

The decolonization process shows us a typical
example of what is called the acceleration of history.
It took a considerable period of time for the white
people in Canada, Australia and New Zealand to obtain
their independence. The same holds true for the
peoples in India, Ceylon or Indonesia, all countries
with a civilization which up till the eighteenth century was equivalent, if not superior, to the west
both in its material and its spiritual aspects. If
one then compares this with the situation in Africa
and especially the decolonization processes of the
last few years, it is clear that the attainment of
independence is becoming increasingly easy and that
the independence of new states is more the fruit of
an international mentality and processes outside the
country than of the determined will of an élite
shouldered by the masses. If Sukarno can rightly
claim that the Indonesian people struggled for their
independence and were victorious, the words "struggle"
and "victory" take on another dimension when one
looks at Ghana, and still another when looking at
the Congo (Leopoldville). In this regard one can
say that independence today is accorded to the
people in inverse proportion to their efforts to obtain it, and perhaps their ability to make good use
of it. This is the result of three processes which
have taken place on the international plane:

(a) The growth of an international public opinion
    increasingly opposed to colonialism. The U.N.
    has been the most important single voice in this
    process.

(b) The existence of the "cold war" since the Second
    World War and the efforts by the two big powers
    to keep or win over the alliance of young na-
    tions.

(c) Changes in the economic situation which made
    colonial countries less and less sources of in-
    come but rather sources of expenditure for the
    metropolitan countries.

The first two processes in particular have, to
a great degree, affected the élite in the developing
countries. Some of the present-day leaders, especially in Africa, have been internationalist before
becoming nationalist. I refer to the Pan-African
movement (see Chapter 4) which has affected a personality such as Nkrumah even up to the present day.
But in general, all the western-educated élite have
been influenced by international concepts and slogans. The whole independence movement started under
the battle cry of liberty, of the U.N. concept for
self-determination of the people, of the rights of
man, of the right of citizenship which meant, for
each man, one vote. In this it found a sympathetic
hearing in the world and especially before the U.N.
If it had not been for the pressure put upon the
Dutch by the United Nations, Indonesian independence
would not, in fact, have been granted in December
1949; in addition, the role of the U.N. in the decolonization of Africa is a phenomenon we can still
watch daily.

But if independence was fought on the basis of
the principle of liberty, after independence the
sacred principle became that of equality. The weapon
of equality is used internally and explains the socialist tendencies of the new states. It is also
used externally to play a role on the international
level. In this, the United Nations has offered
unique opportunities by giving each country the same

voting power. It is this same tendency of equality
again which has led to efforts to bring the developing nations together under one force and so to be
able to play a more equal role on the international
plane. Examples of this have been the famous Asian-
African Conference of Bandung (April 1955); the Pan-
African Conference of Accra (December 1958), and the
inter-African Conference of Liberia. These efforts
towards greater political unity have remained very
much verbal so far. This can be explained to a great
extent by the differences of opinion among the élites
of the different countries. As long as such meetings
are platforms for denouncing colonialism and imperialism, everybody agrees. The moment, however, some effective form of collaboration has to be worked out,
the difficulties start at who shall lead whom. The
problem of the western-educated élite versus the
mass leader appears here all over again. Countries
which are led by a western-educated élite and which
are following democratic processes find the same
difficulties in sitting at the table with countries
led by mass leaders following autocratic processes.
Nehru and Chou En-lai trying to chart a course for
common action in Bandung ran into the same differences of opinion as the PSI and PKI leaders in Indonesia trying to discuss national politics. The only
result of Bandung could be a charter which does not
go much further than stating lofty principles which
demand a lot of the U.N., such as the setting up of
a U.N. fund for economical development and the application of self-determination, but are very clear,
nevertheless, in not touching in any way the sovereignty of the nations. For instance, Article 2
speaks of the respect for the sovereignty and territorial integrity of all nations; Article 4 of the
abstention of intervention or interference in the
internal affairs of another country; Article 6 of
abstention by any country from exercising pressure
on another country; Article 7 of refraining from
acts or threats of aggression.

It would be wrong, however, to consider that
the Bandung Conference had no result at all. Firstly, it came as a kind of a shock to the western
world, who for the first time saw the emergence of a

new bloc in the field of international politics.
Secondly, it greatly strengthened the self-confi-
dence of the leaders of the young nations who slowly became aware that they did represent a certain
power and that by uniting themselves they could at
least force the pace of the decolonization process.

But if the Afro-Asian bloc is not likely to survive long after the end of the decolonization process, there also is not much hope for the realization of Pan-Asianism or Pan-Africanism in the near
future. Here again unity can only be found on the
bases of anti-colonialism, but the friendship which
reigns between Nigeria or Ghana as between India and
Pakistan is of the same order as that of France and
Germany before the Second World War.

To this should be added another factor: the
African élite has been educated either in English or
French style. The influence education has had is
tremendous, and to watch a discussion between French-
educated Africans or English-educated Africans, even
if they are from neighboring countries such as Ghana
and the Ivory Coast, is, in a sense, the same as
watching French and English students discuss. The
same longing for theoretical logical schemes on the
part of the student from the Ivory Coast, the same
disdain for principles but interest in practical details on the part of the Ghanaian. If the word "intellectual" is not much appreciated in London or
Lagos, the word "muddle-through" is not understood
in Bordeaux or Brazzaville. This holds true also
for the élite. The efforts of Nkrumah and Sekou
Toure to link their countries in a union (23rd November 1958), which was later extended to Mali (26th
December 1960) have remained a paper construction.
The whole staff at the Guinean Embassy in Ghana remains restricted to three persons,[10] and nobody in
Accra took this union seriously, apart from feeling
that the Ghanaians were losing money heavily on it.
Smythe, during his research among the Nigerian élite,
noted: "Even Pan-Africanism is not much talked about
by the élite, and the Afro-Asian conferences of Bandung and Cairo as well as continental meetings in
Accra, Tunis and Monrovia, were all received without

excitement."[11] Political unity in Africa, it seems,
therefore, will remain restricted to a negative atti-
tude--anti-colonialism, anti-racism, anti-imperialism.
Closer collaboration, however, on the economic level
might well develop and form a prelude for greater
political unity.

Among the mass leaders, there is certainly a
bond which has been established during the struggle
for independence and which makes them help each
other. A typical example is the letter which Nkrumah
wrote to Patrice Lumumba on 12 September 1960 (see
Appendix 9). Here is a former revolutionary leader
advising his friend in difficulties. He counsels
prudence.

> Do not force Kasabubu out now. It will
> bring too much trouble especially in
> Leopoldville, when you want calm there.
> Do not make an issue of his treachery
> now, or even of Tshombe's treachery.
> The time will come to deal with them.
> [And further]: I must repeat with all
> emphasis here, namely, that you must not
> push the United Nations troops out until
> you have consolidated your position and
> then you can ask them to leave.

The letter further contains advice on how to set up
an administration with an inner cabinet and a technical assistance committee in all details.

> I have added Foreign Affairs to your
> portfolio. But look out for two trusted
> comrades, one to be Deputy Minister of
> Defence and the other to be Deputy Min-
> ister of Foreign Affairs, both under you.

The letter is not without some paternalistic over-
tures:

> As regards the external work, especial-
> ly concerning the security council and
> UNO, leave that to me [and] whenever in
> doubt consult me.

But here are comrades in arms writing to each other.
"Brother, we have been in the game for some time now
and we know how to handle the imperialists and the
colonialists," and "Brother, have implicit faith in
me; I shall not let you down." One must not forget
that Patrice Lumumba's star started to rise after
the Accra Conference in December 1958, like that of
Tom Mboya of Kenya and Julius Nyerere of Tanganyika.
The question remains open, however, as to whether or
not Lumumba would have continued to follow Nkrumah's
lead once he had become the leader in the Congo.
Nyerere no longer follows the same lines as Nkrumah,
just as Nkrumah has not followed Azikewe of Nigeria,
from whom he learned a lot in younger days. The
same holds true for the relationship of Sekou Touré
with Houphouet Boigny, whose former lieutenant he
was.

If regional cooperation shows the differences
between the élite, an even clearer example lies in
their attitude towards foreign aid. In a general
sense, the western-educated élite has shown a willingness to continue to collaborate with the West
and to allow foreign aid or foreign capital to enter
the country. The mass leaders, however, and especially the trade union leaders, took a much more
distrustful attitude. Because of their education
they mistrusted any form of capitalism, especially
that of the West. In Indonesia the PSI, the Natzir
wing of the Masjumi, some elements of the PNI, the
Christian parties and a personality such as Vice-
President Mohammed Hatta, for instance, were willing
to find an arrangement with the Dutch and to allow
Dutch capital to continue to work in Indonesia.
Parties such as the Nahdatul Ulama, PKI and part of
PNI, as well as President Sukarno, took another attitude and strove for confiscation of Dutch property
and were distrustful of American aid. In the first
group we find the western-educated élite at the helm,
in the second the mass leaders, as I have shown in
Chapter 6.

In Ghana a similar split occurred in 1961.
After introducing an austerity budget which included

extra taxes for the population, without any psychological preparation of the masses, the President and
a great part of the government left for a visit to
east and west Europe. The reaction of the workers
was unfavorable and strikes broke out which the
union leaders could not prevent. Instead of seeking
the blame where it really lay, that is on the insuf-
ficient psychological preparation of the population,
the mass leaders blamed it on the imperialistic de-
signs of foreign capital which fomented unrest. The
western-educated leaders such as Gbedemah and Botsio
who did not approve of such tactics as they rightly
feared the psychological reaction on the part of
foreign capital, were dismissed and used as scape-
goats. It must be added, however, that the way
western aid has been given has never helped the
western-educated élite in the developing countries.
Western aid has unfortunately been granted for other
purposes than the aim to help democratic forces in
developing areas.

        The question of neutrality or non-alignment is
not so much a source of disunity among the élite in
the developing countries as is believed in the west.
At least they all want to remain neutral in the cold
war which is going on between the power blocs, and
for very good reasons. The existence of the cold war
has been one of the greatest blessings for the developing countries both during the process of decolonization and after independence. On the purely
political side, there is no advantage in choosing
sides in a permanent way. To play off one bloc
against the other, to obtain the necessary economic
aid is, as Nasser has shown, a difficult but reward-
ing art. We find a democratically-led country such
as India doing so just as much as a dictatorially-
led country as Egypt.

        If so-called neutral countries find it sometimes
easier to be less neutral towards the USA than Russia,
this again is not their fault, but can be explained
by the typical American attitude which is also apparent in American foreign policy--to need to be liked
and to dislike criticism from any dubious side very
very much.[12]

If the western-educated élite is more pro-
western in its thinking and the mass leaders are beginning to tilt more towards the Communist bloc in
their thinking, both groups have discovered that for
neither the USA or Russia or England or France is
this a very important factor in deciding whether aid
should be given or not. The West with all its pre-
tensions regarding the superiority of democratic systems, has not shown any great consistency in this
matter as far as foreign alignment is concerned. The
Russians, one should add, show the same inconsistency
for which the Chinese rightly reproach them.

George Washington once gave a perfect definition
of non-alignment:

> Europe has a set of primary interests
> which to us have no or a very remote
> relation. . . . Why should we, by inter-
> weaving our destiny with that of any part
> of Europe, entangle our peace and prosper-
> ity in the tails of European ambition,
> rivalry, interest or caprice.

As Sukarno once rightly remarked: "Substitute the
word 'Big Powers' for Europe and you find a descrip-
tion of the attitude of the élite in developing
countries."[13]

Footnotes to Chapter 8

1.   Padmore, Pan-Africanism or Communism, p. 289.

2.   Ibid., p. 329.

3.   Other front organizations, as for instance:
World Peace Council (1948); Women's International
Democratic Federation (1945); World Federation of
Scientific Workers (1946); International Organiza-
tion of Journalists (1946); International Medical
Organization (1950); International Radio and Televi-
sion Organization (1946).

4.   Such festivals were organized in Prague 1947,
Budapest 1949, Berlin 1951, Bucharest 1953, Warsaw
1955, Moscow 1957, Vienna 1959, Helsinki 1962.

5.   From Sukarno's address, Marhaen and Proletarian.

6.   From a broadcast at the third anniversary
of independence day, cited by Nkrumah in I Speak of
Freedom, p. 209.

7.   For instance: Presidents Nkrumah of Ghana,
Senghor of Dakar, Kasavubu of Congo, Nyerere of Tanganyika, Youlou of French Congo, all went to Catholic
Schools.   Presidents Azikiwe of Nigeria, Prime Minister Kenyata of Kenya and the Prime Minister of Nyasa-
land, Dr. Hastings Banda, were educated in Protestant
schools.

8.   A typical example has been Ceylon, where until a few years ago, practically all top positions in
the Civil Service, in the forces or other important
institutions were held by Christians.   In Indonesia,
however, too, the number of Christians among the
élite is out of all proportion to the actual number
of Christians.   The existence of two Christian parties which have managed to draw a great number of
non-Christian votes is another indication.

9.   One of the reasons was that the missionaries in English or French speaking territories were
often of a different nationality than the colonizing
power and therefore greatly handicapped in educational matters on an advanced level.   For instance, most
Catholic missions in Ghana were run by Dutch or American fathers.   A large number in Uganda were run by
French Canadians, and in the Sudan by Italian fathers.

10.   A typical example is that practically nobody in the foreign office in Accra could tell me in
1961 where the Guinean Embassy was, which I did not
find so astonishing once I had located the place,
consisting of four shabby rooms.

11.   Hugh Smythe and Mabel M. Smythe, The New Nigerian Elite (Stanford, Calif.:   Stanford University Press, 1960), p. 119.

12.   That the Russians have no such fears was most clearly demonstrated by the resumption of Russian nuclear testing on the eve of the Belgrade Conference of neutral nations.   Very little criticism was heard then as leaders of those countries were well aware that such criticism falls on deaf ears.

Another example is the French attitude. The Bizerta incident does not seem to have hurt De Gaulles' popularity in Africa.

13.   Sukarno quoted this text of Washington at an address before the Council for World Affairs, Los Angeles, California, 21 April 1961.

CHAPTER **9** THE NEW ELITE
AND THE CHALLENGE
OF THE FUTURE

In the previous chapters, we have tried to
sketch the emergence and the role of the élite in
two developing countries.

We have seen in the developing countries that
the élite of today, in the sense of the term as outlined in Chapter 1, is the political élite. This
political élite is a typical outcome of the social
changes which have taken place during the colonial
era. It has generally come forward from a new group,
the middle class, which, with the growth of the cities, the development of trade and commerce, of the
liberal professions and of administration, has
sprung up in the colonies during the nineteenth and
twentieth centuries (Chapters 2 and 3). Another
typical feature of this élite is that it is the product of western education (Chapter 8). After having
sparked the nationalistic feelings in their countries, the members of this élite have ridden the
crest of the nationalistic wave towards independence
(Chapters 4 and 5).

Strongly western in orientation and thinking
after independence, the élite installed governments
based on a parliamentary democratic system. It
turned against the old indigenous aristocratic élite
which held great power during the colonial regime
through the indirect system of government applied by
the Dutch in Indonesia and the British in Ghana.
However, because of this, the aristocratic group was
accused of being the stooge of colonialism and it
lost out against the better educated, more revolutionary younger elements. It continued, nevertheless, to play an important if not spectacular role
in the civil services of the countries and made

possible the transition from a colonial regime to an
independent state. The new élite after independence
has destroyed the political power of the old aristocratic élite--Prijaji in Indonesia, and chiefs in
Ghana--and is now also trying to take away from them
the social prestige which they still hold (Chapters
4 and 5).

The new western-educated élite is, however, menaced itself by a newer group, the mass leaders led
by the charismatic national hero--Sukarno in Indonesia, Nkrumah in Ghana. The mass leader in general
is not so well educated, nor so western in outlook,
but is in closer contact with the population. He
has come forward from the mass organizations, either
trade unions, youth groups or the army (Chapter 6).
This élite, being more revolutionary in outlook, out-
bids the western group in its stand against the European élite. If the latter has been content with
breaking the European élite's political strength, it
was still willing to let it hold on to a great deal
of its economic power, and imitated its style of
life. The former, however, is against European economic power in which it sees a form of neo-colonial-
ism (Chapter 6). The same difference exists in regard to international relations and international
aid. The mass leader has taken non-alignment as his
doctrine (Chapter 8). This victory has been greatly
influenced by the attitude of the national hero
(Chapter 6). This has led in Indonesia to the complete disappearance of the European Dutch élite and
is causing growing difficulties for the Chinese ele-
ment--the second largest holder of economic power.
In Ghana it is causing a growing uneasiness among
the European and Middle Eastern--Syrian and Lebanese--
elements. This struggle for power still, however, is
not finished and on its outcome will depend greatly
the future orientation of the developing countries.
The battle for power is clearly not taking place in
a closed vacuum, but international relations and
world philosophies play a great role (Chapter 8).

It is difficult to predict the outcome, but in
this last chapter, I have tried to give some of my
ideas about a possible course of events. The future

lies in the first place, of course, with the élite
in the countries concerned. Will they strive for
some form of democracy or will the tendency towards
monolithic governments led by a national hero deepen?
If a western democratic parliamentary system does not
seem to work, are there other forms of government
which can promote the democratic principles of human
dignity and the common good? These are some of the
questions we have to pose.

But, if the future of these countries rests in
the first instance in the result of the decisions
taken by their élite, this does not mean that the
rest of the world--and certainly the West--is not
interested in its outcome or incapable of doing anything else but watching. The socio-economic development of those countries is the direct concern of the
West. Has the western aid program--as carried out
so far--been able to promote the democratic tendencies existing in developing countries and, if not,
can they do something in this field? That is the
challenge the western democracies will have to face.

Finally, closely linked to this is the need for
the development of a world-wide social philosophy
which can promote the peaceful but rapid development
of countries which are lagging behind. In the previous chapter, we have talked about two concepts, that
of Communism and that of Christianity. The preten-
sion of Communism to being a united world force with
clear conceptions of the paths to be followed to ensure human happiness and world peace is quietly being given up. This, however, is not true for Christianity. Has it still a role to play and can it
play it?

THE CHALLENGE OF DEMOCRACY

The term "democracy" since the Second World War
has become one of the most venerated words in the
political vocabulary of a world grasping for unity
based on equality. This to a point where regimes
which do not respect the principles of democracy prefer to call themselves peoples' democracies and

attempts to install dictatorships are covered with
the cloak of "basic democracy" or "guided democracy."

This general tendency towards democratic forms
of government has also been noticeable in the newly
independent states. As we have seen, however, in
the case of Indonesia and Ghana, there is a trend
away from western parliamentary democratic systems
towards "strong governments" led by a national hero.
Is this new orientation responding to the ideals and
desires of the new political élite? The question is
difficult to answer for a western European. It
would be necessary to look into the minds of the
political élite of those countries and especially of
their national heroes.

We have shown in Chapter 8 that a Sukarno or a
Nkrumah is not in favor of a parliamentary democracy,
but it is not so easy to discern whether they have
any other clear conception except their desire for
absolute power. Through discussions with the actual
Asian or African leaders, or through reading their
statements, I could not escape the impression that
they are in general satisfied with vague terms as
"the African road to socialism," "Nkrumahism,"
"guided democracy," as expressions of political
ideals which are not further developed.

In justice we should not forget, however, that
the actual leaders are facing enormous problems: of
changing leadership, of the growth of new social
groups and classes who clamor for a rightful place
in society, for developing an economic and a foreign
policy adapted to the needs of their countries. All
this in a period when the unity and enthusiasm of
the national struggle fades away. Small wonder then
that the national leaders have little time for philosophical reflections and are on the lookout for pre-
cepts they might follow. One that holds great attraction today is that of dictatorships and the
argument often used by the political élite in the
developing countries as well as in the west in favor
of this is the assertion that dictatorial governments enjoy a built-in advantage in developing
countries.

Independence, so goes the argument, demands a
change in outlook on the part of the people from de-
fiance of authority as represented by colonial governments to acceptance of authority as represented
by the new regime. This is a difficult process and
one national party is more capable of guiding the
transformation than are several parties, all making
a bid for the national vote.

> The modernizing élite, which is in con-
> trol of most of the newly independent
> African nations, looks around for in-
> tegrating institutions, mechanisms which
> are intermediate between the citizen and
> the state but national in orientation;
> mechanisms which can attract the neces-
> sary loyalty more rapidly and turn this
> loyalty into service of the nation.[1]

The best institutions for this are considered to be
a national party and a national hero. The role of
the hero is, essentially, to be the new symbol of
the nation. "He legitimizes the state by ordaining
obedience to its norm and loyalty to his person."[2]

The existence of several parties is not possible because there exists a confusion between the notions of opposition and secession and therefore,
"the choice has not been between one-party and multi-
party states, it has been between one-party states
and either anarchy or military regimes or various
combinations of the two."[3] The conclusion then
drawn is that "the one-party system in the African
continent is often a significant step toward the
liberal state, not a first step away from it."[4]

It seems to me that such reasoning is just as
superficial and erroneous as the belief of western
parliamentarians that, provided general elections
are held and parliament is installed after independence, the future of democracy in the developing
countries is assured.

As we have seen in our study, the system of
western parliamentary democracy was introduced be-

cause the élite, educated in the West, felt this to
be the best possible system. If it did not work
well right from the start, this can be explained by
the fact that the great mass of people was not accus-
tomed to such a system, since colonial rule had been
essentially authoritarian and no opportunity had
been given the lower levels to practice democracy.
As we have seen, the notion of a democratic opposition
party was alien to national traditions. This did not
mean, however, that a system of parliamentary democracy would be unworkable in the long run. The cases
of India and the Philippines show the contrary. The
reason for failure must be sought in the fact that
the élite was not unified on how to carry a system
of parliamentary democracy to its practical conclusions. As the examples of both Indonesia and Ghana
show, parliamentary democracy was abolished because
the mass leaders and the national heroes did not
want the system to function. They wanted all the
power in their own hands.

The argument that a dictatorship is better capable of assuring a socio-economic revolution is not
yet proven by history.[5] Economic development in
Indonesia did not improve after 1957. On the contrary; and the same can be said for Ghana's evolution in the last few years. Moreover, the whole
history of Latin America is a proof of the extent to
which small oligarchies and dictatorial regimes can
hinder the development of the masses.

The usefulness of a national leader in a newly-
born country as symbol of the new nation cannot be
denied, but, if the national hero becomes a dictator,
he is likely to lose the support of a significant
element of the population--the students and western-
educated élite. Nehru's popularity among the masses
has not been diminished because he is criticized
from time to time in Parliament or by the press, and
Nkrumah has not heightened his popularity among the
masses by a cult of personality and adulation. This
has only harmed his image among the educated elements. All efforts, therefore, to justify authoritarian tendencies on the basis of the Asian or African way of life, or as a necessary stage of develop-

ment, are a posteriori explanations which do not
take into account reality--a reality which is based
on a blatant drive for power among the élite, and
especially the mass leaders.

The mass leader who tries to ensure a strong
government based on one party, with one youth movement, or one trade union controlled by the party,
and who wants to orient the mass media of communica-
tion is not taking into account Asian or African
traditions any more than the western-educated élite
was when it drew up the modern constitutions of
their states. Both have been looking for examples
in the west; the first in communistic or fascist
countries, the second, as we pointed out before, in
democratic countries.

The main question, however, is not whether system a, b or c will be followed, but whether democratic principles will survive. If we define democracy
as a political system which recognizes and promotes
human dignity and where every member is depended
upon to look beyond his own interest and work for
the common good, then certainly it is the system for
which developing countries must strive. In theory,
a strong government based on an unique party system
and a benevolent despotic leader can guarantee the
formation of democratic principles just as well as a
government based on a multi-party system. But, in
the absence of opposition parties, one must look for
other organisms which can introduce checks and bal-
ances against encroachments on human rights or the
mistreatment of minorities. There are five institutions which can play a particularly important role:
(a) an independent judiciary; (b) an autonomous university; (c) a free press; (d) independent, as far
as state control is concerned, trade unions, and
(e) voluntary organizations of all sorts, from student unions to women's clubs, from church organizations to sports associations. Each in its sphere
can play the role of counsellor to the government
and, at the same time, watchdog to ensure that human
rights and the common good are safeguarded. None of
them, with the possible exception of the trade
unions, is so powerful that the government might

consider it a menace, but each has an important role
to play in the promotion of the welfare of the state
and its citizens. Also each can contribute greatly
to the education of the citizen through democratic
processes. It can help give the citizen that sense
of civic responsibility and patriotism so urgently
needed, without falling into exaggerated nationalism.

States which do not recognize as valuable or
workable the western form of parliamentary democracy,
but respect and promote the institutions and organizations mentioned above, might be termed democratic.
However, states which hamper such institutions are
in real danger of skidding down the road to dictatorship. Unfortunately, Indonesia and Ghana show signs
of the latter. What will the future be? If the tendency towards fullfledged dictatorship continues, it
is difficult to see any other future than that of
political plots and revolutions. All the developing
countries are with good reason giving a great deal
of attention to education. This education is still
based on western concepts. The number of educated
élite is therefore steadily growing. These people
will not be content to play on the political level
the same role the colonial regimes wanted their fore-
fathers to play--to see no evil, speak no evil and
hear no evil. If they are not allowed to develop
their leadership talents; if they cannot, through
normal channels, express their opinions and ideas,
the developing countries will not only lose a very
valuable source of talent; they will also create a
group of frustrated leaders who can only be silenced
through jails or exile. Also, under dictatorial governments, the inner circle in power is very restricted and tends to form a closed shop. The jockeying
for position is, however, constant and this might
lead to an era of pronunciamentos of which Latin
America has for so long given such a sordid example.
The national hero in those countries is still a popular figure, not easy to topple, but when opposition
is stifled, the bullet, the knife or the bomb takes
its rights. It is not a very encouraging forecast,
but history teaches that it is a realistic one.[6] In
the final analysis, the future will depend on the
attitude of the western educated élite, whose members

are still growing. It is here that student and
youth organizations, western-style trade unions and
women's organizations take on their value. As we
have pointed out above, it is in such organizations
that leadership qualities are developed and notions
about democratic procedures are imparted. More attention should be given in the West to such training
grounds for democracy. More effort should also be
made by the international organizations to start
branches in young countries. The value of international exchanges of young people has been under-
estimated for too long. If we give young people the
possibility of a training in democracy, we will build
a powerful element which can still turn the tide of
their countries in the right direction.

     Moreover, as we have seen in our study of Ghana,
the western-educated element tends more and more to
go into the field of education and therefore will be
able to influence a large portion of the new generation. This new generation, not having been active
in the struggle against colonialism, with probably
less inborn attachment to the national party or
national hero who led the country to independence,
and more critical of outlived slogans, will in future be a powerful element in the new countries.
If it will strive for democratic institutions, the
future will be a hopeful one.

                    THE CHALLENGE TO THE WEST

     The developing countries have arrived at the
moment of expectations and no élite can hope to remain in power with the consent of the masses unless
it tries as quickly as possible to raise the standard of living of the people. For this it needs outside help. As we have seen before, the western-
educated élite tended to turn solely to the West,
and the West--especially the United States--was willing to give aid for political motives. This, as is
shown in the case of Indonesia, was one of the reasons for division among the élite and it offered an
opportunity to the mass leader to condemn the
western-educated element as neo-colonialist. The

mass leader, however, is himself just as much obliged
to ask for foreign aid although he might prefer to
receive it from both sides.

This dependence on foreign aid forms for the
West both a challenge and an opportunity--a challenge in the sense that it must convince its citizens that foreign aid is a good thing, a challenge
also in that it must see to it that foreign aid is
effective. At the same time, however, it gives the
West the opportunity of realizing its mission to
spread the democratic ideals which it claims to have
fought two world wars for within a half century:
respect for human dignity and freedom and the
achievement of social justice and peace.

Nevertheless, an impartial observer cannot fail
to note that, so far, the West has not been able to
meet this challenge and use this opportunity in an
adequate way. This is due greatly to the absence of
a philosophy of aid with clearly defined principles,
methods and aims.

After the Second World War and with the advance
of the decolonization process, the western world has
slowly been awakened to the realization that the existing gap between the developed and developing
countries must not be allowed to grow bigger, and if
possible should be filled.

However, up until today, the aid programs have
been bedevilled by the cold war and on the western
side by the fear of the spread of communism. The
aim of such aid programs, therefore, was and still
is the buying of alliances or at least to prevent
the advance of Russian aid. Scant attention was
given to the orientation of the political élite in
power, whether they were democratically orientated
or not. American aid therefore was for a long time
more plentiful to dictatorships such as those in
South Korea or South Vietnam than to a democracy
like India. Russian aid now follows suit and we
note that Moscow gives more aid today to a democracy
like India than to "brother-states" such as North
Korea or China. The United States is not even

logical in its aid policy as countries who have
shown--to say the least--a not too friendly attitude
towards the United States or the West, receive more
aid than solid friends like the Philippines or Thailand.[7]

This failure of a clear doctrinal line in aid
on the side of the West, has singularly favored the
prestige of the political élite in the developing
countries who came out for a neutralist attitude; it
has at the same time diminished the prestige of the
western-educated élite.[8]

The irony of it all is, that cases like Guinea
show that Communist aid does not always favor the
prestige of the Communist bloc. The same holds true
for the growing number of students of developing
countries now studying in Russia. Extensive discussions during a fortnight with a group of 25 Asian
and African students studying in Russia in 1962,
showed me that only two were convinced Marxists,
five were influenced in their socio-economic thinking by Communist teaching but did not agree with
Communist policies, while the others were clearly
not interested in Communism and many (nine) had become positively anti-Communist.[9]

The West would be well advised to rethink its
whole aid program. A double approach would be
necessary:

(1) To launch an aid program designed to bolster the
    democratic forces in the various developing na-
    tions. Such an "Alliance for Democracy" should
    concentrate on giving more aid to educational
    programs in the developing countries, by provid-
    ing schools, cheap educational material and
    teachers, university equipment, scholarships--
    specifically for advanced studies--abroad.[10]
    But, especially, such an aid program should give
    aid to voluntary organizations in the field of
    youth, student and trade union activities,
    church activities in the social field, etc.
    Such aid does not necessarily always have to
    pass from government to government. The inter-

mediate institutions, such as non-governmental
organizations, are just as likely to come forward with interesting and worthwhile programs,
and the money spent that way has often less
chance of getting lost by the wayside. The Communists have already been using this system for
years, as we have pointed out in Chapter 8.

(2) To launch a new trade program which would:
(a) Try to stabilize the prices of raw materials
on the world market at such a level that the developing countries could be assured that their
main export products on which they depend to
earn hard currency, could be sold to a certain
volume, at fixed prices for a certain number of
years. The downward trend of the terms of trade
which we have been able to observe from 1955 to
1962 has meant a considerable loss to most developing countries. In some cases it annulled the
benefit of money received through foreign aid.[11]
The objection that the rich countries give with
one hand (aid) and take with the other (through
the deterioration of the terms of trade) holds
therefore a good deal of truth. A willingness
on the part of the West to follow such a policy
would certainly augment singularly the attraction of the West for the developing countries.

(b) To allow more semi- or fully-manufactured
products from developing countries to enter the
western markets. It is true that the myth of
industrialization often haunts the government of
the new nations. It also is true that their industrialization schemes which they propose are
inefficient and do not always achieve any useful
purpose, but one must not forget also that they
are often hampered by the difficulties of com-
peting on the western market.[12]

A policy as outlined above would be more realistic than a good part of the bilateral aid programs
now going on. The slogan "trade, not aid" is a
false one, but undoubtedly a new trade policy aimed
at helping the new nations could replace part of the
aid programs now going on. Aid could then be concen-

trated on more basic problems. The developing countries need, in the first place, investment in human
beings, through literacy campaigns, programs for agricultural cooperatives, the setting up of technical
schools and universities, etc. They also need education in citizenship, in honest government, in democratic principles, in the possibilities of private
enterprise. Only when such a human infrastructure
has been created is the country ready for a "take-
off stage" on the economic level.

On the economic level the big problem for all
developing countries is that of capital saving,
which can never be fully provided by outside capital.
The necessary capital saving is often calculated at
10 to 15 percent of the national income if a country
wants to obtain a sustained growth of the economy.
Capital saving can be forced down the throats of the
citizens by dictatorial measures, as the Communist
regimes prove. It can also be achieved by developing entrepreneurial talents, which is one of the
most effective forces in the production of greater
wealth as the history of the West has shown. The
absence of an indigenous entrepreneurial class forms
one of the greatest handicaps in the developing countries, and foreign firms have a great responsibility
to draw local interest into partnership, encourage
local stockholders to invest, and to train local
technicians and managers. Their negligence in these
fields explains to a great extent the phobia against
foreign private enterprise existing in many countries.

More urgent even for economic development is
the need for agricultural reform, as the bulk of the
population in those countries lives on the land and
the greater part of the wealth generally comes from
agricultural products. In this field, however, as
the example of Russia, Eastern Europe and China
shows, dictatorial measures only tend to foster a
passive resistance. No state-run agriculture any-
where in the world reflects the productivity of
Japanese, American or Dutch agriculture, and the
Ghana peasant farmers have become the largest cocoa
producers in the world on the simple incentive of
cash. For the starting of a cooperative in the

agricultural field or the launching of courses dealing with managerial techniques, the government does
not have to be the sole initiative taker.

It is for these reasons that aid should not be
given exclusively from government to government.
The supra-national specialized organizations (F.A.O.,
UNESCO, W.H.O.), each in its field, are doing inval-
uable work. So also could the non-governmental organizations, in the field of university education or
education for farmers, in the realm of youth or
trade union activities, women's and civil rights
clubs, do much more with less money if they were
given the chance. This is what the "Alliance for
Democracy"should concentrate on and there is no
doubt that it would make a much greater appeal to
people in the West, who certainly are just as eager
to contribute to the spread of the fundamental
ideals in which they believe than to the slogan that
foreign aid means protection at home. There is no
doubt either that such a program would give a very
strong push to all the democratic forces in the developing countries and would singularly enhance the
future of democracy in those areas.

THE CHALLENGE TO CHRISTIANITY

In the previous chapter we outlined the importance of Christianity in the developing countries,
especially insofar as its preoccupation with education is concerned. The Catholic Church certainly
has built an élite in the form of priests, brothers
and nuns, but can one say the same thing for the lay
people? This will be of particular importance with
regard to leadership in political or mass movements.
Because of the revolutionary character which such
movements have often shown in the past, church leaders have been hesitant to encourage Catholics to try
and play an active role. It is in this aspect that
international Catholic organizations, by analogy
with the Communist ones, are playing an increasing
role. Organizations such as "the International
Christian Trade Unions," "Young Christian Workers,"
"Pax Romana," "UNIAPAC," etc. have proved themselves

capable of building such an élite. The Christian
concepts of social justice, of the solidarity of man-
kind, of cooperation among the classes--as opposed
to the Marxist concept of class struggle--of the dignity of women and of the importance of the family as
the basis of society, have greatly influenced the
élite in developing countries. It was more than a
hollow phrase when Nkrumah stated: "for I do not
care what anyone says; this country must develop into a Christian country,"[13] and Sukarno was making a
point any Christian would make when he remarked:
"We Indonesians have seen that the American Declaration of Independence does not contain social justice
and socialism, and we have also seen that the Communist Manifesto still needs an element of the sublime
form, the belief in God the Almighty."[14] Both leaders, the one with a Catholic schooling, the other
with a Muslim one, are typical of a great segment of
the élite. Although they are not what one would
call practicing Catholics or devout Muslims, their
thinking is marked by Christian concepts and they
show a great sympathy towards the Church.[15]

It will be necessary, however, for more competent Christian laymen to be trained, willing to
enter political life, because:

> When men are only interested in technical
> progress, and in raising the standard
> of living, Christianity cannot supply
> any solution. But when they undertake
> to arrange relations between the indi-
> vidual and society, when they set values
> which can give a meaning and nobility to
> human life, when they strive to discover
> the ways in which they can accomplish
> their vocation, then the Christian ought
> to begin acting.[16]

In this regard, much more attention should be
given in Catholic institutions to Christian social
teaching. I found it revealing during a trip to
West Africa in 1961 to note that a Minister in
Ghana and a high civil servant in Guinea explained
to me how much they had learned from the encyclical

Mater et Magistra. Yet none of the missionaries or
Catholic students whom I encountered mentioned this
encyclical and at a meeting of Ghanaian graduates, I
discovered that only a few had heard about it, let
alone read it. Nevertheless, especially in Africa
where all political leaders are speaking about the
necessity of finding a system of development adapted
to the African mentality, Mater et Magistra and
Pacem in Terris could give food for thought. But
this will mean that the Catholic schools must pay
more attention to the social teachings of the Church.
It means also that the Church must try to overcome
the tendency to consider politics a "shady business"
in which the faithful had better not engage, apart
from fulfilling their voting obligation. Christianity could help foster a democratic development. According to Christian doctrine, political authority
stems from divine origin but is based on the common
good and linked with it. Actions taken by this
authority which go against the common good have no
value. It is inherent in the common good to be a
common good of persons, but this implies that the
subject of the common good, and therefore of authority, is the people. It follows therefore that those
who have the mission to exercise authority can only
do so while respecting the nature of this good, that
is to say, basing itself on the general adhesion of
the people. This consent will be better assured the
more the people are called upon to take active part
in political life and notably in the designation and
control of those in power. In Pacem in Terris, we
can therefore read:

> It must not be concluded, however, be-
> cause authority comes from God, that
> therefore men have no right to choose
> those who are to rule the state, to de-
> cide the form of government and to de-
> termine both the way in which authority
> is to be exercised and its limits. It
> is thus clear that the doctrine which
> we have set forth is fully consonant
> with any truly democratic regime.
> (My underlining.)

But, while each truly democratic regime can be
acceptable to Christians, it means that those which
are not truly democratic are, to say the least, more
difficult to accept and that the Christian must
strive for democracy. It might be true that Christianity does not need democracy to fulfil its mission, but democracy may need Christianity to survive
and it still is the system in which Christianity can
best flourish. The Christian active in political
life has often in the past suffered from the fact
that Church authorities are hesitant to speak out
against regimes which are not democratic in nature
but which pretend to defend Church rights. Much
harm could be avoided if in the developing countries,
a clearer stand, for which Pacem in Terris seems to
give a basis, could be taken.

It is therefore the task of the Christian to
come out openly in favor of systems which guarantee
human dignity and social justice, which fulfil the
basic material needs of each and every citizen as
well as the needs of their souls, and against political systems which do not recognize and foster these
ideals, whether these systems are run by persons who
call themselves Christians or Communists. But to be
able to do this, a Christian political élite must be
created.

Christianity has also an important role to play
in the field of international assistance, first of
all by awakening Christians in the West to the need
for international social justice. There are hopeful
signs that the campaigns launched by the hierarchies
in European countries, generally during the Lenten
period, to give to people in developing countries,
are finding an increasing response. Only through an
awakening of the conscience of the masses in Europe
can our democratic governments launch generous aid
programs without political strings attached. But
there is more to be done. Long before the existence
of the United Nations, and before the development of
technical assistance, the missionaries were at work
fighting misery and poverty, building hospitals and
schools. An enormous amount of experience has gone
into this, and a great number of experts has been

formed in this way. It would be useful, therefore,
if this experience could be pooled and if the missionary Orders could work more closely together by
creating, for instance, a central research institute
on methods of technical assistance. It would also
be useful if closer collaboration could be established between the Catholic and Protestant missions
on the one hand and the governmental or international
offices dealing with such problems as health and education, community development, etc. on the other.
This would be useful to both sides, for development
also has a spiritual aspect and Christianity has a
responsibility not only for the souls but also the
bodies of the people in Asia and Africa. It is not
true that

> once people have achieved their politi-
> cal independence, once they have obtained
> economic plenty and once they have
> brought about social justice, the spirit
> will then take care of itself. This is
> the greatest fallacy of the present age;
> that the mind, the spirit, the soul of
> man, the fundamental bent of his will,
> is derivative from and subordinate to a
> function of his economic and social ex-
> istence.[17]

Finally, a great élan exists among Christian
youth in the West to go and work in developing countries. In the Catholic field the number of organizations founded in the last few years to cater to
such people is countless. Alas, very little, if any,
international coordination exists; in some countries
there is not even any on the national scale. This
is regrettable, since nearly everyone could profit
from each other's experiences. The role which the
young technician, teacher, social worker or university professor could play in the developing countries, provided he is well prepared--technically as
well as psychologically--could be tremendous as he
would be able to carry another image of the western
way of life to the people of those areas. It is
true, probably, that for the Asian or African élite,
European life as demonstrated in the past by the

Europeans in their countries, was identical with
"high life." The following remark of a government
official in Eastern Nigeria is very significant:

> All the political offices are filled
> by people whose only standard is an
> acquisitive one. Can this condition
> be due to something inherent in colon-
> ial rule? The [British] officials here
> lived well, in good homes, had servants,
> cars, long vacations and all the rest
> of it. Our people watched all this and
> no doubt came to the conclusion that
> people in power should do the same
> thing as a right: that, since the Bri-
> tish did it when they were the masters,
> then this must be the thing to do once
> you get into authority yourself.[18]

Another significant remark was made by a
Ghanaian teacher whom I interrogated about the American Peace Corps, some members of which were teaching in his district. He was very pleased with them
but could not understand why one of them used to
bicycle to school. "Why doesn't the American government give them cars? It is so un-European to use a
silly bicycle and I myself feel awkward if I pass
him on the road in my car."

The feeling among the élite in developing countries that it is a privileged class which must have
a very high national standard of living and show its
position through big houses, big cars, membership of
many clubs, is understandable.[19] Nevertheless, it
has certain dangerous aspects, especially if it is
combined with a feeling of disdain for the people in
less privileged circumstances. Moreover, it often
leads those in power into corrupt practices, further
pushed by their families who not only expect them to
live well but also to take care of the material
needs of their relatives. The new western élite going out to the developing countries could make a
powerful impact on the young people in those countries who will be tomorrow's élite there.

For, in judging the future, we must have pa-
tience. The problems of developing countries cannot
be solved in the life span of one man or one generation. The political élite of today is faced with
enormous problems. That so many of them want to
solve them through democratic principles is an amazing fact, if one thinks that this élite grew up during the authoritarian colonial era. Their sons,
however, can and will go a step further. It is the
new generation now entering the universities who
will be just as important as the élite who are in
power today. They have a better opportunity to see
democracy at work, than their fathers, in the developing countries. The example of some developing
countries in which the western-educated élite has
remained in power and where true progress along
democratic lines has been achieved--as in India or
Malaya in Asia, and Nigeria in Africa--might serve
as a powerful source of attraction. But we must
never forget that between the Magna Charta and the
actual democracies in Western Europe there lie eight
hundred years of trial and feeling our way. We must
help this future élite to find its own way, but we
can give it certain principles on which to base itself, so as to build the future together.

Notes to Chapter 9

    1.   Immanuel Wallerstein, <u>Africa--The Politics
of Independence</u> (New York: Vintage, 1961), pp. 93-94.

    2.   <u>Ibid</u>., p.99.

    3.   <u>Ibid</u>., p. 96.

    4.   <u>Ibid</u>., p. 163.

    5.   The Communists and also many people in the
West point to Russia as an example. This in my opinion is a mistaken viewpoint since Russia, insofar as
education and industrial development were concerned,
had at the time of the Revolution arrived at the so-
called "take-off stage" and cannot be compared with

the developing countries, as is shown clearly by
W. W. Rostow, Economic Growth--A Non-Communist Manifesto (Cambridge: Cambridge University Press, 1960).

    6. The elimination of the National Heroes in
Togoland, Dahomey, Congo, Brazzaville, as well as
the different attacks on the life of both President
Sukarno and Nkrumah, are recent examples of this
reality.

    7. The French foreign aid program, since de
Gaulle's ascendance to power, is a bit more logical
as it places its political aims more clearly to the
fore. Countries which do not want to accept a certain degree of French predominance on the economic
and cultural levels do not receive any aid at all,
as the case of Guinea shows.

    8. The case of Indonesia is a typical example
of this. The Dutch government, by refusing after
independence to discuss the Irian question with the
Indonesian government, put the pro-western leaders
in a very difficult position. In this way it helped
the mass leaders and Mr. Sukarno to launch a popular
drive against the Dutch and thus implicate the western élite. The result has not been very encouraging
for the Dutch. After having first lost all its economic assets in Indonesia, it later lost Irian as
well.

    9. The interview took place as follows. An in-
vitation was addressed to five African students in
Moscow to visit the West for a fortnight during
their holidays. They were told they could ask
friends or relations to apply. 135 applications
were received from African and Asian students studying in Russia or Eastern Europe. Of these, 25 were
selected. The selection was based on a desire to
have as many different countries as possible represented, with a preference for Africans. The countries represented were: Sierra Leone, Mali, Congo
(Leopoldville), Nigeria, Tanganyika, Cameroun, Ghana,
Basutoland, Somalia, Uganda, Togo, Kenya, Nepal,
Ceylon, Syria and Indonesia. With two exceptions
only, they all studied at Moscow, either at the

State University or the Friendship University. The
two exceptions were a student from Lwow and one from
Prague. They had all spent at least one year in
Eastern Europe and some already three to four years.
They all held Russian scholarships with the exception of one Indonesian and three Ghanaians who were
on scholarships from their own governments. During
the fortnight they visited the Netherlands, Belgium,
Luxembourg, France and Germany, where they were put
in contact with international or national institutions, industries, cooperatives, student clubs, etc.

     10. A mistake the West has often made is to
provide a great number of scholarships for foreign
students, but then not· to bother about them once
they were installed in their universities. Anyone
having dealt with Afro-Asian students knows about
the tremendous difficulties of adaptation they come
across and how easily they can become disgusted with
western life. A worthwhile aid program must try to
allow the Afro-Asian student to do his first years
of study in his home country and bring only those
who want to further their studies abroad; but then,
it must also look after them during their stay in
the foreign country.

     11. According to calculations made by CEPAL,
the deterioration of the terms of trade for Latin
America during the period 1955-60 caused a loss in
earning power of $7,300 million. The net influx
of foreign capital in Latin America for the period
1950-55 was $7,700 million. (Taken from Commerce
extérieur et Sous-développement, by Guy de la
Charrière [Paris: Presse Universitaire de France,
1964], p. 12.)

     12. It should also be admitted that Western
firms often contribute singularly to such unrealis-
tic projects. They are interested in selling their
products. This may mean the building of an oil re-
finery, a sugar factory or other plants, even though
they often know that no technicians are there to run
the factory once it is built or that no suitable
selling organizations exist to market the products
in and outside the country. Moreover, they are

quite willing to pay huge bribes to get their plants
sold. In nearly every developing country, both in
Asia and Africa, I found examples of this.

13.   In his address to a Pax Romana meeting in
Ghana, December 1957, Africa, a Christian Continent
(Pax Romana publication, 1957), p. 36.

14.   From the August 17th, 1960, address by
President Sukarno.

15.   With regard to President Sukarno, this sympathy is often explained as a result of the contact
he had with Catholic missionaries during his exile
in Flores. They were the only Dutch people who
treated him well and he often had long discussions
with them.
        Church-state relations up to the present
have been very satisfactory both in Ghana and Indonesia, and the educational role of the Church has
until now not been hampered. On the contrary, especially in Indonesia, a great deal of government
aid is given to it.

16.   From an address to a Pax Romana meeting in
Fribourg (August 1961) by the former French Prime
Minister, Pierre Pflimlin.

17.   From the address of Mr. Charles Malik to
the meeting of the World Council of Churches in
Evanston in 1954.

18.   Smythe, op. cit., p. 133.

19.   I saw a typical example of this while visiting a new palatial residence which a Ghanaian government Minister had built. A sign of wealth was to
have a big fountain in the garden. But, as the Minister entertained rather often and lavishly, and he
did not want to have his neighbors see this, he had
a big wall built around the garden. However, such a
wall prevented the neighbors from noting that he had
a fountain. He therefore built a fountain with a
base three metres high so it would be noticeable
from the outside even if no water was spouting from
it.

APPENDIXES

APPENDIX 1

EDUCATIONAL LEVEL OF INDONESIAN POLITICAL DECISION-MAKERS (in percentages)

Educational Level Obtained	Cabinet Members Total 146		Members of Parliament Total 234		High Civil Service Total 61	
University:	68		27		87	
fully trained		58		19		67
partially trained		10		8		20
Secondary:	32		64		13	
senior cert.		15		32		13
junior cert.		17		32		0
Primary cert.:	0		9		0	
Total	100%		100%		100%	

COUNTRY OF EDUCATION OF INDONESIAN POLITICAL DECISION-MAKERS (in percentages)

Country of Education	Cabinet Members		Members of Parliament		High Civil Service	
Indonesia	73		93		50	
university		42		19		44
non-university		31		74		6
Netherlands	25		5		42	
university		24		5		42
non-university		1		0		0
Other countries	2		2		8	
university		2		2		2
Total	100%		100%		100%	

NEW ELITE IN ASIA AND AFRICA

APPENDIX 2

NON-POLITICAL OCCUPATION OF INDONESIAN POLITICAL DECISION-MAKERS
(in percentages)

Occupation	Cabinet Members		Member of Parliament		High Class Civil Servant	
	Pre-war	Japanese Occupation	Pre-war	Japanese Occupation	Pre-war	Japanese Occupation
Civil Service	37	48	34	42	62	83
Civil Administration	4	8	6	9	15	24
Other Civil Service	33	40	28	33	47	59
Professions	45	35	40	36	23	8
Government teachers	4	5	10	10	3	0
Non-Govt. teachers	15	10	16	12	10	2
Newspapermen	11	8	9	8	0	1.5
Lawyers	9	6	5	6	5	1.5
Physicians	5	5	0	0	3	1.5
Engineers	1	1	0	0	2	1.5
Private Occupations	4	4	16	16	8	7
Landowners or small business	3	3	10	13	5	0
Employers	1	1	6	3	3	7

APPENDIX 2 (Continued)

Occupation	Cabinet Members		Member of Parliament		High Class Civil Servant	
	Pre-war	Japanese Occupation	Pre-war	Japanese Occupation	Pre-war	Japanese Occupation
Labor	0	0	2	2	0	0
Not Occupied	6	5	3	1	7	2
Unknown	8	8	5	3	0	0
Total	100%	100%	100%	100%	100%	100%

APPENDIX 3

AGE GROUP OF INDONESIAN DECISION-MAKERS
IN THE POLITICAL SPHERE
(in percentages)

Age Group	Cabinet Ministers	Members of Parliament	Top Civil Service
Under 30	1	7	8
31 - 35	13	18	17
36 - 40	21	28	33
41 - 45	25	27	26
46 - 50	18	12	14
Over 50	16	8	2

APPENDIX 4

SOCIAL BACKGROUND OF STUDENTS, HIGH SEMINARY, CAPE COAST (GHANA)

Occupation of Father	Schooling for Father			For Mother		Total
	No Schooling	Primary School	Secondary School	Literate	Illiterate	
Farmer	19	6			25	25
Secondary School Teacher			1		1	1
Catechist		1			1	1
Blacksmith	1				1	1
Clerk or Civil Servant		4	1	1	4	5
Businessman		1	2	3		3
Trader		2			2	2
Bricklayer	1				1	1
Electrician	1				1	1
Information not given*	4	2			6	6
Totals	26	16	4	4	42	46

*Most of those who did not give this information stated that their fathers were dead.

APPENDIX 5

SAMPLE. SOCIAL BACKGROUND AND ASPIRATIONS OF STUDENTS APPLYING FOR ADMISSION TO THE UNIVERSITY OF GHANA, 1962

Position Held by Father	Application for				Profession Wanted						
	B.A. Gen.	B.Sc. Gen.	Certificate of Education	Law	Economist	Teacher	Civil Servant	Lawyer	Doctor	Diverse*	Unknown
Accountant	1				1						
Trader	3	3		1	1	3	1			2	
Clerk	2	1		1		1	1				2
Laborer	1			1			1	1			
Farmer	9	6	10	1	1	15	3			2	4
Civil Servant	2	4	2	1	1	5			1	2	
Carpenter	2					1					1
Restaurant Owner	1										1
Teacher	2	4	3	2		8	1		1		1
Lawyer		2								2	
Storekeeper			2			2					
Photographer			1			1					

APPENDIX 5 (Continued)

Position Held by Father	Application for				Profession Wanted						
	B.A. Gen.	B.Sc. Gen.	Certificate of Education	Law	Economist	Teacher	Civil Servant	Lawyer	Doctor	Diverse*	Unknown
Goldsmith			1			1					
Minister of Religion				2		1		1			
Member of Parliament				1				1			
Unemployed**				1				1			
Not Given (Deceased)	2		1			3					
Totals	25	20	20	10	4	41	7	4	2	8	9

* Among "diverse," we find professions mentioned such as Statistician, Politician, Member of the Diplomatic Corps, Member of Parliament.

**This is the case of someone imprisoned for political reasons.

APPENDIX 6

ASPIRATION AND BACKGROUND OF SAMPLE OF GHANA STUDENTS FROM
WELL-TO-DO PARENTS STUDYING IN LONDON

Profession of Father	Schooling received by father			Field of study or profession	What is considered most important job	Whether student would want wife to have had education
	Primary	Secondary	University			
Businessman	Yes	No	No	Domestic Science	Teacher	Yes (husband)
Businessman	Yes	Yes	No	Architecture	Architecture	No answer
Civil Servant	Yes	No	No	Chemistry	Teacher	Yes
Civil Servant	Yes	Yes	No	Law	Lawyer	Yes
Civil Servant	Yes	Yes	No	Law	Lawyer	Yes
Doctor	Yes	Yes	Yes	Domestic Science	Teacher	No answer
Doctor	Yes	Yes	Yes	Engineering	Teacher	Yes
Teacher	Yes	Yes	No	Engineering	Teacher	No answer
Supreme Court Judge	Yes	Yes	Yes	Engineering	Teacher	Yes

APPENDIX 7

THE MOST IMPORTANT NEWSPAPERS EXISTING
IN INDONESIA IN 1957

Name	Party Papers	Independent but in favor of a certain party or group	Independent
Abadi		Pro Natsir wing, Masjumi	
Bintang Timur		Pro PRN till Sept. 1955; since Nov. 1956 pro PKI	
Daily Telegraph			Chinese language
Djawa Post			Of Chinese interest; Conservative
Duka Masjarakat	Nahdatul Ulama		
Haluan		Pro PSI	
Harian Limbaga		Pro Masjumi	
Harian Rakjat	PKI		
Harian Unum		Pro PSI	
Indonesia Raya			In 1957 anti-government, pro army
Indonesian Observer		English language; usually pro PNI	
Kedaulatan Rakjat		Pro PNI	
Keng Po			Often inclined to PSI
Kuang Po			Independent
Marhaen		Pro PNI	
Merdeka		Pro PNI	
Nasional			Independent
Nieuwsgier			Dutch language, liberal; pro government

APPENDIX 7 (Continued)

Name	Party Papers	Independent but in favor of a certain party or group	Independent
Pedoman	PSI		
Pemandangan		Pro Masjumi	
Pendorong		Pro PKI	
Perdamaian		Pro Sukarno	
Pikiran Rakjat			Independent
Sin Mi		Pro Sukarno	
Sin Po		Chinese and Indonesian edition; pro PKI and Sukarno	
Suluh Indonesia	PNI		
The Sumatra Times			Independent; Chinese language
Tay Kong Sian Poo			Independent; Chinese language
Trompet Masjarakat			Independent; Radical left
The Times of Indonesia			Independent; English language
Warta Harian Pengkela Rakjat		Pro pasindo	
Waspada		Pro PNI	

APPENDIX 8

SAMPLE OF 85 CATHOLIC PERSONS, HOLDING A UNIVERSITY
DEGREE--DIVISIONS MADE ACCORDING TO THE
PROFESSIONS EXERCISED IN 1960

Ministries and Departments	Diverse
5 Ministry of Health*	1 National Assembly
1 Ministry of Agriculture	2 Lawyers
1 Ministry of Housing	1 Engineering Firm
11 Ministry of Education	2 Diamond Market
2 Ministry of Local Government	Total: 6
1 Ministry of Finance	
1 Ministry of Transport and Communications	Teaching Profession
3 Ministry of Information	6 University Teachers
3 Ministry of Foreign Affairs*	
2 Government Hospitals	30 Secondary School Teachers ***
3 Law Chamber*	
1 Ghana Census Office	Total: 36
4 Department of Mines and Geology	
1 Ghana Supply Commission	
1 Social Welfare and Community Development	
3 Local Magistrates**	
Total: 43	

*   Amongst whom was one woman.
** Amongst whom were two women.
*** Amongst whom were six women.

APPENDIX 9

P R E S I D E N T

Accra
12th September, 1960

My dear Patrice,

Enclosed are two releases to gladden your heart
in this your dire hour--the first about General Alex-
ander, my Army Chief, and the other, my Note to the
Security Council concerning the diabolical attempt
to dethrone you and the lawfully constituted Government of the Congo of which you are the legal head.

My emissaries Mr. Botsio and Mr. Welbeck returned from Leopoldville yesterday to inform me of
what has been happening there. I am sending back
Mr. Welbeck with this note regarding the lines to be
followed to safeguard your position and save the
unity of the Congo.

The first point I would like to bring to your
attention again is that considering the fact that
you had to form a very wide Coalition Government,
and considering the fact that you have the Tsombe
problem, the Kalonji problem, the Kasavubu problem
and other similar problems so far concealed now, and
considering the fact that the colonialists and imperialists are doing their utmost to retrieve their lost
ground in the Congo, you cannot afford, my Brother,
to be harsh and uncompromising. Do not force Kasavubu out now. It will bring too much trouble especially in Leopoldville, when you want calm there
now. Do not make an issue of his treachery now, or
even of Tsombe's treachery. The time will come to
deal with them.

Let sleeping dogs lie. Leave these people
alone now. In the same way, please, DO NOT COME OUT
WITH ANY NEW CONSTITUTION NOW. It will jeopardise
your position. It will give the whip to Tsombe and

APPENDIX 9 (Continued)

the separatists to stir up trouble again. Be "as
cool as a cucumber," establish the administration
and consolidate your position before you take the
next step. I would be the last person to advise you
to compromise on any matter of principle; but the
very critical situation in the Congo demands your
adopting what I call "tactical action." That is,
you should so adopt your methods, without sacrific-
ing any principles, that you work even with your
bitterest political enemies in order to give you
time TO CONSOLIDATE YOUR POSITION--organisationally,
i.e., governmental and party, both with regard to
the Central Government as well as in the Provinces,
before you take the next step.

     Allied to this is what I have sent to tell you
before and I must repeat with all the emphasis here,
namely, that you must not push the United Nations
troops out until YOU HAVE CONSOLIDATED YOUR POSITION,
and then you can ask them to leave. I know the difficulties you are having with the United Nations and
we are not sparing them at all, as you can find from
my enclosed note to the Security Council. But if
the United Nations troops move out now, you will not
be able to cope with the confusion that will ensue,
fomented by the colonial powers, Belgian and other
imperialists working with the reactionaries at home.

     The third important point is that you must
quickly establish your administration so that people
may feel secure and get work to do: Immigration and
Customs should also be established immediately at
all sea and air ports. Fortunately, the United Nations are there with plenty of funds to help you and
you must set up the organisation you announced at
your Press Conference two days ago to make use of
the aid offered. Get hold of the aid and control it.
Whatever the political squabbles with your opponents,
the hungry unemployed people will not continue to
stand by and go hungry; they will soon act, and will
respond to whoever will be able, or even promise, to
give them "bread and games," as the ancient Romans
put it.

APPENDIX 9 (Continued)

My dear Patrice, the above are my three basic
and urgent suggestions. The position is critical;
if you act quickly on them, the position will be
saved; if you delay, anything may happen. Please,
pay heed to my suggestions and tackle the internal
situation which you alone can remedy, provided you
pay heed to my suggestions. As regards the external
work, especially concerning the Security Council and
UNO, leave that to me. You can be sure that on any
issue, I shall mobilise the Afro-Asian block and
other friendly nations to support you as in the case
of the present attempt to dethrone you.

Now, a few other suggestions:

Firstly, your Cabinet is too big but it will
not be wise to cut it down at this time. In the
meantime the best thing is to establish a sort of
inner Cabinet, called for instance The Cabinet Committee, to deal with urgent issues. A good excuse
for setting it up is the present emergency facing
the country, when urgent decisions have to be taken
quickly as in war time.

I suggest the membership of this Committee be
as follows:

CABINET COMMITTEE:

    1. Prime Minister & Minister of
        Defence and Foreign Affairs...Chairman
    2. Deputy Premier................Vice-Chairman
    3. Minister of the Interior......Member
    4. Minister of Local Government..Member
    5. Minister for Technical
        Assistance...................Member
    6. Commander of the Forces.......Member
    7.)
    8.) Three other Ministers........Members
    9.)

APPENDIX 9 (Continued)

CABINET COMMITTEE

Purpose:

1. To deal with the emergency.
2. For political, military and airports matters.
3. The Katanga and Kasai questions.
4. Relations with the United Nations.
5. Technical Assistance - approval of policy
    and programme.
6. Any urgent business.

You will see that because of the emergency and
your having a lot to do with the United Nations and
the Security Council, etc., I have added Foreign Affairs to your portfolio. But look out for two trust-
ed comrades, one to be Deputy Minister of Defence and
the other to be Deputy Minister of Foreign Affairs,
both under you.

You may hold ordinary Cabinet meetings with all
your Ministers once a week for ordinary Government
business but the inner Cabinet, i.e. The Cabinet Committee, should meet every day. You should however
keep Cabinet informed of decisions and executed.
Some important matters dealt with by the Cabinet Committee have to be referred to the whole Cabinet for
approval in order to get the full backing of your
Ministers.

Your Technical Assistance Committee may be composed as follows:

TECHNICAL ASSISTANCE COMMITTEE:

1. The Deputy Premier.................Chairman
2. Minister for Technical Assistance..Member
3. Minister of Local Government.......Member
4. Minister of Establishment.........Member
5. Minister of Labour.................Member
6. Minister of Public Works..........Member
7. Minister of Industries............Member
8. Minister of Mines and Natural
    Resources........................Member
9. Minister of Communications........Member

APPENDIX 9 (Continued)

TECHNICAL ASSISTANCE COMMITTEE

Purpose:

To co-operate with the United Nations and other agencies and countries for the speedy and effective use of any technical assistance offered.

The Committee is to have weekly joint meetings with United Nations representatives to plan programmes for the approval of Cabinet before execution.

The Minister for Technical Assistance, as the Chief Executive for this programme is to be given adequate authority for effective and speedy action within approved policies and programmes.

Now, Patrice, I come to the question of the Force Publique. I admire them for what they have done and I would not have them disarmed. But it needs to be officered properly and trained to suit your requirements.

I urge you not to force out the United Nations troops until you have conditioned the Force Publique. Their provincial loyalties are too strong and groups of them are inclined to follow Ministers from their areas. At the moment, too, you have not got adequate rations, supplies, etc. Considering therefore what the imperialists are pumping into Katanga, considering also the Kalongi, Kasavubu and other menaces, Brother, it is ABSOLUTELY UNSAFE to depend entirely upon the Force Publique AT THIS CRITICAL TIME.

It is imperative to have your officers trained without delay and so let me have your reply to my offer concerning the training of your officers here in my Military Academy.

Finally, a word from you on the radio calling on all Congolese to bury their differences and come together in the interest of the nation will have an electric effect in bringing the people together and

APPENDIX 9 (Continued)

thus establishing your own position and the peace
necessary for the development of the Congo. Brother,
mark my advice.

Whenever in doubt consult me. Brother, we have
been in the game for sometime now and we know how to
handle the imperialists and the colonialists. The
only colonialist or imperialist that I trust is a
dead one. If you do not want to bring Congo into
ruin, follow the advice I have given. Brother, have
implicit faith in me; I shall not let you down.
Your stand for United Congo and for African unity
commend you dearly to me. Your friend, Mr. Djin, is
there to help you in every way possible; you cannot
have a better admirer and supporter than Djin. Trust
him as you did heretofore and he will serve you well.

Patrice, I have surveyed the position in the
Congo very very carefully. If you fail, you have
only yourself to blame and it will be due to your
unwillingness to face the facts of life or as the
Germans called "real politique." Your failure will
be a great blow to the African liberation movement,
and you cannot afford to fail. Your policy "to do
away with your enemies now" will fail; you must
adopt "TACTICAL ACTION." Remember the forces pitched
against you are legion. But the odds are in your
favour, and you will succeed if only you handle the
situation carefully and tactfully.

God bless.

Yours affectionately,

Sd: Kwame Nkrumah.

BIBLIOGRAPHY

BIBLIOGRAPHY - GENERAL

Books

Abdoulaye, Ly. Les Masses Africaines et l'Actuelle
    Condition Humaine. Paris: Editions Présence
    Africaine, 1956.

Aron, Raymond. L'Opium des Intellectuels. Paris:
    Calmann-Lévy, 1955.

Birket-Smith, Kaj. Geschichte der Kultur. Zurich:
    Urell Füssli Verlag, 1946.

Boll, Marcel and André. L'Elite de Demain. Paris:
    Calmann-Lévy, 1948.

Busia, K. A. The Challenge of Africa. London:
    Pall Mall Press, 1962.

Cameron, James. Die Afrikanische Revolution.
    Cologne: Du Mont Documente, 1961. [The Afri-
    can Revolution. New York: London House, 1961.]

de la Charrière, Guy. Commerce extérieur et Sous-
    développement. Paris: Presse Universitaire de
    France, 1964.

Considine, John J. Africa, World of New Men. New
    York: Dodd, Mead and Company, 1954.

Cornevin, R. Histoire de l'Afrique des Origines à
    nos jours. Paris: Payot, 1956.

Desai, A. R. Social Background of Indian National-
    ism. Bombay: Bombay University Press, 1948.

Dia, Mamadou. Nations Africaines et Solidarité
    Mondiale. Paris: Presses Universitaires de
    France, 1960.

Djilas, Milovan. La Nouvelle Classe dirigeante.
     Paris: Plon, 1957.

Duboiss, Cora. Social Forces in S.E. Asia. St. Paul:
     University of Minnesota, 1951.

Duverger, Maurice. Political Parties, Their Organi-
     sation and Activities. London: Methuen, 1954.

Fortes, M., and Evans, Pritchard. African Political
     Systems. Oxford: Oxford University Press, 1958.
     Fifth Impression.

Geiger, Th. Aufgaben und Stellung der Intelligenz in
     der Gesellschaft. Stuttgart: Enke, 1949.

Gunther, John. Inside Africa. London: Hamish
     Hamilton, 1955.

Hodgkin, Thomas. Nationalism in Colonial Africa.
     3rd ed. London: Frédéric Müller, 1960.

van Hulzen, Johan. Onze Westindische Geschiedenis.
     den Haag: W. van Hoeve, 1946.

Italiaander, Rolf. Der Ruhelose Kontinent. Dussel-
     dorf: Econ. Verlag, 1958.

_____. Die Neuen Männer Afrikas. Dusseldorf:
     Econ. Verlag, 1960.

Jennings, Ivor W. Democracy in Africa. Cambridge:
     Cambridge University Press, 1963.

Knight, Maxwell E. The German Executive 1890 - 1933.
     Stanford: Stanford University Press, 1952.

Kolabinska, Maria. "La Circulation des Elites en
     France. Etude Historique depuis la fin du XIe
     siècle jusqu'à la Grande Révolution." Thesis,
     Lausanne, 1912.

Kuper, Hilda. An African Aristocracy--Rank Among
     the Swazi. Oxford: Oxford University Press,
     1947.

Laswell, Harold. The World Revolution of Our Time--
    A Framework for Basic Policy Research. Stan-
    ford: Stanford University Press, 1951.

Laswell, Harold, Rothwell, Easton, and Lerner, Daniel.
    The Comparative Study of Elites: An Introduc-
    tion and Bibliography. Hoover Institute Studies;
    Stanford, Calif.: Stanford University Press,
    1952.

Lebret, L. J. Suicide ou Survie de l'Occident.
    Paris: Edition Economie et Humanisme, 1958.

Littre, E. Dictionnaire de l'Académie. La Langue
    Francaise. Paris: Hachette, 1873.

Lynton, R. P. The Tide of Learning--the Aloka Ex-
    perience. London: Routledge and Kegan Paul,
    1960.

Mannheim, Karl. Ideology and Utopia. London: Kegan
    Paul and Co., 1936.

_____. Ideologie van onze tijd. Leiden: Sythof,
    1947.

_____. Mensch und Gesellschaft im Zeitalter des
    Umbaus. Leiden: Sythof, 1953.

Melady, Thos. P. Profiles of African Leaders. New
    York: Macmillan, 1961.

_____. The White Man's Future in Black Africa.
    New York: MacFadden-Bartel Corporation, 1962.

Mosca, Gaetano. The Ruling Class. New York:
    McGraw-Hill, 1939.

Murray, J. A New English Dictionary. Vol. III.
    Oxford: Clarendon Press, 1897.

Nasser, Gamal Abdel. La Philosophie et la Révolu-
    tion. Cairo: Dar Al Maaref, 1958.

Padmore, George. Pan Africanism or Communism.
    London: Dennis Dobson, 1956.

van der Post, Laurens. The Dark Eye in Africa.
    London: Hogarth Press, 1955.

Pareto, Vilfredo. The Mind and Society. Edited by
    Arthur Livingston. Vols. 1-4. New York: Jona-
    than Cape, 1935.

Rostow, W. W. Economic Growth--A Non-Communist
    Manifesto. Cambridge: Cambridge University
    Press, 1960.

Roussier, P. de. L'Elite dans la société moderne--
    Son Role. Paris: Librairie Armand Colin, 1914.

Schueller, George K. The Politbureau. Nadir Project;
    Stanford: Stanford University Press, 1951.

Segal, Ronald. Political Africa--A who's who of
    personalities and Parties. London: Stevens
    and Sons Ltd., 1961.

Smith, P. Africa in Transition. London: Frédérick
    Müller.

Smythe, Hugh, and Smythe, Mabel M. The New Nigerian
    Elite. Stanford: Stanford University Press,
    1960.

Sulzer, Peter. Schwarze Intelligenz. Zürich:
    Orell Fusli Verlag, 1951.

Taylor, J. V. Christianity and Politics in Africa.
    London: Penguin African Series, 1957.

Ward, Barbara. The Rich Nations and the Poor Nations.
    Massey lectures inaugural series. Toronto: The
    Hunter Rose Co. Ltd., 1961.

Zahrnt, Heinz. Probleme der Elite Bildung. Hamburg:
    Furche Verlag, 1956.

Zischka, A. E. Afrika--smeltkroes voor Europa. Trans-
    lated by JHR J. Van Kretschmar. Tilburg: Neder-
    lands Boekhuis, 1952.

Articles

Abhayavardhana, Hector. "The Role of the Western-
    Educated Elite," Community - An Independent Bi-
    Monthly, Colombo, IV, No. 1 (1962).

Aron, Raymond. "Remarques sur les particularités de
    l'évolution sociale en France," Transactions of 3rd
    World Congress of Sociology, London, III-IV
    (1956), 42-53.

_____. "Social Structure and the Ruling Class,"
    British Journal of Sociology, No. 1 (1950), 1-16,
    126-143.

Bastide, R. "African Students in France," Interna-
    tional Social Science Bulletin, Paris, VIII,
    No. 3 (1956), 489-492.

Bendix, Reinard, and Hawton, Frank W. "Social Mobil-
    ity and the American Business Elite," British
    Journal of Sociology, No. 9 (1959), 357-369.

Brausch, G.E.J.B. "The Problems of Elites in the
    Belgian Congo," International Social Science
    Bulletin, Paris, VIII, No. 3 (1956), 452-458.

Clifford-Vaughan, Michelina. "Some French Concepts
    of Elites," British Journal of Sociology, No. 2
    (1960), 319-329.

Eisenstadt, S. N. "Changes in Patterns of Stratifi-
    cation Attendant on Attainment of Political In-
    dependence," Transactions of 3rd World Congress
    of Sociology, London, III-IV (1956), 32-41.

Geiger, Th. "An Historical Study of the Origins and
    Structure of the Danish Intelligentsia, British
    Journal of Sociology, No. 1 (1950), 209-220.

Goldthorpe, J. E. "An African Elite--a Sample Sur-
    vey of Fifty-two Former Students of Makerere
    College in East Africa," British Journal of
    Sociology, No. 6 (1955), 31-47.

Guttsman, W. L.   "Aristocracy and the Middle Class
    in the British Political Elite 1886-1916,"
    British Journal of Sociology, No. 5 (1954),
    12-32.

_____.   "The Changing Social Structure of the
    British Political Elite 1816-1935," British
    Journal of Sociology, No. 2 (1959), 122-134.

_____.   "Social Stratification and Political
    Elite," British Journal of Sociology, No. 2
    (1960), 137-150.

Hoffner, J.   "Colonialism and Christian Ethics,
    World Justice, II, No. 3 (March, 1961), 298-313.

Leith, Ross S.   "The Rise of a new Elite amongst the
    Women of Nigeria," International Social Science
    Bulletin, Paris, VIII, No. 3 (1956), 481-488.

Levi, Werner.   "The Fate of Democracy in South and
    South-East Asia," Far Eastern Survey (February,
    1959), 25-29.

Mercier, P.   "Evaluation of Senegalese Elites," In-
    ternational Social Science Bulletin, Paris,
    VIII, No. 3 (1956), 441-452.

Moreira, A.   "The Elites of the Portuguese Tribal
    Provinces," International Social Science Bulle-
    tin, Paris, VIII, No. 3 (1956), 460-481.

Nadel, S. F.   "The Concept of Social Elites," Inter-
    national Social Science Bulletin, Paris, VIII,
    No. 3 (1956), 413-420.

Ngcobo, S. Bangani.   "African Elite in South Africa,"
    International Social Science Bulletin, Paris,
    VIII, No. 3 (1956), 431-440.

Peeters, F. L.   "L'Anticolonialisme en Politique
    Mondiale," Justice dans le Monde, IV, No. 2
    (1962), 161-180.

Senghor, L. S. "Eléments Constructifs d'une civili-
    sation d'inspiration négro-africaine," Présence
    Africaine (February-May, 1959), 249-279.

Zizzamia, Alba. "Catholicism and Internationalism,"
    Papal Anthology, reprinted from "Thought,"
    Fordham University Quarterly, XXVIII, No. 11.

                        Reports

Asian Nationalism and the West. A symposium based
    on documents and reports of the 11th Conference
    of the Institute of Pacific Relations, New York,
    1953, by W. T. Holland, George McT. Kahin,
    Philippe Devillers, Th. Sileoek, Ungku Azir.

Aspects sociaux de l'industrialisation et de l'urban-
    isation en Afrique au sud du Sahara. UNESCO,
    1956.

The Common Christian Responsibility Towards Areas of
    Rapid Social Change. A Study of the World Coun-
    cil of Churches.Progress Report, 1955-1958.
    Geneva, 1958.

Dilemmas and Opportunities, Christian Action in Rapid
    Social Change. Report of an International
    Ecumenical Study Conference, Thessalonica,
    Greece, Division of Studies, World Council of
    Churches. Geneva, 1959.

Economic Bulletin for Africa. U.N. Publication.
    Addis Abeba, June 1962, III, No. 2.

Economic Factors Affecting Access to the University.
    World University Service. Studies on the Uni-
    versity scene in 35 countries. Geneva, 1961.

Economic Survey of Africa Since 1950. U.N. Depart-
    ment of Economic and Social Affairs. New York,
    1959.

"Education for National Management in Kenya." An un-
    published report to the Minister for Commerce,
    Industry and Communications, by J. C. Roche,
    September, 1961.

Nigeria 1960. A special issue of Nigeria Magazine.
    Lagos, October, 1960.

Report on the Alliance for Progress 1963. By Hubert
    H. Humphrey to the Committee on Appropriations
    and the Committee on Foreign Relations, United
    States Senate, Washington: U.S. Government
    Printing Office, 1963.

Report on the Social Situation of the World. U.N.
    Document E/CN 5/346.

U.N. Economic Commission for Asia and the Far East
    1959, A Preliminary View of the ECAFE Region
    in 1959. Bangkok, 1960.

U.N. Report on the Definition and Evaluation of
    Standards of Living. E/CN 3/179; E/CN 5/299.

BIBLIOGRAPHY - INDONESIA

Books

Anderson, Benedict R. O'G. Some Aspects of Indonesian
    Politics under Japanese Occupation 1944-1945.
    Series Modern Indonesia Project. Ithaca:
    Cornell University Press, 1961.

Benda, Harry, and McVey, Ruth T. (eds.). The Commun-
    ist Uprisings of 1926-1927 in Indonesia. Key
    Documents. Series Modern Indonesia Project.
    Ithaca: Cornell University Press, 1960.

Benda, H. The Crescent and the Rising Sun--Indonesian
    Islam under the Japanese Occupation. The Hague:
    W. van Hoeve, 1958.

Berg, C. C. Hoofdlijnen der Javaansche Literatuur
    Geschiedenis. Inaugural lecture University,
    Leiden. Groningen: Bos, 1929.

Bunnell, Frederick P. American Reactions to Indo-
    nesia's Role in the Belgrade Conference. Modern
    Indonesia Project. Ithaca: Cornell University
    Press, 1964.

Elsbree, Willard H. Japan's Role in South East
    Asian Nationalistic Movements 1940-1945.
    Harvard: Harvard University Press, 1953.

Feith, Herbert. The Indonesian Elections of 1955.
    Interim Reports Series. Modern Indonesian Pro-
    ject. Ithaca: Cornell University Press, 1957.

_____. The Wilopo Cabinet 1952-1953, A Turning
    Point in Post Revolutionary Indonesia. Ithaca:
    Cornell University Press, 1958.

Fromberg, P. H. Verspreide Geschriften. Leyden:
    Verzameld door Chung Hwa Hui, Chineesche
    Vereniging in Nederland, 1926.

Furnivall, J. S. Colonial Policy and Practice--A
    Comparative Study of Burma and the Netherlands
    Indies. Rev. Ed. New York: New York Univer-
    sity Press, 1956.

Ganda Subrata, S. M. An Account of the Japanese
    Occupation of Banjumas Residency, Java, March
    1942, to August 1945. Translated by Leslie
    Palmer. Data Paper No. 10. Ithaca: Cornell
    University Press, 1953.

Hal, Dr. C.J.J. van. Insulinde Werk en Welvaart.
    Naarden: In den Tooren, 1942.

Helsdingen, W. H. van, and Hoogenberk, H. Daar werd
    wat Groots Verricht, Nederlandsch Indie in de
    XXste eeuw. Amsterdam: Elsevier, 1941.

Kartini, E. B. Lettres de Raden Adjing Kartini, Java
    en 1900. Paris et La Haye: Mouton et Co., 1960.

Kielstra, E. B. De Vestiging van het Nederlandse
    gezag in den Indischen Archipel. Haarlem: De
    Erven F. Bohn, 1920.

Krom, N. J. Hindoe--Javaansche Geschiedenis. Den
    Haag: Nyhoff, 1931.

Legge, J. D. Central Authority and Regional Autonomy
    in Indonesia: A Study in Local Administration,
    1950-1960. Ithaca: Cornell University Press,
    1961.

van Leur, J. C. Indonesian Trade and Society. The
    Hague: W. van Hoeve, 1955.

Moukerjis, Radha Kumund. Indian Shipping, A History
    of the Seaborne Trade and Maritime Activity of
    the Indians from the Earliest Times. London:
    Longmans and Co., 1912.

Niel, R. van. The Emergence of the Modern Indonesian
    Elite. The Hague: W. van Hoeve, 1960.

Pringgodigdo, A. K. The Office of President in Indo-
    nesia as Defined in Three Constitutions in
    Theory and Practice. Series Modern Indonesia
    Project. Ithaca: Cornell University Press,
    1957.

Rouffaer, G. P., and Yzerman, J. W. De Eerste Schip-
    vaart der Nederlandens Naar Oost Indie onder
    Cornelis de Houtman, 1545-1597. Journalen, Docu-
    menten en Andere Bescheiden. 2 vols. The Hague:
    Linschoten Vereniging, 1924.

Sjafruddin, Prawiranegara. Politiek dan Revolusi
    Kita [Politics and our Revolution]. Djakarta:
    Department of Information, 1948.

Sjahrazad. Indonesische Overpeinsingen. Djakarta:
    Pembagnunan, 1950.

Stapel, F. W. Geschiedenis van Nederlandsch Indie.
    Amsterdam: J. M. Meulenhoff, 1943.

Tedjasukmana, Iskander. The Political Character of
    the Indonesian Trade Union Movement. Ithaca:
    Cornell University Press, 1958.

Vlekke, Bernard H. M. Geschiedenis van den Indischen
    Archipel. Roermond: Romen en Zonen, 1947.
    [The Story of the Dutch East Indies. Cambridge,
    1948.]

Wertheim, W. F. Indonesian Society in Transition, A
    Study in Social Change. The Hague: W. van
    Hoeve, 1956.

Willmott, Donald Earl. The Chinese of Semarang--A
    Changing Minority Community in Indonesia.
    Ithaca: Cornell University Press, 1960.

                        Articles

Bone, Robert C. "The Future of Indonesian Political
    Parties," Far Eastern Survey (February, 1954),
    17-23.

Bretton, H. L. "Current Political Thought and Prac-
    tice in Ghana," American Political Science Re-
    view, No. 52 (March, 1958), 46-63.

Budiardjo, Miriam S. "The Provincial Parliament in
    Indonesia," Far Eastern Survey (February, 1956),
    17-23.

Compton, Boyd R. "The Indonesian Election Law," Far
    Eastern Survey: Part I (April, 1954), 62-64;
    Part II (May, 1954), 74-77.

Fryer, D. W. "Indonesia's Economic Prospects," Far
    Eastern Survey (December, 1954), 177-182.

Higgins, Benjamin. "Development Problems in the
    Philippines--A Comparison with Indonesia," Far
    Eastern Survey (November, 1957), 161-169.

Higgins, Benjamin. "Indonesia's Five Year Plan,"
    Far Eastern Survey (August, 1956), 122-123.

Kroef, Justus M. van der. "Disunited Indonesia,"
    Far Eastern Survey: Part I (April, 1958), 49-63;
    Part II (May, 1958), 73-80.

_____. "The Dutch Position in Indonesia Today,"
    Far Eastern Survey (June, 1954), 88-94.

_____. "Guided Democracy in Indonesia," Far East-
    ern Survey (August, 1957), 113-124.

_____. "Indonesia's Economic Difficulties," Far
    Eastern Survey (February, 1955), 17-24.

_____. "Instability in Indonesia," Far Eastern
    Survey (April, 1957), 49-52.

_____. "Minority Problems in Indonesia," Far
    Eastern Survey: Part I (September, 1955), 129-
    133; Part II (September, 1956), 165-172.

Lubis, Mochtar. "The Indonesian Communist Movement
    Today," Far Eastern Survey (November, 1954),
    161-168.

Moes, John E. "Trade Unionism in Indonesia," Far
    Eastern Survey (February, 1959), 17-24.

Mysberg, H. James. "The Indonesian Elites," Far
    Eastern Survey (March, 1957), 38-42.

Pauker, Guy J. "The Role of Political Organisation
    in Indonesia," Far Eastern Survey (September,
    1958), 129-142.

Roeslan, Abdulgani. "Indonesia's National Council,
    The First Year," Far Eastern Survey (July, 1958),
    97-109.

Soemardi, Soeloeman. "Some Aspects of the Social
    Origin of Indonesian Political Decision-Makers,"
    Transactions of the 3rd World Congress of
    Sociology, London (1956), 338-348.

Tinker, Irene, and Walker, Millidge. "The First Gen-
    eral Elections in India and Indonesia," Far
    Eastern Survey (July, 1956), 97-110.

_____. "Indonesia's Panacea, 1959 Model, Guided
    Democracy," Far Eastern Survey (December, 1954),
    177-182.

                        Reports

A Bibliography of Indonesian Government Documents
    and Selected Indonesian Writings on the Govern-
    ment in the Cornell University Library. Data
    Paper 31. Ithaca: Cornell University Press,
    1958.

Handbook on the Political Manifesto--Two Executive
    Directions of Manipol. Djakarta: Department
    of Information, 1961.

The History of the Armed Forces of the Republic of
    Indonesia. Djakarta: Department of Informa-
    tion, 1961.

Keterangan Pemerintah, Atas Program Kabinet Wilopo.
    Kementerian - Penerangan, Djakarta, 1952.
    (Gov. Statement by Wilopo on his Cabinet's
    Policy.)

Kepartaian dan Parlementarian Indonesia. Kemen-
    terian - Penerangan, Djakarta, 1954. (Informa-
    tion on political parties and their activities
    in Indonesian Parliament.)

Pergerakan Keme Sedjarah Kilat Pergerakan Kermer-
    dekaan Indonesia. Kementerian - Penerangan
    1948. (A Brief History of the Interdependence
    Movement in Indonesia from 1908-1948.)

Political Manifesto Republic of Indonesia--17 Aug.
    1959. Djakarta: Department of Information,
    1959.

Preliminary Checklist of Indonesian Imprints during
the Japanese Period (March 1942 - August 1945).
John M. Echols. Modern Indonesia Project.
Ithaca: Cornell University Press, 1963.

Udang (2) Dasar Sementara R. I. dan Pendjelasan -
The Official Provisional Constitution and its
Clarification. Act No. 7, 1950. Gazette Indo-
nesia 1950 No. 56.

                        Addresses

Aidit, D. N. Djalan Ke Demokrasi Rakjat Bagi Indo-
      nesia Oct. 1953. (The Road to People's Democ-
      racy for Indonesia.) Address at Plenary Session
      of Central Committee of PKI, October, 1953.
      Djakarta: Department of Information, 1953.

Hatta, Mohamed. Past and Future, Nov. 27, 1956.
      Modern Indonesia Project. Translation Series.
      Ithaca: Cornell University Press, 1960.

Sukarno. Marhaen and Proletarian. Bandung, July
      1957. Modern Indonesia Project. Translation
      series. Ithaca: Cornell University Press,
      1960.

_____. For Liberty and Justice. California, 21
      April 1961. Djakarta: Department of Informa-
      tion, 1961.

_____. From Non-Alignment to Coordinated Accumu-
      lation of Moral Force Toward Friendship, Peace,
      and Social Justice among Nations. Belgrade
      1 September, 1961. Djakarta: Department of
      Information, 1961.

_____. The Rediscovery of our Revolution. 7 Aug-
      ust, 1959. Djakarta: Department of Informa-
      tion, 1959.

_____. Het Ontstaan van de Pantjasila. (The
      Birth of Pantjasila.) Information Service in
      Indonesia, Den Haag, 1962.

BIBLIOGRAPHY - GHANA

Books

Apter, D. E. The Gold Coast in Transition. Prince-
    ton: Princeton University Press, 1955.

Beckett, W. H. Akokoaso: A Survey of a Gold Coast
    Village. London: Humphreys and Co., 1944.

Bourret, F. M. Ghana, the Road to Independence.
    Oxford: Oxford University Press, 1960.

Boyon, Jacques. Le Ghana, Naissance d'un Etat afri-
    cain. Paris: A. Colin, 1958.

Busia, K. A. The Position of the Chief in the Modern
    Political System of Ashanti. Oxford: Oxford
    University Press, 1951.

_____. Report on a Social Survey of Secondi
    Takoradi. London: Crown Agents, 1950.

Fage, J. D. An Introduction to the History of West
    Africa. Oxford: Oxford University Press, 1956.

Guggisberg, Sir Gordon. The Gold Coast. A Review of
    Current Events 1920-1926, and the Perspectives
    for 1927-1928. London: Bureau of Current Af-
    fairs, 1927.

Hailey, Lord. An African Survey. Revised Edition.
    London: Oxford University Press, 1956.

Hanna, A. J. European Rule in Africa. London: Cox
    and Wyman Ltd., 1961.

Nkrumah, Kwame. Ghana. Edinburgh: Thomas Nelson
    and Sons, Ltd., 1959.

_____. I Speak of Freedom. Accra: Heinemann,
    1961.

Padmore, George. The Gold Coast Revolution--The
    Struggle of an African People from Slavery to
    Freedom. London: Dennis Dobson, 1953.

Wallerstein, Immanuel. Africa--the Politics of Inde-
    pendence. New York: Vintage, 1961.

Warner, Douglas. Ghana and the New Africa. London:
    Frederick Muller Ltd., 1961.

                        Articles

Ady, P. "The Ashanti Survey, 1945-1946: An Experi-
    ment in Social Research," Geogr. Journal C x 4/6
    (1948), 149-180.

Briggs, Asa. "People and Constitution in the Gold
    Coast," West Africa, March 29, 1952.

Busia, K. A. "The Present Situation and Aspirations
    of Elites in the Gold Coast," International
    Social Science Bulletin, Paris, VIII, No. 3
    (1956), 426-431.

Jahoda, Gustav. "The Social Background of a West
    African Student Population," British Journal of
    Sociology: No. 5 (1954), Part I, 355-356; No. 6
    (1954), Part II, 71-79.

Little, Kenneth. "The Role of Voluntary Associations
    in West African Urbanisation," American Anthro-
    pologist, LIX (1957), 579-596.

_____. "Two West African Elites," International
    Social Science Bulletin, Paris, VIII, No. 3
    (1956), 495-498.

Omari, Peter T. "Changing Attitudes of Students in
    West African Society Towards Marriage and Family
    Relationships," British Journal of Sociology,
    No. II (1960), 197-208.

Reports

Africa, a Christian Continent. Fribourg: Pax Romana
    Publication, 1958.

Africa in Transition. By K. A. Busia, published by
    Department on Church and Society, World Council
    of Churches, 1959.

Development of the Volta River Basin. Accra: Cocoa
    Marketing Board, 1952.

The Development Plan 1951. Accra: Cocoa Marketing
    Board, 1951.

Final Report of the Exploratory Commission on Educa-
    tional Policy for Africa of the World Confedera-
    tion of Organisations of the Teaching Profession.
    Washington, D.C., July 31, 1959.

Gold Coast (Constitution) Order in Council. Accra,
    1954.

Report of the (WATSON) Commission of Enquiry into
    Disturbances in the Gold Coast. Colonial No.
    231. London, 1948.

Survey of High Level Manpower in Ghana 1960. Accra:
    Ministry of Information, 1961.

University College Report. Register of Students of
    the University College of Ghana awarded Degrees
    and Certificates. Accra, September 1961.

Women's Role in the Development of Tropical and Sub-
    Tropical Countries. Report of the 31st Meeting
    of the International Institute of Differing
    Civilizations, Brussels 17-20 Sept., 1958.
    Brussels, 1959.

Addresses

Nkrumah, Kwame. Address on Motion for Approval of
the Government's Revised Constitution Proposals.
12 November 1956. Accra: Hansard Society, 1956.

_____. Christmas Broadcast to the Nation. Accra:
Ghana Information Service, 1957.

_____. Government's Policy for National Develop-
ment. Address to the Assembly. 20 February
1958. Hansard Society.

_____. Opening Address, First Conference of Inde-
pendent African States, April 15, 1958. Accra:
Ghana Information Service, 1958.

_____. Welcome Address Conference on Positive
Action and Security in Africa. April 7, 1960.
Accra: Ghana Information Service, 1960.

_____. Address to the U.N. General Assembly.
Friday, September 23, 1960. Ghana Information
Service.